Understanding Algebra I

Mathematical Reasoning™ Series

📖 Beginning 1 📖 Beginning 2
📖 Level A 📖 Level B 📖 Level C 📖 Level D
📖 Level E 📖 Level F 📖 Level G
📖 Understanding Geometry 📖 Understanding Algebra I
📖 Grades 2-4 Supplement 📖 Grades 4-6 Supplement
📖 Middle School Supplement (Grades 7-9)

Written by
Terri Husted

Graphic Design by
Chip Dombrowski

Edited by
Joe Walker
Chip Dombrowski

© 2015
THE CRITICAL THINKING CO.™
www.CriticalThinking.com
Phone: 800-458-4849 • Fax: 541-756-1758
1991 Sherman Ave., Suite 200 • North Bend • OR 97459
ISBN 978-1-60144-711-1

Arithmetic
a poem by Carl Sandburg

Arithmetic is where numbers fly like pigeons
   in and out of your head.

Arithmetic tells you how many you lose or win
   if you know how many you had before you lost or won.

Arithmetic is seven eleven all good children go to heaven —
   or five six bundle of sticks.

Arithmetic is numbers you squeeze from your head
   to your hand to your pencil to your paper
   till you get the answer.

Arithmetic is where the answer is right and everything is nice
   and you can look out of the window and see the blue sky —
   or the answer is wrong and you have to start all over and
   try again and see how it comes out this time.

If you take a number and double it and double it again
   and then double it a few more times, the number gets
   bigger and bigger and goes higher and higher and
   only arithmetic can tell you what the number is
   when you decide to quit doubling.

Arithmetic is where you have to multiply — and you carry the
   multiplication table in your head and hope you won't lose it.

If you have two animal crackers, one good and one bad, and
   you eat one and a striped zebra with streaks all over him
   eats the other, how many animal crackers will you have
   if somebody offers you five six seven and you say No no no
   and you say Nay nay nay and you say Nix nix nix?

If you ask your mother for one fried egg for breakfast and
   she gives you two fried eggs and you eat both of them,
   who is better in arithmetic, you or your mother?

Table of Contents

About the Author

Terri Husted, formerly Terri Santi, has been teaching math for over 30 years. She taught middle school math for many years and is curently an algebra and geometry teacher at Ithaca High School in Ithaca, N.Y. Terri was the Math Coordinator for the Saturday Science and Math Academy, a program for elementary minority students, that was run by Cornell University and later Ithaca College.

In 1995, she was chosen as one of two New York state finalists for the Presidential Award for Excellence in Science and Math Teaching. Her life and work have been included in the book *Young People's Lessons in Character* (1998) Young People's Press. Besides giving many workshops to teachers in her district, Terri loves writing about math and including multicultural math in her math lessons.

Terri firmly believes that math can be made clear and simple for everyone and that critical thinking is not only necessary, but also fun! Terri is also the author of *Math Detective*®, *Math Ties*®, and *Understanding Geometry* (The Critical Thinking Co.™). She holds teaching certificates in Math 7-12, Reading 7-12, Biology 7-12, Elementary Education K-12, and has a Bachelor of Science in Mathematics and a Masters of Science in Reading. Her specialty areas are reading in the content area of math, overcoming math anxiety, and multicultural math. She is a member of the National Council of Teachers of Mathematics.

3/11

What Is Algebra?

Algebra is generalized arithmetic. By this we mean that in algebra you use all the rules of arithmetic to find the unknown values needed to solve real world problems. Unknown values in algebra are represented by letters or symbols we call *variables*. To date, in arithmetic you have been taught how to use operations like addition, subtraction, multiplication, and division to find the answers.

$$6 \times 4 = ?$$

You use algebra when you need to work backwards to find missing and unknown numbers.

$$6 \times ? = 24$$

Algebra is a powerful tool. The more algebra you know and the better you understand it, the better you will do in future math courses. You will also become more confident in solving problems; not just in math but in other fields that utilize math.

The word "algebra" is a Latin variation of the Arabic word "al-jabr," which was taken from the title of a book written around AD 825 by the Arab mathematician known as al-Khwarizmi. The translation of the book's title is *The Book of Restoration and Balancing*. It's interesting that later the word "algebra" began to be used as a term for a surgeon or anyone who restores bones. A barber in medieval times called himself "algebrista," since barbers did bone setting and bloodletting on the side. That is why the barber poles have red and white stripes on them!

The first step to understanding algebra is to review concepts from our system of numbers and learn the proper use of set notation. This book will teach you to translate from words to math expressions and equations, as well as give you some great new strategies to succeed at solving word problems.

Algebra also involves learning how to change patterns into equations to predict outcomes. You will learn how to view geometric ideas algebraically and how to use algebra to solve geometric problems. After you learn several algebra concepts, and only then, will a graphing calculator (TI-83 or TI-84 is suggested) enhance your understanding of those concepts.

3/12

Chapter 1

Our Number System – Sets, Operations, and Properties

Our number system is composed of different sets of numbers. We need to review these sets and later study their properties to be successful at solving problems.

Our number system is composed of the set of **real** numbers and the set of **imaginary** numbers. In this book we will concentrate only on the set of reals. You will later learn in future courses that the set of reals and the set of imaginary numbers together comprise the set of **complex** numbers.

Study the chart on page 5 and starting on the *bottom* of the page, see how the sets build upon each other. Some are **subsets** of other sets. Study the relationships of these sets so you can gain a better understanding of their properties.

Sets and Set Notation

A **set**, as you may already know, is a collection of objects or numbers. We call the members of the set the **elements** of the set. The symbol ∈ means "is an element of" (The symbol ∉ means "is NOT an element of"). You can describe a set by using **braces** { }. Do not use parentheses ( ) or brackets [ ] when describing sets. Here's the set of even numbers. It is an infinite set. Some sets are finite and some are infinite.

infinite goes on for ever   *finite*

Even = {0, 2, 4, 6, 8,...}   Primes less than 12 = {2, 3, 5, 7, 11}

begins   *ends*

You can describe a set by making a list or **roster**, or by a **rule**. A rule is a written description of a set. Some sets cannot be written by a roster because they are impossible to list. For example, how could you make a list of the set of fractions?

Also, some sets are well-defined and others are not. If you can easily define its elements then we say the set is well defined. For example, the set of best pizza restaurants may vary according to different opinions, so the set of best pizza restaurants is not a well-defined set.

A set may also be empty, meaning that it has no elements. We use the symbol ∅ or { } to define the **empty set**. Do NOT use both symbols together like this, {∅}, as this would be a set that has the empty set symbol in it so it's no longer empty!

Remember the empty set is also not this set, {0}, as this is the set that contains the element 0, so it has one element in it.

If a set is COMPLETELY contained inside another set it is said to be a **subset** of that set. For example: the set {-3, 4} is a subset of the set {-3, 4, 8, 10}. Notice that the set {-3, 4} is NOT a subset of the set {-3, 8, 10} since the element 4 is not an element of that set. The symbol for subset is ⊂, whereas the symbol ⊄ stands for "not a subset of." For example: List the subsets of the set {R, Q, S}. The answer is {R}, {Q}, {S}, {R, Q}, {R, S}, {Q, S}, {R, Q, S} and { }. Notice the original set or **improper set** is always a subset of the given set and the empty set is a subset of every set as well.

You may also be asked to find the **complement** of a set. If you have a subset of a larger set, the complement of the subset is the set of elements in the larger set that are NOT in the subset. For example, if Set A = {3, 7, 10} is a subset of Set B = {3, 4, 7, 10, 33, 45}, the complement of Set A is {4, 33, 45}. The symbol for complement of subset A is A^c or $\tilde{}A$.

John Venn (1834-1923), an English mathematician developed Venn diagrams to represent sets. Here's a picture of a set and its subset and how you find the complement.

The complement of the set of cats is the set of all the animals that are not cats.

animals

cats

B = {3, 4, 7, 10, 33, 45}
A = {3, 7, 10}
~A = {4, 33, 45}

B
33
4
A 3
7 10
45

The order in which you list the elements of a set is not important, so the set {4, 6, 10} is the same set as {6, 10, 4}. We call these sets **equal**. Two sets are **equivalent** if they have the same number of elements in them. You can match equivalent sets by creating a **one-to-one correspondence**. For example: {A, Q, 7, -67} is equivalent to {-3, 4, 8, 10}, since both sets have 4 elements. See the drawing on the next page.

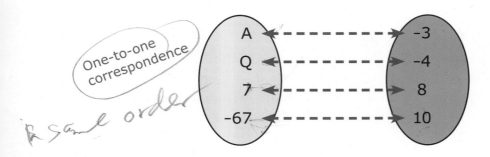

One-to-one correspondence

in same order

You can join or unite sets together. We call that the **union** of sets. The symbol for union is "U." For example: Find the union of set A = {-2, 8, 6} and set B = {-2, 4, 8, 10, 34}. It can be written as A ∪ B. The answer is {-2, 4, 6, 8, 10, 34}. Notice, you don't need to worry about the order in which you write your answer and you don't need to repeat the elements -2 or 8.

Now, when we need to find what elements two or more sets have in common we find the **intersection** of sets. The symbol for intersection is "∩" (upside down U). For example: Find the intersection of A and B or A ∩ B, if A = {0, 5, -10} and B = {0, 5, 34, 101}. The answer is to A ∩ B = {0, 5} because those are the elements that both sets have in common.

If two sets have no elements in common, they are called **disjoint** sets.

Here's a representation of a Venn diagram for the union and intersection of two sets. In the picture on the left, both sets are included in the answer. In the picture on the right, only the overlapping area is the answer.

$A = \{0, 5, -10\}$ $B = \{0, 5, 34, 101\}$

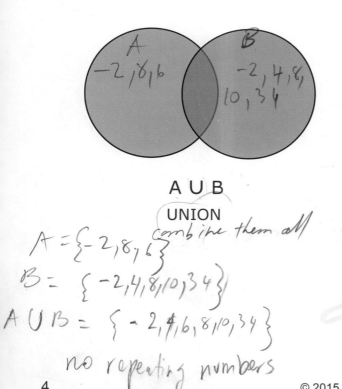

A ∪ B

UNION

combine them all

$A = \{-2, 8, 6\}$

$B = \{-2, 4, 8, 10, 34\}$

$A \cup B = \{-2, 4, 6, 8, 10, 34\}$

no repeating numbers

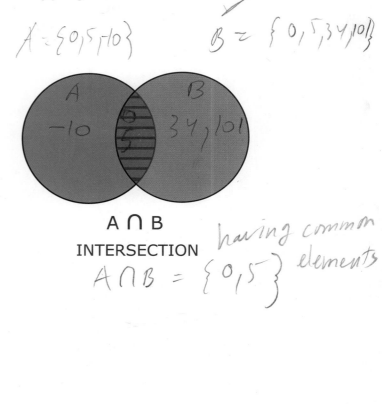

A ∩ B

INTERSECTION

having common elements

$A \cap B = \{0, 5\}$

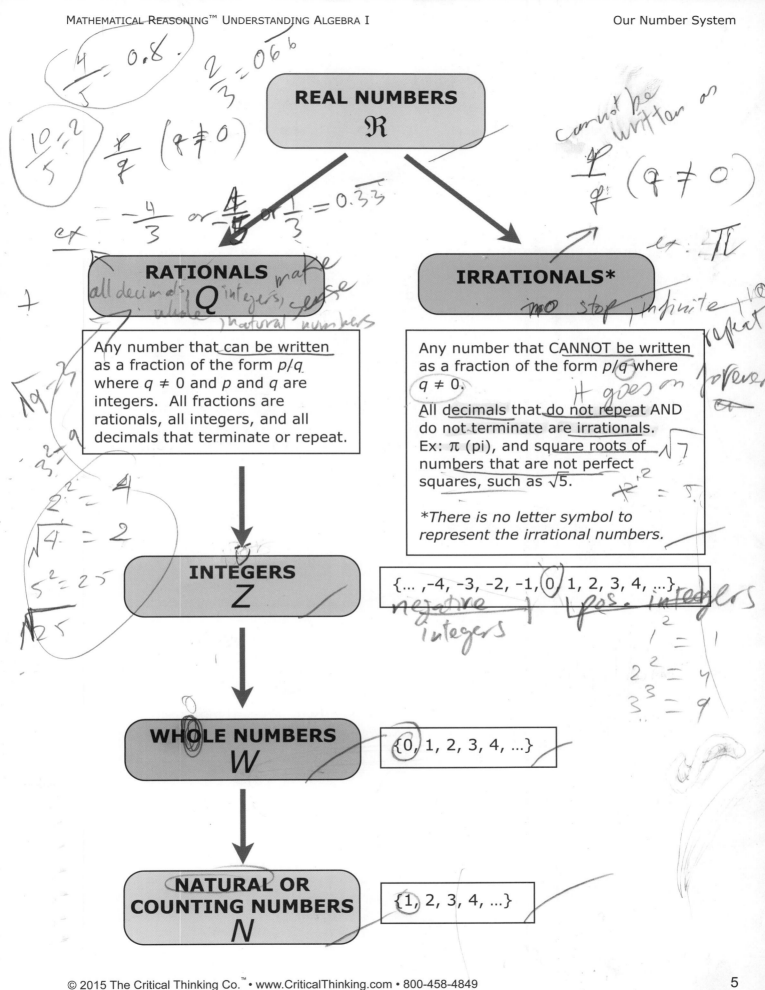

REAL NUMBERS
$\mathfrak{R}$

RATIONALS
Q

Any number that can be written as a fraction of the form p/q where $q \neq 0$ and p and q are integers. All fractions are rationals, all integers, and all decimals that terminate or repeat.

IRRATIONALS*

Any number that CANNOT be written as a fraction of the form p/q where $q \neq 0$.

All decimals that do not repeat AND do not terminate are irrationals. Ex: π (pi), and square roots of numbers that are not perfect squares, such as $\sqrt{5}$.

*There is no letter symbol to represent the irrational numbers.

INTEGERS
Z

$\{\ldots, -4, -3, -2, -1, 0, 1, 2, 3, 4, \ldots\}$

WHOLE NUMBERS
W

$\{0, 1, 2, 3, 4, \ldots\}$

NATURAL OR COUNTING NUMBERS
N

$\{1, 2, 3, 4, \ldots\}$

These are other important sets you should know in this course.

PRIMES	PERFECT SQUARES
{2, 3, 5, 7, 11, 13, 17, ...}	{1, 4, 9, 16, 25, 36, 49, 64, ...}

Here's a **rule** to describe the primes: {any whole number divisible only by one and itself}. So the primes can be listed as a roster as well as by a rule.

Answer the following questions based on the concept map on page 5.

1. Is the set of *N* (Natural numbers) ⊂ *W* (Whole numbers)? _Yes_ Explain your thinking.

   because starting with 1, I see the same numbers

2. Are the Even numbers ⊂ Natural numbers? _Yes_ Explain your thinking.

   There are Even numbers in Natural numbers

3. Why is the number 5 an element of the Rational numbers? Hint: Review the definition of rationals. Explain your thinking.

   _____

4. Write a rule for the Perfect Squares. *A whole number multiplies its self*

5. Are all square roots rational or irrational? Explain your thinking.

   _____

6. Is the fraction $\frac{22}{7}$, which is commonly used to represent π, rational or irrational? Explain your thinking. Hint: Divide 22 by 7 without a calculator.

   _____

> Remember: the number 1 is not a prime number.

If Set A = {-5, 0, 3, 7, 22}, Set B = {-5, 0, 8, 9, 22}, and Set E = {-5, 4}, answer the following questions.

7 What is A ∪ B? _____

8 What is A ∪ B ∪ E? _____

9 Is E ⊂ A? __No__ Explain your thinking. _____

_____

10 **a** What is A ∩ E? __-5__   **b** What is A ∩ B ∩ E? __-5__

11 Are set A and B equivalent or equal? Explain your thinking.

_____

12 If set F = {12, 24}, find E ∩ F. ____Non____

13 Describe the numbers 0, 1, and 2 by listing the sets they belong to.

0	**1**	**2**
not prime!	not prime!	prime
even	odd	even
not natural	natural	natural
whole	whole	whole
integer	integer	integer
rational	irational	rational
real	real	real

14 List the subsets of {S, T, A, R}.

{S, T} {S, A} {S, R} {S, A}

{S, T}

_____

_____

More Practice

Do these problems on a separate paper.

1   State if **true or false** and be ready to support your answer.

     a   Whole numbers are not rationals because they are not fractions.

     b   The number $.\overline{6}$ is rational.

     c   The square roots of all perfect squares are rational numbers.

     d   0 is not a real number.

     e   1 is prime.

     f   The roster for the set of primes between 13 and 29 is {17, 19, 23}.

     g   The set of rationals and irrationals make up the set of reals.

     h   The positive even numbers are a subset of the set of whole numbers.

     i   {51, 57} is a subset of the set of Primes.

2   Draw a Venn diagram if T = {triangles}, P = {polygons}.

     a   Is $T \subset P$?;   b   Is $P \subset T$?;   c   What is ~T?

3   If A = {5, 6, 7}, B = {10, 11, 12},   a   find $A \cup B$,   b   find $A \cap B$.

4   Write a roster for the set of odd numbers.

5   Write a rule for the set of odd numbers.

6   Is the $\sqrt{121}$ rational or irrational? Explain your thinking.

7   Raffi thinks the fraction $\frac{22}{641}$ is irrational because when he changed it to a decimal he couldn't get it to repeat or terminate. Is he right?

8   Write a roster for the set {the whole numbers between 12 and 15 inclusive}. Hint: **Inclusive** means that you include 12 and 15.

9   Explain if the set {0, 1, 2, 3, ..., 100} is finite or infinite.

10   Give an example of the intersection of set and its subset. What is the result?

11   Find a pattern for the number of subsets a set can have. A set of one element has two subsets (the improper and the empty set), a set of two elements has four subsets. What about a set of three elements? Four elements? Explain your thinking.

The Number Line and Graphing Sets

To graph on a number line means to put a point or points on the number line. It's important to remember that every **point** on the number line corresponds to a **real** number and that every **real** number has a **point** on the number line. That means that the irrational numbers can also be graphed on the number line (approximately).

Review the symbols below.

> **>** is greater than
>
> **≥** is greater than or equal to
>
> ● dark circle means "include"

< is less than

≤ is less than or equal to

○ open circle means "do not include"

Examples

1 Graph {whole numbers less than 6}.

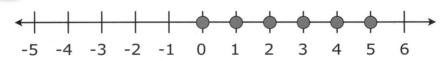

You can put an open circle on 6 but you don't need to.

2 Graph {real numbers less than 6}.

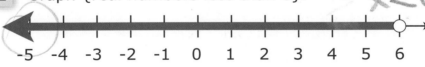

Here you do need an open circle on 6. Notice the dark arrow head pointing to the left.

3 Graph all the real numbers between –2 and 3 including –2 but not 3.

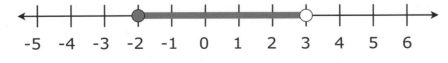

4 Graph the set of integers less than or equal to 5.

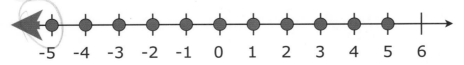

Another way of writing this set is $x \le 5$, where $x \in$ {integers}.

In Example 3 on page 9, there are two inequalities happening at the same time: the real numbers less than 3 AND the real numbers greater than or equal to -2. When two inequalities are put together, such as $x < 3$ and $x \geq -2$, a **compound inequality** is created. A compound inequality could also be an OR statement, such as $x > 14$ OR $x < 2$.

An AND compound inequality can be written in one statement: $-2 \leq x < 3$. This reads: -2 is less than or equal to x and x is less than 3. AND always means at the same time. Notice how the solution x, which stands for the real numbers in this example, is between both of those numbers on the number line, including -2. It can also be written in reverse order: $3 > x \geq -2$.

Preserving the order of the number line with -2 going first is a good idea when you are just learning compound inequalities for the first time.

This is incorrect: $-2 \geq x < 3$. Always keep both symbols facing in the same direction.

Graph the following sets. Make sure to review the examples on page 9.

1 Graph the set of positive odd numbers. Don't forget this set is infinite.

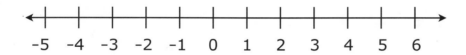

2 Graph the set of integers between -4 and 4.

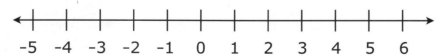

3 Graph the set of reals greater than -2.

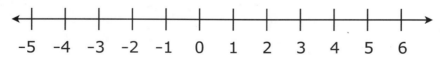

4 Graph the set of reals greater than -2.5 and less than or equal to 4.

5 Write a compound inequality for problem #4 above. _____

6 Which of the following compound inequalities using the set of reals represents the graph below? Select the correct letter, and then write your choice in words.

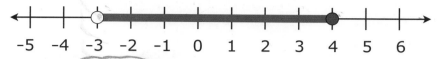

-5 -4 -3 -2 -1   0   1   2   3   4   5   6

   a   -3 < x < 4; x ∈ reals   _____

   b   -3 < x ≤ 4; x ∈ integers   _____

   c   -3 ≤ x ≤ 4; x ∈ reals   _____

   d   -3 < x ≤ 4; x ∈ reals   _____

7 Write a compound inequality for this statement. The set of reals less than 10 and greater than or equal to 0. _____

8 The following graph shows an <u>OR statement</u>. x is less than –1 OR x is greater than or equal to 3. Explain why this set of two inequalities cannot be written in one statement (with only one x as in problem #6).

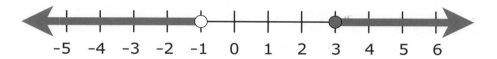

-5 -4 -3 -2 -1   0   1   2   3   4   5   6

_____

_____

9 Another type of notation looks like this: {x | x < 10; x ∈ reals}.
                                                    ← This is read as "such that."

This translates to all the real numbers (represented by the variable x) such that they are less than 10. Use this type of notation to write the following using a variable (maybe the first initial of your name).

The set of real numbers greater than or equal to 12 and less than 15.

_____

10 Graph the primes greater than 54 but less than 74. Hint: It's okay to put a **break** on the number line but always show **0** on the number line.

0   54   74

> Note: There will be more about inequalities later.

More Practice

Do these problems on a separate sheet of paper.

1   Write an inequality for the graph shown below.

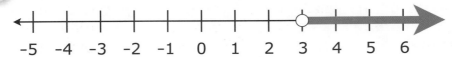

2   Write a compound inequality for the graph shown below.

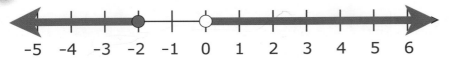

3   Write a compound inequality for the graph shown here.

4   What is wrong with this compound inequality: $-5 > x < 5$?
Explain your thinking.

5   Paulo said: "My real number is between 3 and 10." Write a compound
inequality to represent his statement.

6   Use a roster to represent a subset of the set of primes with six elements.

7   If Set R = {-3, 4, 8} and Set Q = {-3, 4, 5, 8, 10}, find ˜R. Graph ˜R
by using a number line. Remember to always show the number 0 on the
number line.

8   Venn diagrams can be used to solve problems. A school has 127
students taking math classes. Of those, 88 take Algebra I, 75 take
Geometry, and 36 take both Algebra I and Geometry. How many take
Algebra I but not Geometry?

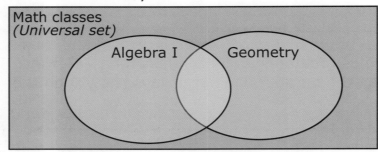

9   Make a Venn diagram for our number system. Refer to page 5.

10   Create four sets, where *A* is a subset of *B*, the intersection of *A* and *C* is
the empty set and the intersection of *B* and *C* is set *D*. Why is *D* a subset
of both *B* and *C*? Explain your thinking.

Enrichment Problems

Do these problems on a separate sheet of paper.

11 The compound inequality -3 < x ≤ 5, where x ∈ reals, represents an interval on the number line which can also be written with the interval notation (-3, 5]. The parenthesis here means "do not include the 3," and the bracket means "include the 5." Write an interval notation for these sets.

   a -9 ≤ y < 10   b 0 < w ≤ 3   c 4 < p < 100

12 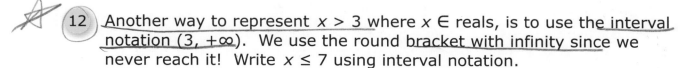Another way to represent x > 3 where x ∈ reals, is to use the interval notation (3, +∞). We use the round bracket with infinity since we never reach it! Write x ≤ 7 using interval notation.

13 How would you write all the real numbers using interval notation?

14 Write a compound inequality for the following: (-∞, -3] ∪ (2, +∞). Hint: It's an OR statement.

15 Write the compound inequality and the interval notation for the graph below.

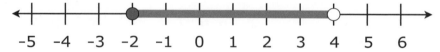

-5 -4 -3 -2 -1 0 1 2 3 4 5 6

16 Connie has 8 small blue buttons that are round. She has 3 large buttons that are blue and square. 5 buttons are blue and square and also small. She knows she has 28 buttons that are small and a total of 26 that are blue. 2 buttons are red, small, and also square. If in total she has 50 buttons, how many are large, square but not blue? Use a Venn diagram to find the answer.

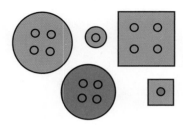

17 Write a word problem where the intersection of A and B has 7 elements, the union of A and B has 23 elements and B has 17 elements.

18 Use a Venn diagram to show if this statement is valid or not valid. No X is in Y. Every Q is an X. Therefore, no Q is a Y. What is the relationship between Q and X?

Operations and Properties of Rational Numbers

In this section we will review operations ($+ - \cdot \div$) with rational numbers. Remember to use the number line to help you. Later, you will use your graphing calculator to speed the arithmetic process, but it's important to understand the concepts so you know if your answers make sense.

Addition of Rationals

When adding two numbers, if the signs are the same, add and keep the sign.

| 1 | $5 + 10 = 15$ | 2 | $-3 + (-4) = -7$ | 3 | $-\frac{1}{2} + \left(-\frac{3}{4}\right) = -1\frac{1}{4}$ |

Handwritten: $-\frac{2}{3} + \left(\frac{-4}{4}\right) = \frac{1}{1}$

Handwritten: $-3 - 4 = -7$

Parentheses are used to help you read the problem.

Handwritten: $-\frac{1}{2} - \frac{3}{4} = 1$

Remember that to add (or subtract) fractions a common denominator is needed.

When adding two numbers, if their signs are different, subtract the two numbers and keep the sign of the number farthest away from 0. This is the number with the larger **absolute value**.

Remember: the **absolute value** of a number is written like this $|5|$ and the answer is **always positive**. $|5| = 5$ and $|-5| = 5$.

| 4 | $-5 + 8 = 3$ | 5 | $-10 + 4 = -6$ | 6 | $-6 + 6 = 0$ |
| 7 | $-\frac{1}{2} + \frac{3}{4} = \frac{1}{4}$ | 8 | $2.04 + (-5.46) = -3.42$ | | |

Property 1: Addition Property of Zero
Add **0** to any real number to get the same number. Zero is the identity for addition.

$$n + 0 = n$$

Property 2: Additive Inverse Property
Two numbers whose sum is 0 are called additive inverses.

$$n + -n = 0$$

Thinking Strategies

When more than two rational numbers are added, a good strategy is to combine the numbers with the same signs first.

9 −3 + 12 + (−7) + 10
Add −3 plus −7 first, which is −10, and then add 12 plus 10, which is 22. Then −10 plus 22 is 12.

Always read the entire problem first. When there is a long string of numbers to add, some may cancel and save you a lot of work.

10 −246 + 899 + 246 + 5,002 + −899

~~−246~~ + ~~899~~ + ~~246~~ + 5,002 + ~~−899~~ so the answer is 5,002.

Using a separate sheet of paper, practice adding rationals without a calculator.

1 −9 + (−10) = _____

2 12 + (−88) = _____

3 −15 + 15 = _____

4 −95 + 5 = _____

5 −3.5 + 0 + (−3.5) = _____

6 −4 + 12 + (−8) + 20 = _____

7 ____ + (−24) = −100

8 $\frac{1}{2} + -\frac{1}{2} + \frac{3}{8}$ = _____

9 −199 + 200 + 348 + (−1) = _____

10 3.75 + _____ = −5

11 −67 + 90 + 67 + (−90) = _____

12 −9 + _____ = −9 + 34 + (−36)

13 28 + (−52) = _____

14 200 + (−400) = _____

15 −6 + $2\frac{1}{3}$ = _____

16 17 + (−9) + (−1) + 18 = _____

17 11 + (−21) + 21 = _____

18 $-2\frac{2}{3} + (-5\frac{1}{2})$ = _____

19 8 + (−9) + 5 + (−1) = _____

20 100 + (−56) + (−2) = _____

21 _____ is the identity for addition.

22 −Q + Q + Q = _____

23 What's the additive inverse of one million? _____

Subtraction of Rationals

Subtracting two numbers is the same as adding the inverse of the number that follows the subtraction sign.

1   6 – 4 is the same as 6 + (–4) which also equals 2.

Change the subtraction sign to an addition sign and then change the sign of the number that follows the subtraction sign.

$$a - b = a + (-b)$$

2   8 – ⁺9 is the same as 8 + ⁻9 or –1.

3   –1 – 3 = –4 means: –1 **subtract** a positive 3. Make two changes: –1 + (–3) which equals –4.

4   –2 – 6 – 3 – 5 = –16 means: –2 + (–6) + (–3) + (–5) which is the same as adding four negative numbers.

5   –7 – (–3) = – 7 + 3 = –4.

Using a separate piece of paper, practice subtracting rationals without a calculator.

1.   5 – (–5) = _____

2.   0 – 6 = _____

3.   6 – (–8) = _____

4.   –7 – 13 = _____

5.   –9 – 2 = _____

6.   70 – 60 = _____

7.   –9 – (–4) = _____

8.   4 – 12 = _____

9.   –12 – 3 – 5 = _____

10.   10.5 – 33.458 = _____

11. $-\dfrac{1}{2} - \dfrac{3}{4} - \dfrac{1}{3} =$ _____

12.   2.3 – 6 = _____

13.   –10 – (–22) = _____

14.   –9 – 91 = _____

15.   0 – (–7) = _____

16. $\dfrac{1}{6} - \dfrac{4}{5} =$ _____

Multiplication and Division of Rationals

To multiply or divide rationals follow the rules below. The symbol ×
for multiplication is replaced by · or ( ). If you see a number times a
variable, like 5y, it means 5 times y and wy means w times y.

same signs = +

different signs = -

Multiplication Rules

$$+ \cdot + = +$$
$$+ \cdot - = -$$
$$- \cdot + = -$$
$$- \cdot - = +$$

Division Rules

$$\frac{+}{+} = + \qquad \frac{+}{-} = -$$
$$\frac{-}{-} = + \qquad \frac{-}{+} = -$$

Same signs = +

different signs = -

Examples

1. $-5 \cdot 6 = -30$
2. $(-7)(8) = -56$
3. $(-4)(-5) = 20$
4. $0\,(-5) = 0$
5. $-20 \div 5 = -4$
6. $-100 \div -2 = 50$

7. $(-5)^3 = -125$ Remember that $(-5)^3$ means $(-5)(-5)(-5)$.
8. $\frac{100}{-200} = -\frac{1}{2}$
9. $0 \div 5 = 0$
10. $5 \div 0 = \emptyset$ See the next page to understand examples 9 and 10.

Property 3: Commutative Property for Addition and Multiplication
The order in which you add two numbers does not change
the sum. The order in which you multiply two numbers does
not change the product.

$$a + b = b + a$$

$$a \cdot b = b \cdot a$$

Remember:
the word
"commute"
means to move.

The commutative property does NOT work for subtraction or division.
$5 - 4 \neq 4 - 5$ and $6 \div 3 \neq 3 \div 6$

Property 4: **Associative Property of Addition and Multiplication**
The way you **group** when you add or multiply does not
affect the answer.

$$(a + b) + c = a + (b + c)$$

$$(a \cdot b) \cdot c = a \cdot (b \cdot c)$$

$$(-3 + 5) + 8 = -3 + (5 + 8)$$
$$2 + 8 = -3 + 13$$
$$10 = 10 \checkmark\checkmark$$

$$-5 \cdot (-6 \cdot 4) = (-5 \cdot -6) \cdot 4$$
$$-5 \cdot -24 = 30 \cdot 4$$
$$120 = 120 \checkmark\checkmark$$

The associative property does NOT work for subtraction or division.
$$(9 - 4) - 3 \neq 9 - (4 - 3) \text{ and } (8 \div 4) \div 2 \neq 8 \div (4 \div 2)$$

Property 5: **Division Property of Zero**
Zero divided by any number (except 0) is always 0.
Remember you may never divide by zero. Zero in the
denominator results in the empty set.

We know that $\frac{12}{3} = 4$ because 4 (quotient) times 3 (divisor) equals 12
(dividend). Now, $\frac{0}{3} = 0$ because 0 (quotient) times 3 (divisor) equals
0 (dividend). What about $\frac{3}{0} = $? If you say the answer is 0, it won't
check because 0 times 0 is not 3. No answer will work, so the answer is
$\emptyset$ or **undefined**. The same is true of $0 \div 0$. (While some will argue the
answer is ∞ or $-\infty$, it's recommended you write $\emptyset$ or **undefined**.)

Property 6: **Multiplication Property of One**
Any number multiplied by 1 equals the same number.
One is the **identity** for multiplication.

$$n \cdot 1 = n$$

Property 7: **Multiplicative Inverse Property**
Any two numbers that multiply to 1 (the identity for
multiplication) are called **multiplicative inverses**
(reciprocals).

$$\frac{a}{b} \cdot \frac{b}{a} = 1; \text{ as long as } a \neq 0 \text{ and } b \neq 0.$$

Practice

Using a separate sheet of paper, practice multiplying and dividing rationals. Review your properties before you start. Make sure to simplify your answer.

1 $(5)(-6) = $ _-30_

2 $3.2 \cdot -10.5 = $ _____

3 $(-11)^2 = $ _121_

4 $\frac{144}{-12} = $ _-12_

5 $0 \div 29 = $ _0_

6 $\frac{4}{5} \cdot \frac{5}{4} = $ _1_

7 $-5 \cdot -6 \cdot 3 = 3 \cdot -6 \cdot$ _-5_

8 $\frac{8}{0} = $ _0_

9 $-\frac{2}{3} \cdot -\frac{3}{2} = 1$

10 $100 \div -5 \div -4 = $ _-5_

11 $\frac{8}{9} \cdot -\frac{9}{8} = $ _-1_

12 $-2,000 \div -2,000 = $ _1_

13 Using this example, show why the commutative property doesn't work for subtraction.

$$10 - 3 \neq 3 - 10$$
$$7 \neq -7$$

14 Using this example, show why the associative property doesn't work for subtraction.

$$(-5 - 6) - 10 \neq -5 - (6 - 10)$$
$$-9 - 10 \neq -5 - (-4)$$
$$-19 \neq -1$$

15 Using this example, show why the associative property doesn't work for division.

$$(200 \div 50) \div 2 \neq 200 \div (50 \div 2)$$
$$4 \div 2 \neq 200 \div 25$$
$$2 \neq 8$$

16 Is $3 + (5 + 4) = 4 + (3 + 5)$? Which property or properties support your answer? Explain your thinking.

Associative; the answer is still the same, even if you reverse the numbers

Property 8: Distributive Property of Multiplication Over Addition or Subtraction

Multiply the outside number by each of the numbers inside the parentheses.

$$a\,(b + c) = ab + ac \qquad a\,(b - c) = ab - ac$$

Remember *ab* means $a \cdot b$ and *ac* means $a \cdot c$

$$5\,(9 + 3) = 5 \cdot 9 + 5 \cdot 3$$
$$5 \cdot 12 = 45 + 15$$
$$60 = 60 \checkmark\checkmark$$

$$-3\,(7 - 4) = (-3 \cdot 7) - (-3 \cdot 4)$$
$$-3 \cdot 3 = -21 - (-12)$$
$$-9 = -9 \checkmark\checkmark$$

$5(9 + 3)$ is the same as $(9 + 3)5$ because of the commutative property for multiplication, so you can also distribute if the 5 is on the other side. The distributive property only holds if you are multiplying a parenthesis that has addition or subtraction inside.

$$10 \div (10 \div 5) \neq (10 \div 10) \div (10 \div 5)$$
$$10 \div 2 \neq 1 \div 2$$

Using a separate sheet of paper, practice the distributive property.

1   $8(-2 + 3) = -16 + \underline{\hphantom{xxx}}$

2   $(9 - 4) \cdot -4 = -36 + \underline{\hphantom{xxx}}$

3   $-5(3 - 6) = \underline{\hphantom{xxx}} + \underline{\hphantom{xxx}}$

4   $\underline{\hphantom{xxx}}(3 + 7) = -15 - 35$

5   $\frac{1}{4}(-16 + \underline{\hphantom{xx}}) = \underline{\hphantom{xxx}} + 8$

6   $18 + 28 = (-9 - 14)\underline{\hphantom{xxx}}$

7   $\underline{\hphantom{xxx}}(-10 + 34) = -5 + 17$

8   $a\,(b - c + d) = ab - \underline{\hphantom{xxx}} + \underline{\hphantom{xxx}}$

9   $-3(\underline{\hphantom{xxx}} + 9) = 30 - 27$

10   $100(-2 + \underline{\hphantom{xxx}}) = -200 + 50$

More Practice

Using a separate sheet of paper, practice all operations and properties without using a calculator.

1. $5 \cdot -4 =$ _____

2. $-10 + -10 =$ _____

3. $|6| =$ _____

4. $|-6| =$ _____

5. $\frac{-144}{-12} =$ _____

6. $4.2 \div 0 =$ _____

7. $\frac{-18}{0} =$ _____

8. $-5 - (-7) =$ _____

9. $11 - 28 =$ _____

10. $0 - (-11) =$ _____

11. $(2)(-3)(5) =$ _____

12. $-13 \cdot 13 =$ _____

13. $\frac{-36}{72} =$ _____

14. $-(-13) =$ _____

15. $(-2)^3 =$ _____

State which property is illustrated.

16. $8 + (-9 + 2) = (8 + (-9)) + 2$

17. $8 \cdot 1 = 8$

18. $-10 + 0 = -10$

19. $-3 + 5 + 10 = -3 + 10 + 5$

20. $9(10 - 4) = 90 - 36$

21. $\frac{3}{4} \cdot \frac{4}{3} = 1$

22. $89 = 0 + 89$

23. $(2 + 12)(-3) = -6 - 36$

24. $5 \cdot \frac{1}{5} = 1$

25. $9 \cdot (10 \cdot 2) = (9 \cdot 10) \cdot 2$

26. $(-8 \cdot 10) \cdot 3 = 3 \cdot (-8 \cdot 10)$

Read the following and answer the questions.

27. Ms. Cochran has 15 students in her first class. She gives each of her students in that class 5 crackers. In her second class she has 20 students. She gives each of them 5 crackers. To determine how many crackers were handed out, Luis wrote: $5(15) + 5(20)$ and Jocelyn wrote: $5(15 + 20)$. Who is correct and why?

28. Helen was asked to find the multiplicative inverse of .0865. Her answer was $\frac{2{,}000}{173}$. Is she correct? Why or why not?

29. What shortcut can you use to find the answer to $(-2.65)(-10{,}000)$?

30. Find the multiplicative inverse of $-5\frac{2}{5}$. Prove that your answer is the multiplicative inverse.

Order of Operations

An **expression** is any mathematical statement that does not have an equal or inequality symbol. The expression $5 \cdot 4 - 2$ can result in two different answers without the order of operations rules. One answer is 10 by subtracting first and then multiplying (5) by $(4 - 2)$ and the other answer is 18 by multiplying first and then subtracting $(5 \cdot 4) - 2$. In order to avoid confusion, follow these rules to simplify expressions. To **simplify** means to find the answer in its simplest form. If your answer is a fraction, it should be reduced.

Do the operations inside the parentheses first. From inside out do the exponents.	$5 \cdot (3 + 1) - 2$ $5 \cdot 4 - 2$
Do multiplication OR division, whichever operation is first, from left to right.	$5 \cdot 4 - 2$ $20 - 2$
Do addition or subtraction, whichever operation is first, from left to right.	$20 - 2$ 18

Examples Using Funnel Outlines

1
$$9 - 8 \cdot 4 + 7$$
$$9 - 32 + 7$$
$$9 - 32 + 7$$
$$-23 + 7$$
$$\boxed{-16}$$

2
$$(3^2 - 5)(4 + 2)^2 + 8$$
$$(9 - 5)(6)^2 + 8$$
$$4 \cdot 36 + 8$$
$$144 + 8$$
$$\boxed{152}$$

3
$$\frac{[(80 + 4) \div 4]}{(49 \div 7 \cdot 1)}$$
$$\frac{[84 \div 4]}{(7 \cdot 1)}$$
$$\frac{21}{7}$$
$$\boxed{3}$$

Simplify the numerator and denominator completely **before** doing any division! <u>Never</u> drop any grouping symbols until each operation is completed.

4
$$\frac{1}{2} - \frac{1}{2} + \frac{1}{4}$$
$$0 + \frac{1}{4}$$
$$\boxed{\frac{1}{4} \text{ or } .25}$$

Remember to simplify left to right.

Brackets and braces are also used as parentheses. They are inclusion symbols. Work from the inside out.

Simplify the following expressions. Follow the order of operations rules and use the funnel outline.

1   -20 ÷ 5 · 2

2   -4 · 2 − 3 · 4 + 2 · 0

3 $|-5| - |9| + |-20|$

4   27 − 9 + 6 · 2 · (-1)

5   (39 + 3) ÷ 2

6   -100 + 24 ÷ 3

7 $7 \cdot 4^2 + 3^2 \cdot 5$

8 $\dfrac{-13 + (4 \cdot 3) + 13}{-6}$

9   -2 + 3(8 + 8)

10   23 + [22 − 3(4 + 1)]

11 $(3^2 - 5)^2 + 1^3$

12 $8(2 - 3)^3 + 2^5$

More Practice

Use a separate sheet of paper to do these problems.

1 $|-6| + |6|$

2 $9(-19 + 2)$

3 $(2 + 4) \cdot 7$

4 $(7 - (-3)) + 2^3$

5 $-10 \div 2 \cdot 3 - 7 + 3 \cdot 4$

6 $\dfrac{5 - (4 + 9)}{10}$

7 $5(4 + (10 - 3) - 1)$

8 $3 + 2(5)^2 + (2 \cdot 5)^2$

9 $18 \div 2 \cdot 2 \div 2 + 4$

10 $\dfrac{3}{4} + \dfrac{1}{4} - 2 + 5$

11 $\dfrac{(9 - 12)(-2)}{16 - 42}$

12 $(20 - 4 + 18) \div (-2)$

13 $8 \cdot \dfrac{3}{4} + \dfrac{1}{4} \cdot 4$

14 $\dfrac{(10 - 7)(10 + 7)}{100 - 49}$

Enrichment Problems

15 Magda says that $(-1)^{19} = -19$ and Marisa says it equals -1. Who is right? Explain your thinking.

16 The "11" problem: $-11 \div -11 \cdot 11 - 11 + 11$

17 The most nested "3" problem: $3\{3 \cdot [3 - (3 + 3) + 3]\}$

18 Add as many parentheses or other inclusion symbols as you need to make this expression simplify to 0.

$$3 - 3 \cdot 5 + 4 - 3$$

19 Add as many parentheses or other inclusion symbols as you need to make this expression simplify to 28.

$$18 + 3 \cdot 3 - 4 + 3 \cdot 5$$

20 Add as many parentheses or other inclusion symbols as you need to make this expression simplify to 126.

$$5 + 3^2 - 8 + 10 \cdot 9 + 3$$

Chapter Review

Use a separate sheet of paper to do these problems.

1　If $A = \{1, 3, 5, 7\}$, $B = \{1, 4, 9, 16\}$ and $C = \{9, 16\}$, answer these questions.

　　a　Is Set $A \subset$ {prime numbers}? Explain your thinking.
　　b　Is Set $B \subset$ {perfect squares}? Explain your thinking.
　　c　Are sets A and B equal or equivalent? Why?
　　d　$C \subset B$. Find the complement of C?
　　e　What is $A \cup B$?
　　f　What is $A \cap B$?

2　If a real number n is between –3 and 5,
　　a　Write this statement using a compound inequality.
　　b　Write the same statement using interval notation.

3　Why is .035 a rational number? Explain your thinking.

4　What is larger, $(-5)^3$ or $(-5)^5$? You may use a calculator (see p. 51).

5　Use =, >, or < to make each statement true.

　　a　-5 _____ $\left|-5\right|$
　　b　$9 + (-10)$ _____ $-1 + 2$
　　c　$\frac{0}{8}$ _____ -20
　　d　$8(2 + 3)$ _____ $(2 + 3)8$
　　e　$(10 \cdot 2) \cdot 5$ _____ $2 \cdot (5 \cdot 10)$

　　f　$\frac{-144}{12}$ _____ $-16 - 4 \cdot 2 + 12$
　　g　$\sqrt{100}$ _____ 50
　　h　$[3(8 + 2 \cdot 5)]$ _____ $5^2 + 29$
　　i　$-7(3 - 4)$ _____ $-21 + 28$

6　Use a Venn diagram to solve this problem.
　　In an algebra class, 16 students are in band, 7 play sports, and 3 students participate in both activities. Nine are not in band AND do not play sports. How many students are in the algebra class?

7　Two sets that have no elements in common are called <u>disjoint</u> sets. Create your own example of two disjoint sets and show their union and intersection.

8　Write an inequality for this graph. The graph starts halfway between 0 and –1.

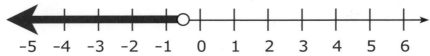

The Rhind Papyrus

Thinking Problem From the History of Mathematics

Rhind Papyrus

The Rhind Papyrus contains ancient Egyptian problems that may date back to around 2600 BCE. Here's problem 79 found in that collection.

> There are 7 houses and in each house there are 7 cats. Each cat kills 7 mice. Each mouse has eaten 7 grains of barley. Each barley would have produced 7 hekat.* What is the sum of all the items listed here?

*A hekat is a unit of volume approximately 1.3 gallons.

Write an expression for the above problem and use the order of operations to simplify.

The Closure Property

A set of numbers is said to be **closed** for a specific operation if the result obtained when an operation is performed on any two numbers in the set is itself a member of the set. If a set of numbers is closed for a particular operation, then it is said to possess the closure property for that operation.

Given the set {-1, 1} and the operation division, notice that dividing any element in the set by any element in the set results in an element in the set. This set is said to be **closed under** division.

$$-1 \div 1 = -1; \quad 1 \div -1 = -1; \quad -1 \div -1 = 1; \quad 1 \div 1 = 1$$

Examples

1   Is the set {-1, 0, 1} closed under multiplication?

If all the elements of the set are multiplied with each other and each element by itself, the answer is always in the set, so this set is closed under multiplication.

$$-1 \cdot -1 = 1; \quad -1 \cdot 0 = 0; \quad -1 \cdot 1 = -1; \quad 0 \cdot -1 = 0; \quad 0 \cdot 0 = 0;$$
$$0 \cdot 1 = 0; \quad 1 \cdot -1 = -1, \quad 1 \cdot 0 = 0; \quad 1 \cdot 1 = 1.$$

2   Are the even numbers closed under multiplication?

$$\{0, 2, 4, 6, 8, ...\}; \cdot$$

Yes, if any even number is multiplied by itself or by another even number in the set, the answer is always an even number.
$$24 \cdot 46 = 1{,}104; \quad 4 \cdot 12 = 48; \quad 0 \cdot 88 = 0$$

3   Is the set {-1, 0, 1} closed under division?

No. This set is not closed under division because none of the numbers can be divided by 0.

4   This table shows results for the operation "Smiley Face."
Is the set closed? Can you find the identity for the set?

☺	M	A	T	H
M	H	M	A	T
A	M	A	T	H
T	A	T	H	M
H	T	H	M	A

Yes, every letter in the table is an element of the original set {M, A, T, H}.

The identity is A because
A ☺ T = T and A ☺ any element of the set gives you the element you started with.

Answer the following questions.

1   Is the set {0, 2, 4} closed under subtraction? Explain your answer.

_____

_____

2   Is the set of reals closed under the operation of addition? Explain your answer.

_____

_____

3   Are the odd numbers closed under the operation of addition?
How about multiplication? Give examples to explain your answers.

_____

_____

4   Are the irrational numbers closed under addition? Give at least one example to explain your answer.

_____

_____

5 Paulo's new speaker has five settings: Off, Low, Medium, High, and Super Loud. The dial only turns clockwise. This is the chart he made to represents where the needle ends up depending on the number of turns.

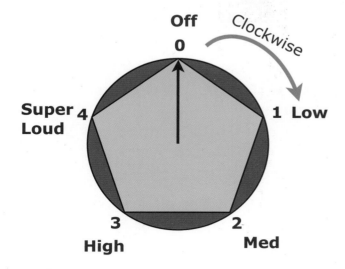

🎼	0	1	2	3	4
0	0	1	2	3	4
1	1	2	3	4	0
2	2	3	4	0	1
3	3	4	0	1	2
4	4	0	1	2	3

a What is the symbol for the operation? _____

b Find 3 🎼 4 = _____. (Start at 3-High and turn the dial four times clockwise.)

c Find 4 🎼 3 = _____. (Start at 4-Super Loud and turn the dial three times clockwise.)

d Is the operation commutative? _____ (Hint: Did you get the same answers for a and b?)

e Does this "mathematical system" representing Paulo's speaker dial have closure? Explain your answer.

_____

f Is there an identity element in the chart? Show with an example. Explain your answer.

_____

g Is (2 🎼 3) 🎼 4 = 2 🎼 (3 🎼 4)? _____ Is 🎼 associative?

Explain your answer. _____

Chapter 2

Evaluating **Expressions** and Solving **Equations**

What are Expressions, Equations, and Inequalities? Look at the following chart.

EXPRESSIONS	EQUATIONS	INEQUALITIES
Hi Maria!	Maria is 14 years old.	Maria is more than 13 years old.
$8 + 20$	$8 + 20 = 28$	$8 + 20 \geq 28$
$a^2 + b^2$	$a^2 + b^2 = c^2$	$a^2 + b^2 < c^2$
$\dfrac{3(x + 8)}{2}$	$18 = 2(x + 8)$	$18 > 2(x + 8)$
-19	$-19 + x = 0$	$-19 \neq 19$
$(a + 3)(a - 3)$	$(a + 3)(a - 3) = 0$	$-3 < w \leq 3$

An **expression** is a mathematical statement or phrase that has no equal or inequality symbol. You can **evaluate** an expression only if you are given **values** for the variables in the expression. An **equation** is any sentence where two sides are separated by an equal sign. When you **solve** an equation you are looking for the value (or values) that make the equation true. Some equations have one answer, others have no answer, and yet others can have many answers as you will soon see. **Inequalities** have an inequality symbol ($<$, $>$, $\leq$, $\geq$, or $\neq$) separating the left and right sides. We will study how to solve inequalities in Chapter 5.

Evaluating Expressions

To **evaluate** an expression means to **substitute** (plug in) the given values and then **simplify**. Do not skip the substituting step.

1　Evaluate $-2ab$ if $a = 3$ and $b = 5$.
　Show the substitution step.

　Remember to use the order of operations.

　$-2(3)(5)$

　$\boxed{-30}$

2　If $y = -4$, evaluate these three expressions.

　Use parentheses here.

a　$5y^2$
　$5(-4)^2$
　$5 \cdot 16$
　$\boxed{80}$

b　$(5y)^2$
　$(5 \cdot -4)^2$
　$(-20)^2$
　$\boxed{400}$

Do not drop the parentheses here.

c　$-y$
　$-(-4)$
　$\boxed{4}$

In the following exercises, $x = -3$, $y = 4$, and $z = -1$. Evaluate these expressions. Remember to show the substitution step.

Remember this means x times y times z.

1　xyz

5　$x^3 + z - y$

2　$5x + 7y - z$

6　$yz^2 + (yz)^2$

3　$x^2y + z^2$

7　$\dfrac{-y - z}{x}$

4　$x(y + z)$

8　$(xyz)^2$

Find the Error

The following problems show common errors made by students. What did the students do wrong? Explain your thinking and then write the correct answer.

1 If $x = 5$, evaluate $3x$. Student wrote: 8.

_____

_____

2 If $a = -5$, evaluate a^2. Student wrote: -25.

_____

_____

3 Evaluate $3a - c$ if $a = 4$ and $c = 2$. Student wrote: -24.

_____

_____

4 Evaluate $|r + s|$ if $r = 10$ and $s = 2$. Student wrote: -12.

_____

_____

5 If $a = 0$ and $b = -3$, evaluate $b \div a$. Student wrote: 0.

_____

_____

6 If $x = 32$ and $y = -4$, evaluate $y \div x$. Student wrote: -8.

_____

_____

7 Evaluate x^3 if $x = 2$. Student wrote: 6.

_____

_____

Equations – A Balancing Act!

An **equation** (sometimes called an **open sentence**) is a sentence with an equal (=) sign separating two expressions, the left side of the equation from the right side of the equation. An **equation** is a **balance**. You must be careful to maintain its balance by doing the same operation to each side of the equation.

Let's take a look at this balancing act. Suppose you have the scale below.

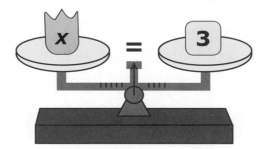

If you double the x bag (you're adding another bag with x), what would you have to do to the right side? Do you see that you would need to double the 3 as well to preserve the balance?

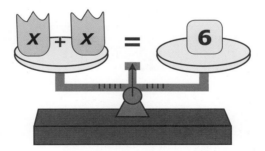

We can now write $2x = 2 \cdot 3$ or $2x = 6$. To **double** means to multiply by 2. What if we now add 4 to the left side? We would have to add 4 to the right side to preserve the balance.

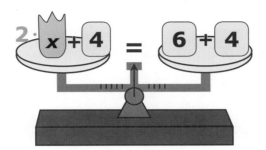

The equation $2x + 4 = 10$ is the same as $2x = 6$ and $x = 3$, because we have preserved its balance. In this chapter we will learn how to start with a longer equation and work backwards to find the value of the variable (or symbol) which we call the **solution** to the equation.

Suppose you have this equation, $x - 5 = 7$, on the balance. This is what would happen if someone were to add 5 to the left side, but nothing to the right side. The equation would no longer be balanced.

What would you have to do to the right side? Yes, you would need to also add a 5 to the right side. This is the most important part of solving equations. Whatever you do to one side of an equation must be done to the other side.

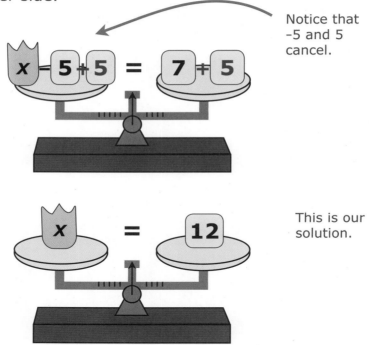

Notice that –5 and 5 cancel.

This is our solution.

Remember to keep each equation balanced.

Steps for Solving Equations

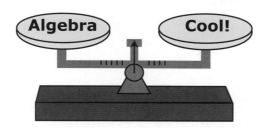

1 **Distribute**.

2 **Combine** all like terms on each side.

3 **Move** variables to the same side.

4 **Undo** + and − (additive inverse).

5 **Undo** · and ÷ (multiplicative inverse or reciprocal).

These steps will become automatic the more you practice. Knowing how to solve equations is the key to solving real life word problems. Solving equations is the core of algebra and this skill will be a great tool to succeed in other math classes. You will be able to vary the steps as long as you keep in mind the idea of a balance, and you are careful using the additive and multiplicative inverses.

We will start with steps 4 and 5, which are the steps used to solve simple equations. Then we will move onto steps 1-3, which are used together with steps 4 and 5 to solve longer equations. Longer equations are not necessarily harder.

Even though steps 4 and 5 are pretty easy to do in your head, practicing doing the steps will help you become an expert when the equations have more steps.

Later, to make equations with fractions easier to solve, we will learn how to use the least common denominator (LCD) to get rid of all the denominators without changing the balance of the equation. We will also learn a strategy to make equations with decimals easier to solve.

The more you practice and think about every step, the more comfortable you will become!

Step 4 – Solving Simple Equations Using the Additive Inverse

In this section we will learn how to use the **additive inverse** to solve for the variable. Remember, although you may be able to solve most of these equations by doing the work in your head, <u>please</u> show your steps because you will need all these steps to solve longer equations.

1
$$x - 5 = 7$$
$$+5 = +5$$
$$\overline{x + 0 = 12}$$
$$x = 12$$

Start on the side that has the variable. Undo the subtraction by adding 5 (5 is the additive inverse of –5). Remember to add 5 to **both** sides.
You can also cross out –5 and 5 as they cancel.

This line is optional.

2
$$-52 = y + 38$$
$$-38 \qquad -38$$
$$\overline{-90 = y}$$

Start on the side that has the variable. Undo + 38 by subtracting 38 from each side. Be careful not to lose any signs. To join –38 and –52, you will add and keep the sign.

3 Check that –90 is the solution to the equation –52 = y + 38.

Substitute –90 in place of the variable. Does –52 = –90 + 38? The answer is yes. You can always check your answer.

Solve the following equations. Remember to show your steps.

1 $w + 10 = -20$

2 $0 = R + 11$

3 $y - 7 = 6.5$

4 $y - 20 = -10$

5 $15 = x + 19$

6 $-20 = y + 40$

7 $P - 4 = -6$

8 $18 + x = -24$

9 Check your answer to problem 6 here.

10 Check your answer to problem 8 here.

11 $139 + w = 400$

12 $-4.56 = T - 3.1$

Step 5 – Solving Simple Equations Using the Multiplicative Inverse

When a number is multiplying or dividing a variable, you can solve for the variable by using the multiplicative inverse. Remember to start on the side that has the variable.

Remember the expression $3x$ means 3 times x.
The 3 is called the <u>coefficient</u>.

1 $3x = -27$

$$\frac{3x}{3} = \frac{-27}{3}$$

$$x = -9$$

To undo the 3, divide both sides by 3 or multiply by $\frac{1}{3}$ (the multiplicative inverse).

2 $\frac{y}{12} = 3$

$$\frac{12}{1} \cdot \frac{y}{12} = 3 \cdot 12$$

$$y = 36$$

To undo the 12, multiply both sides by 12 (the multiplicative inverse).

3 $\frac{3}{4}w = 120$

$$\frac{4}{3} \cdot \frac{3}{4}w = 120 \cdot \frac{4}{3}$$

$$1w = 40 \cdot 4$$
$$w = 160$$

Instead of dividing by 3 and then multiplying by 4, multiply by $\frac{4}{3}$ (the multiplicative inverse of $\frac{3}{4}$). 3 goes into 120 forty times.

$$\frac{4}{3} \cdot \frac{3}{4} = 1$$

$1 \cdot w$ is the same as w

4 $-y = -50$

$$\frac{-1y}{-1} = \frac{-50}{-1}$$

$$y = 50$$

$-y$ means $-1 \cdot y$, so you can divide each side by -1.

Shortcut:
You can change both signs on each side of the equation. However, in longer equations you will have to change **all** the signs.
Example:
$-y + 2 = -20$ is the same as $y - 2 = 20$.

Practice

Solve the following equations. Remember to start on the side that has the variable. Show the steps.

1 $5y = -100$

2 $8 = 4x$

3 $4 = 8x$

4 $-9 = -y$

5 $-w = 65$

6 $-\dfrac{2}{3}x = 66$

7 $-w = -3.56$

8 $\dfrac{y}{7} = -14$

9 $-\dfrac{y}{3} = -4$

10 $\dfrac{3}{5}y = -15$

11 $90 = 18y$

12 $2 = \dfrac{y}{6}$

13 $-\dfrac{3}{4} = \dfrac{6}{5}w$

14 $-52y = 26$

15 $-18 = -2x$

Steps 4 and 5 Together – Solving Two-Step Equations

Do you remember that to follow the order of operations we always do multiplication or division (left to right) and then addition or subtraction (left to right)? Now since we're trying to solve equations we will be working backwards to find our answer. When solving two-step equations, you must undo addition or subtraction **(step 4)** before the multiplication or division or using reciprocals **(step 5)**. Remember to start on the side that has the variable.

1

$$5x - 6 = 79$$
$$ + 6 \quad + 6$$
$$\frac{5x}{5} = \frac{85}{5}$$
$$x = 13$$

Undo – 6 by adding 6.
Undo the 5 by dividing by 5.

Remember to do the same on each side of the equation.

$1 \cdot x$ is the same as x.

2

$$0 = \frac{4}{5}x - 20$$
$$+ 20 \qquad + 20$$
$$20 = \frac{4}{5}x$$
$$\frac{5}{4} \cdot 20 = \frac{5}{4} \cdot \frac{4}{5}x$$
$$25 = x$$

Undo – 20 by adding 20.

Undo $\frac{4}{5}$ by multiplying by the multiplicative inverse or reciprocal $\frac{5}{4}$.
4 goes into 20 five times and 5 times 5 = 25.

Don't forget you can always check your answer.

$$0 = \frac{4}{5} \cdot 25 - 20?$$

$$0 = 20 - 20? \text{ Yes!}$$

3

$$-\frac{6}{7}w + 8 = 50$$
$$\phantom{-\frac{6}{7}w} - 8 \quad - 8$$
$$-\frac{6}{7}w = 42$$
$$-\frac{7}{6} \cdot -\frac{6}{7}w = 42 \cdot -\frac{7}{6}$$
$$w = -49$$

Undo + 8 by adding -8 (or subtracting 8).

Then undo with the multiplicative inverse of $-\frac{6}{7}$ by multiplying by $-\frac{7}{6}$ on each side.

Remember to watch your signs.

Thinking Questions

Answer the following questions.

1 One of the most common errors students make when solving this type of equation is shown here. Look at where the student wrote the 6 on the left side of the equation. Why is this wrong? Explain your thinking.

$$\frac{w}{6} = 18$$

$$6 \cdot \frac{w}{6} = 18 \cdot 6$$

_____

_____

_____

_____

2 When given the equation $-1\frac{2}{3}x = 60$, Alexis rewrote it as $-\frac{5}{3}x = 60$. Was he correct? Can you solve his new equation?

_____

_____

3 Laura and Gwen were arguing about the easiest way to solve this equation, $.65x = 26$. Laura wanted to change the decimal to the fraction $\frac{13}{20}$ first and then use the reciprocal. Gwen wanted to divide by .65 on both sides. Who is correct? Finish their equations and explain.

Laura's Method	Gwen's Method	
$\frac{20}{13} \cdot \frac{13}{20}x = 26 \cdot \frac{20}{13}$	$\frac{.65x}{.65} = \frac{26}{.65}$	You may use a calculator for Gwen's method if you wish.

_____

_____

_____

④ John solved this equation by using these steps below. Are John's steps correct? Explain your thinking.

$6x + 5 = 11$
$\quad -5 \quad -5$

_____

$\dfrac{6x}{6x} = \dfrac{6}{6x}$

_____

$x = 1$

_____

⑤ Luisa rushed through her math homework one night and she solved this equation, $\dfrac{w}{3} + 7 = 5$, by doing the steps below. Then she checked it and realized that 8 divided by 3 plus 7 doesn't equal 5. What did she do wrong? Explain your thinking.

$3 \cdot \dfrac{w}{3} + 7 = 5 \cdot 3$

_____

$w + 7 = 15$
$\quad -7 \quad -7$

_____

$w = 8$

_____

⑥ Why do you think these equations give you the same answers? Remember what you learned about the balancing scales at the beginning of this chapter. Solve the equations, and then explain your thinking.

$$4x - 6 = 10 \qquad\Big|\qquad 12x - 18 = 30 \qquad\Big|\qquad \frac{1}{2}x - \frac{3}{4} = \frac{5}{4}$$

_____

_____

_____

More Practice

Solve the following equations. Remember to show the steps.

1 $3w - 6 = 12$

2 $-4x + 5 = -15$

3 $0 = 4 - 5y$

4 $8 - y = 10$

5 $\dfrac{w}{7} + 8 = 12$

6 $-\dfrac{4}{5}y + \dfrac{1}{2} = 20\dfrac{1}{2}$

7 $90x + 5 = 45$

8 $6.5 = -3g - 2.5$

9 $\dfrac{4}{9}d - 9 = -45$

10 $45 - \dfrac{3}{5}p = 102$

11 $7 - h = 46$

12 $\dfrac{w}{8} - 34 = 78$

13 $-\dfrac{5}{4}y = \dfrac{5}{4}$

14 $96 = -3x + 6$

15 $3 = \dfrac{w}{2} + 3$

16 $4.5x + 9 = 99$

17 $7a = \dfrac{28}{3}$ Remember, the reciprocal of 7 is $\frac{1}{7}$.

18 $-3x = 0$

Step 3 – Moving Variables to the Same Side

When you have variables on both sides of an equation, you may not know where to start. At first, I suggest that you move the variable terms (groups with variables) over to the left side. The goal is to have **variable** terms on one side and **constants** (numbers without variables) on the other side of the equation.

1

$$5w + 4 = 3w + 10$$
$$\underline{-3w \qquad -3w}$$
$$2w + 4 = 10$$
$$\underline{-4 \qquad -4}$$
$$\frac{2w}{2} = \frac{6}{2}$$
$$w = 3$$

Undo $3w$ by adding $-3w$ ONCE to each side.

You can ONLY combine (join) a **variable** term with a **variable** term and a **constant** with a **constant**.

Notice that you now have a two-step equation.

2

$$-4y + 8 = -8y - 4$$
$$\underline{+8y \qquad +8y}$$
$$4y + 8 = -4$$
$$\underline{-8 \qquad -8}$$
$$\frac{4y}{4} = \frac{-12}{4}$$
$$y = -3$$

To undo $-8y$, add $8y$ ONCE per side.

— Do not lose this negative.

add, keep sign!

Notice that you can solve the same equation by starting on a different side and even starting with the constants first. But, you must undo the operations correctly and undo each term only ONCE per side.

3

$$-4y + 8 = -8y - 4$$
$$\underline{+4y \qquad +4y}$$
$$8 = -4y - 4$$
$$\underline{+4 \qquad +4}$$
$$\frac{12}{-4} = \frac{-4y}{-4}$$
$$-3 = y$$

4

$$-4y + 8 = -8y - 4$$
$$\underline{-8 \qquad -8}$$
$$-4y = -8y - 12$$
$$\underline{+8y \qquad +8y}$$
$$\frac{4y}{4} = \frac{-12}{4}$$
$$y = -3$$

Practice

Solve the following equations.   Remember to show your steps.   Refer to examples 1 and 2.

1 $7c + 8 = 5c + 20$

2 $9w + 7 = -11w - 3$

3 $9 + 3x = 2x - 10$

4 $-8a - 6 = 10 + 8a$

5 $-9w - 8 = -8w + 2$

6 $\frac{1}{2}y + 7 = \frac{5}{2}y + 3$

7 $25 + 25W = 75 + 5W$

8 $Y + 34 = -Y - 36$

9 $18 - y = 23 + 4y$

10 $9x + 9 = 81 + 3x$

Putting All the Steps Together

Now, we're using all the steps because the equations are longer, but not necessarily harder.

Steps for Solving Equations

1. **Distribute**.
2. **Combine** all like terms on each side.
3. **Move** variables to the same side.
4. **Undo** + and − (additive inverse).
5. **Undo** · and ÷ (multiplicative inverse or reciprocal).

---

1 $10(x - 1) + 20 = 5(x - 3)$

$10(x - 1) + 20 = 5(x - 3)$ 1   Distribute.

$10x - 10 + 20 = 5x - 15$ 2   Combine like terms on each side.

$10x + 10 = 5x - 15$ 3   Move variables to the same side.
$-5x -5x$

$\underline{}$

$5x + 10 = -15$ 4   Undo + and −.
$ -10 -10$

$\underline{}$

$\dfrac{5x}{5} = \dfrac{-25}{5}$ 5   Undo · and ÷.

$x = -5$

---

2 $18 - 5(x - 1) = -10 + 3$ 1   Distribute.

$18 - 5x + 5 = -7$ 2   Combine like terms on each side.

     3   Step 3 is not needed here.

$23 - 5x = -7$ 4   Undo + and −.
$-23 -23$

$\underline{}$

$\dfrac{-5x}{-5} = \dfrac{-30}{-5}$ 5   Undo · and ÷.

$x = 6$

3 $15w - (w + 2) = 3w - 5w$

$15w - \mathbf{1}(w + 2) = 3w - 5w$

$15w - w - 2 \quad = -2w$

$14w - 2 \quad\quad = -2w$
$+2w \quad\quad\quad\quad +2w$

$16w - 2 \quad\quad = \mathbf{0}$
$+2 \quad\quad\quad\quad +2$

$\dfrac{16w}{16} \quad = \quad \dfrac{2}{16}$

$w \quad\quad = .125 \text{ or } \dfrac{1}{8}$

1 Distribute. Write "–1" in front of the parenthesis. The entire parentheses is being subtracted.

2 Combine like terms on each side.

3 Move variables to the same side.
It would have been faster to subtract "14w" from each side, but this shows what happens if "2w" is added to each side. You must write 0 on the right side.

4 Undo + and –.

5 Undo · and ÷.

The above examples highlight some of the areas where you need to be careful when you distribute. Math is not about working fast and just getting an answer. Take your time, pay attention to details, and make sure you follow the steps in this section.

Does every equation have an answer? No! Look at these two equations.

4 $8x + 5 = 8x + 5$
$-8x \quad\quad\quad -8x$

$5 = 5$
$-5 \quad -5$

$0 = 0$

5 $3(x + 2) = 3x + 9$

$3x + 6 \quad = 3x + 9$
$-3x \quad\quad\quad\quad -3x$

$6 \quad = \quad 9$

Be careful, the answer is NOT 0. At every stage of the equation, the left side is equal to the right side. Any value for x would work, so this equation has **infinite** answers. This is called an **identity equation**.

You can stop here. There is NO solution to this equation. There is no value that will make it true. You can also say the answer is { } or ∅.

Equation Scramble

Solve the following equations and write the letter that corresponds to the answer below to find out the answer to the riddle.

(s) $3(x - 9) = 2x$

(d) $7x + 3 - 3x = 2 - 5x - 8$

(i) $8(x - 1) = 3(x - 4) - 6$

(h) $-2(x + 3) - 3(x - 1) = -4(x - 5)$

(u) $-2(x - 2) = 2 - 4x + 8$

(t) $8x + 3 - 5x = 3 - 5x$

(p) $-(x - 2) = 5 - 3(x - 2) + x$

(n) $7x - 1 - 7x = 5x + 19$

(o) $11(x - 11) = 6x + 4$

(a) $8(x - 1) = 7(x - 1)$

This Greek mathematician is sometimes called the Father of Algebra. He wrote a collection of books called *Arithmetica,* which contains many equations and applications of algebra. He is thought to have lived between 200-284 C.E.

___ ___ ___ ___ ___ ___ ___ ___ ___ ___
-1   -2   25   9   -23   1   -4   0   3   27

Thinking About Equations

Answer the following questions.

1 Mara thought that the left side and the right side of all identity equations always have to look the same. So when Julia solved this equation and claimed any value for *Y* would work, Mara did not agree because the left side of the equation looked very different than the right side. Solve the following equation. Who was right? Why?

$\frac{1}{3}(3Y - 12) - 18 = 15Y - 14Y - 22$ _____

_____

_____

_____

2 Circle the <u>two</u> mistakes made by this student, then solve the equation.

$4(w + 1) = -3(3w + 4)$ Corrected Work

$$4w + 1 \;=\; -9w + 12 \qquad\qquad 4(w + 1) = -3(3w + 4)$$

$$\underline{+ 9w \qquad\qquad + 9w}$$

$$13w + 1 \;=\; 12$$

$$\underline{- 1 \qquad - 1}$$

$$\frac{13w}{13} \;=\; \frac{11}{13}$$

$$w \;=\; \frac{11}{13}$$

3 Seth did not like working with fractions, so he decided to change $\frac{1}{3}$ to .3 while his friend Paulo kept the fraction. Who's correct? Finish their equations and explain what you discover.

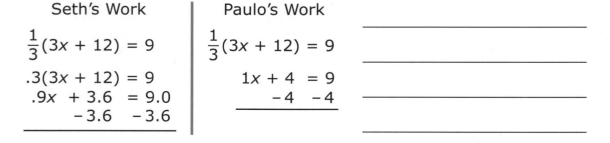

Seth's Work | Paulo's Work

$\frac{1}{3}(3x + 12) = 9$ | $\frac{1}{3}(3x + 12) = 9$

$.3(3x + 12) = 9$ | $1x + 4 \;= 9$

$.9x + 3.6 \;= 9.0$ | $\underline{\quad -4 \quad -4 \quad}$

$\underline{\quad -3.6 \quad -3.6 \quad}$

_____

_____

_____

_____

4   Larry solved this equation and got an answer of 7. Then he rushed through the check, and when he couldn't get his equation to balance, he erased his original work. Solve the equation. Is the answer 7? What was Larry's mistake?

> Most mistakes are made on easy concepts because we tend to work faster on the parts we know how to do.

Solve for y:

$$5y + 10 = 6 + 3(2y - 1)$$

Larry's Check

$$5y + 10 = 6 + 3(2y - 1)$$
$$5 \cdot \mathbf{7} + 10 = 6 + 3(2 \cdot \mathbf{7} - 1) \text{ ?}$$
$$35 + 10 = 6 + 3(8) \text{ ?}$$
$$45 = 30 \text{ ?}$$

Explain the mistake that Larry made.

_____

_____

5   Given the following equation, two students solved it in two different ways. Explain why they both got the same answer. Remember what you know about balancing an equation.

Olga's Way

$$\frac{Y}{5} + 3 = 9$$

$$5 \cdot \frac{Y}{5} + 5 \cdot 3 = 5 \cdot 9$$

$$Y + 15 = 45$$

$$Y = 30$$

Michael's Way

$$\frac{Y}{5} + 3 = 9$$
$$-3 \quad -3$$

$$5 \cdot \frac{Y}{5} = 6 \cdot 5$$

$$Y = 30$$

_____

_____

_____

6   When Kendall tried to solve this equation, he decided there was no solution. Did Kendall do something wrong? What step did he miss? What is the correct answer? Explain your thinking.

Solve for Q: $8Q = 6Q$ _____

$$\frac{8\cancel{Q}}{\cancel{Q}} = \frac{6\cancel{Q}}{\cancel{Q}}$$ _____

_____

$8 = 6$ _____

_____

_____

7   Solve these long equations. Watch out for negatives. The answer to the first one is –7 and the answer to the second one is –5.

a $-2 - (x - 3) + 3 = -5(x + 3) - 9$

b $4(y - 4) + 3(y + 2) - 2(y - 5) + 9 = 2(2y - 1) + 3(y + 2) - 3y$

Equations With Decimals and Fractions

Equations with decimals and fractions can be made much easier to solve by getting rid of the fractions and the decimals. Remember you can always change a fraction to a decimal but do not change any fraction to a decimal if the decimal repeats as you won't get the same answer (see p. 48, problem 3).

To change a decimal to a fraction in your graphing calculator, type the decimal, say .125, then go to (MATH) and press (ENTER) twice. You will get ⅛. If you type a fraction by using the division sign, the calculator will change it to a decimal, but again make sure it's not a repeating decimal. You can also type ⅛, go to (MATH) and down to 2-DEC and it will change it to a decimal.

Use this key to enter exponents.

Remember that to type negatives, you must use the NEGATIVE key (under the number 3) and NOT the subtraction sign.

In this section, we are going to learn how to get rid of decimals and fractions. The use of the calculator will be optional, although it's very handy for checking your work.

---

1 $.03x + .05(1,000 - x) = 34$

Multiply **each** term (group) by 100.

Two decimal places.

$3x + 5(1,000 - x) = 3,400$

$3x + 5,000 - 5x = 3,400$

Notice that nothing inside the parentheses was multiplied by 100, as that entire middle group is one term.

$-2x + 5,000 = 3,400$
$ - 5,000 = -5,000$

$$\frac{-2x}{-2} = \frac{-1,600}{-2}$$

Now, follow the steps for solving equations (p. 45).

$x = 800$

---

2 $.2(y - 1) + .008 = 1$

$200(y - 1) + 8 = 1,000$

$200y - 200 + 8 = 1,000$

$$200y - 192 = 1,000$$
$$\ + 192 \quad\ + 192$$

$$\frac{200y}{200} = \frac{1,192}{200}$$

$y = 5.96$ or $\dfrac{149}{25}$

To get rid of all the decimals you need to multiply each term by 1,000 this time.

Follow the steps for solving equations (p. 45).

Either answer is accepted unless told otherwise, but make sure all fractions are simplified.

Equations with fractions look complicated. If you know how to find the least common denominator (LCD), you'll be able to get rid of all your denominators and make the equation easier to solve. Remember, every term of the equation must be multiplied by the LCD.

1 $\dfrac{y}{5} - \dfrac{y}{10} = 2$

$10 \cdot \dfrac{y}{5} - 10 \cdot \dfrac{y}{10} = 10 \cdot 2$

$2y - y = 20$

$y = 20$

The LCD is 10. Multiply each term of the equation by 10.

5 goes into 10 twice. 10 goes into 10 one time. Then multiply the 2 by 10.

Follow the steps for solving equations (p. 45).

You can see that by multiplying by the LCD, the equation was much easier to solve. Don't forget that you can check any equation you solve.

Check: $\dfrac{y}{5} - \dfrac{y}{10} = 2$ ⟵ When you do a check, copy the equation over.

$$\dfrac{20}{5} - \dfrac{20}{10} = 2$$

$$4 - 2 = 2 \quad \text{Yes!}$$

2

$$\frac{2x+5}{4} - \frac{10x+13}{8} = 2x+1$$

The LCD is 8. Multiply each term by 8.
Be very careful with the negative!

$$\frac{^{8}(2x+5)}{4} - \frac{^{8}(10x+13)}{8} = {}^{8}2x + {}^{8}1$$

It helps to surround the bigger terms with parentheses.

4 goes into 8 twice. 8 goes into 8 once. Multiply 8 times $2x$ and 8 times 1.

$$2(2x+5) - 1(10x+13) = 16x + 8$$

Follow the steps.

$$4x + 10 - 10x - 13 = 16x + 8$$

$$
\begin{array}{rcl}
-6x - 3 &=& 16x + 8 \\
-16x & & -16x \\
\hline
-22x - 3 &=& 8 \\
+3 & & +3 \\
\hline
-22x &=& 11 \\
\overline{-22} & & \overline{-22} \\
x &=& -.5 \text{ or } -\frac{1}{2}
\end{array}
$$

Using a separate sheet of paper, solve each equation for the variable.

1. $-12x - 3 = -27$

2. $2 + 3(y - 1) = 11$

3. $8 - (2a - 1) = 1$

4. $4K - 7 = 2(2K + 3)$

5. $9R = 10R$

6. $-\frac{4}{5}w = -100$

7. $.5 + .06(y - 2) = 1$

8. $.08(4y + 5) - .03(2y - 3) = .36$

9. $-\frac{x+3}{7} = 18$

10. $\frac{3x}{2} + \frac{8-4x}{7} = 3$

11. $\frac{n+5}{12} - \frac{2n-3}{8} = 2$

12. $\frac{2a+3}{9} - \frac{4a-1}{6} - \frac{9-8a}{18} = 0$

Working With Formulas

The more you understand the steps involved in solving an equation with one variable, the better you will do solving for a variable in terms of other variables. Formulas usually have many variables.

The formula to find the area of a triangle is $A = \frac{1}{2}bh.$

Suppose you were given the area (A) and the base (b) of many triangles and had to find the height (h) of each one, you would save time by rewriting the formula as $h = \dfrac{2A}{b}$. Rewriting formulas is a skill you will use not only in math class but in many fields.

1   Solve for h if $A = \frac{1}{2}bh$

Area = 40
base = 10

$$2 \cdot A = \frac{2 \cdot 1}{2}bh$$

Multiply both sides by 2 to get rid of the fraction.

$$\frac{2A}{b} = \frac{b \cdot h}{b}$$

$$\frac{2A}{b} = h$$

Notice that to leave **h** alone on one side you must undo multiplication, so divide by b on both sides.

To find the height of the triangle above really quickly, take the area of 40, multiply by 2, and divide by 10. The height is 8 units.

2   The formula for the area of a trapezoid is $A = \frac{1}{2}h(b + B)$, where h represents the height and b and B the two bases (parallel sides) of the trapezoid. Solve for B (the larger base).

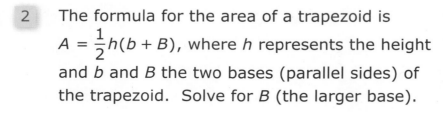

$$A = \frac{1}{2}h(b + B)$$

Multiply both sides by 2 to get rid of the fraction.

$$2A = h(b + B)$$
$$2A = hb + hB$$
$$\underline{-hb \quad -hb}$$

Distribute the h.

$$\frac{2A - hb}{h} = \frac{hB}{h}$$

Subtract hb from each side.

$$\frac{2A - hb}{h} = B$$

Divide by h on each side.

This is the same answer as $B = \dfrac{2A}{h} - b$ if you divide each term by h.

Remember, many times you may end up with more steps, but make sure you are following the inverse operations correctly and keeping your equation balanced.

3   Solve for x.

$$\frac{4}{x} = \frac{a}{b}$$

First, notice the x is in the denominator. $(x \neq 0$ and $b \neq 0)$.

$$\frac{ax}{a} = \frac{4b}{a}$$

Also, notice that this is a proportion equation (a fraction = a fraction), so cross multiply.

Divide each side by a. $(a \neq 0)$

$$x = \frac{4b}{a}$$

A very important formula you will need if you travel to other countries is the Fahrenheit/Celsius formula, unless you carry a conversion chart. Actually those conversion charts were created by using this formula!

4   Solve for F in terms of C.

$$C = \frac{5}{9}(F - 32)$$

Multiply each side by 9 to get rid of the denominator.

$$9C = 5(F - 32)$$

Distribute the 5.

$$9C = 5F - 160$$

Add 160 to each side.

$$\underline{+160 \qquad\qquad +160}$$

Divide by 5 on each side.

$$\frac{9C + 160}{5} = \frac{5F}{5}$$

$$\frac{9C + 160}{5} = \frac{9}{5}C + \frac{160}{5}$$

$$F = \frac{9}{5}C + 32 \quad \longleftarrow$$

If someone had a fever of 40° Celsius, which formula would be better to use? What is the same temperature in Fahrenheit?

_____

Formula Practice

Show your steps.

1   Area of a parallelogram; $A = bh$; solve for h.

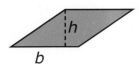

2   Area of a circle; $A = \pi r^2$; solve for π.

3   Einstein's theory of relativity: $E = mc^2$; solve for m. E = energy, m = mass and c = speed of light. This formula was developed by Albert Einstein (1879-1955) to find how much energy would be produced if a quantity of matter could be completely changed into energy.

4   Perimeter of a rectangle; $P = 2(L + W)$; solve for W.

5   Volume of a sphere; $V = \frac{4}{3}\pi r^3$; solve for π.

6   Solve for x: $2x + b = c$

7   Solve for a: $2b - a = d$

Chapter Review

Using a separate sheet of paper, solve the equations. Remember to show your steps.

1   $D = RT$; solve for T.

2   $M = \dfrac{D}{V}$; solve for D; $V \neq 0$.

3   $2 = r - w$; solve for w.

4   $4y = -8x$; solve for y.

5   $3b - b + c = 5a$; solve for b.

6   $I = prt$; solve for t.

7   $d = \dfrac{1}{2} gt^2$; solve for g.

8   $abx = ab$; solve for x.

9   $p = a - prt$; solve for a.

10   $P = \dfrac{W}{r}$; solve for r; $r \neq 0$.

11   $W + L = 3W - 2L$; solve for W.

12   $3x - 7b = 5x$; solve for x.

13   $\dfrac{x}{3} + 8 = x + a$; solve for x.

14   $w + 36 = 1 - 4(w - 5)$

15   $\dfrac{3}{4} w + 23 = -1$

16   $-\dfrac{1}{2} w + \dfrac{3}{4} = w - \dfrac{3}{4}$

17   $69 = 4(w + 5) - (w - 1)$

18   $.03w + .1 = .003$

19   $-18 = \dfrac{-w + 3}{8}$

20   $\dfrac{2w + 3}{9} - \dfrac{4w - 1}{6} = 1$

21   $.01(51w - 2) = -w + 3$

22   $2(w + 5) = 2w + 20 - 10$

23   $\dfrac{1}{w} + 3 = \dfrac{3}{4}$

24   $-(w + 3) = -(w - 3) + 3$

25   $\dfrac{1}{x} = 10$

Fun Equations

Use your knowledge of equations to solve these. Use a separate sheet of paper if you need more space.

1   Solve for the witch's hat.

2   Solve for the apple.

3   Solve for the calculator.

$$\frac{1}{\text{[calculator]}} = \frac{1}{\text{[pencil]}}$$

4   Solve for the owl.

Important Women Mathematicians

Women have made very important contributions to mathematics. Below is a list of women mathematicians. Research these mathematicians online. Write the letter of each mathematician's contribution in the blank.

____ **1** **Emmy Noether**
1882-1935
born: Germany

a Known for her work on number theory and her work on elasticity. She proved that if x, y, and z are integers and if $x^5 + y^5 = z^5$, then x, y, or z must be divisible by 5.

____ **2** **Maria Gaetana Agnesi**
1718-1799
born: Milan, Italy

b Known for her work in mathematics and astronomy. Wrote *Mechanisms of the Heavens*.

____ **3** **Sonya Kovalevskaya**
1850-1891
born: Russia

c Head of the Platonist School in Alexandria. Lectured in mathematics and philosophy. Often called the First Lady of Algebra.

____ **4** **Mary Fairfax Sommerville**
1780-1872
born: Scotland

d Known for her work on abstract algebra and physics. Einstein referred to her as the most important woman in the history of mathematics.

____ **5** **Sophie Germain**
1776-1831
born: Paris, France

e Mathematician, physicist, writer, and advocate for women's rights. Won an award from the French Academy of Science for her paper *On the Rotation of a Solid Body Around a Fixed Point*.

____ **6** **Hypatia**
c. 350-370 – 415 C.E.
born: Greece

f Best known for her curve graph, $y = \dfrac{a^3}{x^2 + a^2}$. Wrote *Analytical Institutions*, a book on algebra and calculus.

Chapter 3

From Words to Algebra – Translating and Solving **Word Problems**

Here are some of the key words to remember that indicate addition, subtraction, multiplication, division, or setting quantities equal.

Addition	**Subtraction**	**Multiplication**	**Division**	**Equal**
add	minus	times	into	is (are)
plus	less	by	quotient	gives
sum*	less than**	product	break into	is the same as
increase	from	of	by	yields
more	difference*	twice	half	becomes
augment	take away	squared		results
exceeds	decrease	cubed		
	diminish			

* The words "sum" and "difference" in a word problem indicate you will need to use parentheses when you translate. Because of the order of operations, when a sum or difference has to be done first, parentheses are used.

**Note the distinction between "less than" for subtraction and "is less than" with all three words together, which means an inequality.

Examples   These problems have been translated into algebraic expressions or equations.

Translated

1	x less y	$x - y$
2	x less than y	$y - x$
3	a from b	$b - a$

Notice how "less than" and "from" reverse the order of the two given variables.

4	twice x plus one	$2x + 1$
5	twice the sum of x plus one	$2(x + 1)$

Notice how the word "sum" requires parentheses since it means the addition must be done before multiplying by 2.

6	eight diminished by w	$8 - w$
7	the product of five and y	$5y$
8	the quotient of x divided by two	$\dfrac{x}{2}$
9	twice the difference of y from eight yields twenty	$2(8 - y) = 20$
10	four from twice x is forty	$2x - 4 = 40$

Translation Practice

Translate the following problems into algebraic expressions.

1   three times *x*   _____

2   four less *y*   _____

3   *w* plus twice *y*   _____

4   eighteen less than *w*   _____

5   twice the difference of *w* less than five   _____

6   the product of *x* and *y* increased by ten   _____

7   ten decreased by twice *x*   _____

8   twenty increased by the quotient of *x* divided by two   _____

9   seven from three times *w*   _____

10   the sum of twice *a* plus eight squared   _____

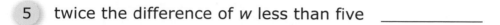

Translate the following problems into algebraic equations.

11   eleven from *w* is equal to twice *w*.   _____

12   twice *a* results in three times the sum of *a* plus one.   _____

13   twice *a* is the same as three times *a* plus one.   _____

14   the sum of *z* plus seven divided by seven becomes fifty.   _____

15   *x* less fifteen yields *x* less than fifteen.   _____

Strategies for Solving Word Problems

Below are ten strategies for solving word problems. You should follow these steps for every word problem.

Word Problem Strategies

1. Read and re-read every problem carefully.

2. Underline or circle key words but keep in mind the order in which the key words appear in the problem.

3. Make a diagram or picture, especially in geometry problems.

4. Make sure you understand what is being asked. Sometimes it helps to say the problem in your own words.

5. Identify the variable. The variable is what you know the least about. If you are using one equation, write the rest of the information in terms of that variable. Include a let statement to indicate what you have identified as the variable. (We will learn how to use two variables later.)

6. Use a chart or table to organize the information.

7. Ask yourself if you can solve a similar, but simpler problem.

8. Find a pattern with numbers to see if you can generalize and arrive at an algebraic equation that represents what is taking place.

9. Once you solve the problem, always ask if your answer makes sense.

10. Make sure you used the correct units and label your answer.

One thing you must not do is quit before you start, or believe that you just can't do word problems. If you are struggling with a word problem, explain your process to another person. Someone else may have a different method to solve the same problem. The more you share your thinking, the stronger a problem solver you will become.

Diagramming Geometry Word Problems

Use a diagram to help you visualize what information is being given and what information is being asked in a geometry word problem. Every time you read a problem that involves geometric concepts, make a diagram.

Examples

1   The width of a rectangle <u>is</u> sixteen <u>less than</u> twice the <u>length</u>. If the <u>perimeter</u> is 40 meters, find the length and the width.

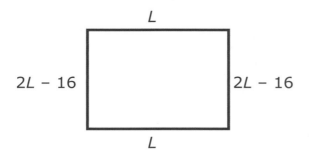

Let statement:

Let length = L

This is how you identify your variable.

Then width = $2L - 16$

Thinking Box

Draw a rectangle. It does not have to be to scale.

<u>Perimeter</u> is the total distance around your shape.

The variable is what you know the least about. You are being told information about the width in terms of the length, so length (word at the end of that sentence) is your variable. Yes, you can rewrite length in terms of width but you don't need to do that in this problem.

Width is 16 <u>less than</u> twice L. Label your picture.

Equation: $L + L + 2L - 16 + 2L - 16 = 40$ Add four sides.

or $2L + 2(2L - 16) = 40$ Either of these two equations can be your starting equation.

Solving the equation:

$$2L + 4L - 32 = 40$$
$$ +32 \ +32$$
$$\overline{}$$
$$\frac{6L}{6} = \frac{72}{6}$$
$$L = 12$$ Now, go back and find the width by substituting. $2L - 16 = 2 \cdot 12 - 16$.

Answer:
length: 12 m
width: 8 m

Check your answer.

Does $12 + 12 + 8 + 8 = 40$? Yes!

2 The Baker family is raising money to surround the community swimming pool with a fence. The <u>perimeter</u> of the swimming pool is 496 feet. The length is two more than twice the <u>width</u>. Find the pool's dimensions.

$$L = 2 + 2W$$

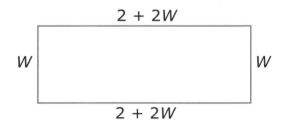

2 + 2W

W   W

2 + 2W

This is NOT an inequality. "is two more than" is not the same as "two is more than."

An inequality has each of the three words (is more than) right next to each other, as we'll see in Chapter 5.

Let statement:
Let W = width
2 + 2W = length

Do not forget to show your let statement.

Thinking Box

Draw a rectangle. It does not have to be to scale.

<u>Perimeter</u> is the total distance around your shape.

Equation: 2W + 2(2 + 2W) = 496
$$2W + 4 + 4W = 496$$
$$6W + 4 = 496$$
$$ -4 -4$$
_____
$$\frac{6W}{6} = \frac{492}{6}$$
$$W = 82$$

The variable is what you know the least about. You are being told information about the length so this time width is the variable.

$2 + 2W$ is the same as $2W + 2$ (commutative property for +)

Answer:
width: 82'
length: 166'

Make sure to label your answer.

3 In △ABC, ∠C is three times the measure of ∠B and ∠A is twenty more than four times the measure of ∠B. Find the measure of <u>each</u> angle.

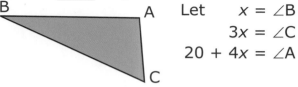

B   A

C

Let $x = \angle B$
$3x = \angle C$
$20 + 4x = \angle A$

Thinking Box

Draw a triangle. It does not have to be to scale.

Equation: $x + 3x + 20 + 4x = 180$
$$8x + 20 = 180$$
$$8x = 160$$
$$x = 20$$

You should be able to follow the last two steps not shown here.

Answers: ∠B = 20°, ∠C = 60°,
∠A = 100°

Remember the sum of the measures of the angles in any triangle is 180°.

What angle should be x?

Geometry Practice

Solve the following word problems. Make sure to identify your variable by showing a let statement.

1 Each of the two equal sides of an isosceles triangle is twenty more than five times the base. If the perimeter of the triangle is 62 feet, find each of the sides of the triangle.

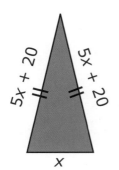

Let x =   base
$5x + 20$ =   one of the equal sides

Equation:

Answers:

2 In a rectangle, the length is two less than three times the width. If the perimeter of the rectangle is 100 meters, find the dimensions.

3 In parallelogram ABCD, AB = $15x - 10$ and DC = $x + 18$. The perimeter of the parallelogram is 58 units. Find all the sides of the parallelogram.

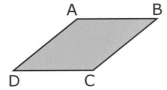

Thinking Box

What is true about the opposite sides of a <u>parallelogram</u>?

Never confuse sides with angles. Angles always add up to degrees, whereas sides add up to feet, inches, meters, or whatever the unit happens to be.

More Practice

Using a separate sheet of paper, solve the following word problems. Be sure to make a drawing and use a let statement.

1 In a right triangle, the larger of the two non-right angles is ten more than three times the smaller angle. Find the smaller angle.

2 Noah and Maggie are making a rectangular picture frame. They want the length of the frame to be three inches longer than the width. If the perimeter is 42", what are the dimensions of their frame?

3 The measures of the angles of a triangle are in the ratio of 2:3:4. What is the biggest angle?

> To be in the ratio of 2:3:4 means that each angle must be a multiple of 2, 3, 4 respectively. Use $2x$, $3x$, and $4x$ for your angles, then substitute.

4 The measures of the angles of a triangle are in the ratio of 2:2:5. What are the measures of all the angles? What type of triangle is this?

5 In a rectangle, the width must be three less than half the length. If the perimeter is 138 inches, find the dimensions of the rectangle.

6 In a parallelogram the measure of opposite angles are equal. If one angle is $(4x - 5)°$ and its opposite angle is $(3x + 3)°$, find all the angles of the parallelogram. Hint: The measures of the angles of any parallelogram add up to 360°.

7 Colleen, who works for a company that designs playgrounds, wants to create a small wading pool shaped like an isosceles trapezoid. She wants the longer base of her trapezoid to be twice the other base. The two equal sides are 8' each. If the perimeter is 46 feet, find the dimensions of the pool.

8 In a scalene triangle the largest angle is twice the smallest angle. The smaller angle is 20 less than the middle angle. Find all three angles.

9 Latarsha is making a sidewalk drawing outside of her school. Her life-long dream is to someday be as good as 3D sidewalk artist Julian Beever. She draws a rectangle with a perimeter of 44 feet. The width of her rectangle is two less than half her length. What are the dimensions of her rectangle?

10 Two vertical angles have measures $(6x + 18)°$ and $(11x + 3)°$. Find their measures. Hint: Vertical angles have equal measures.

Word Problems About Missing Numbers

The following problems are designed to give you practice translating from words to algebra. They are not designed to make you a numbers magician even though many of them are fun to try on your friends.

1   Larry said, "When I subtract a number <u>from</u> ten, I get the <u>same</u> answer as when I multiply <u>twice</u> the <u>difference</u> of 4 from my number. What is my mystery number?"

Let n = the missing number

Equation: $10 - n = 2(n - 4)$

$$10 - n = 2n - 8$$

$$\underline{+n \quad\quad +n}$$

$$\begin{array}{rcl} 10 & = & 3n - 8 \\ +8 & & +8 \end{array}$$

$$\frac{18}{3} = \frac{3n}{3}$$

$$6 = n$$

The key words above are underlined.

Make sure you check the answer.

$$10 - 6 = 2(6 - 4)$$
$$4 = 2 \cdot 2 \; \checkmark$$

2   Kimberly showed Tom a picture of the December 2015 calendar and asked him to choose four dates that form a square, like 4, 5, 11, and 12, and then only tell her the sum of the four numbers he chose. Tom said the sum of his four days was 76 and Kimberly found the four days pretty quickly. How did she do it?

December 2015						
SU	MO	TU	WE	TH	FR	SA
		1	2	3	4	5
6	7	8	9	10	11	12
13	14	15	16	17	18	19
20	21	22	23	24	25	26
27	28	29	30	31		

Kim subtracted 16 from 76 and divided by 4. So, Tom's first day is 15, so the square he picked was 15, 16, 22 and 23.

Kim did it with algebra.
Let **x** = number of Tom's first day
x + 1 = number of the next day
x + 7 = number of the day a week from x
x + 8 = number of the day right after x + 7
Equation: **4x + 16** = 76. Can you see that subtracting 16 and dividing by 4 works every time?

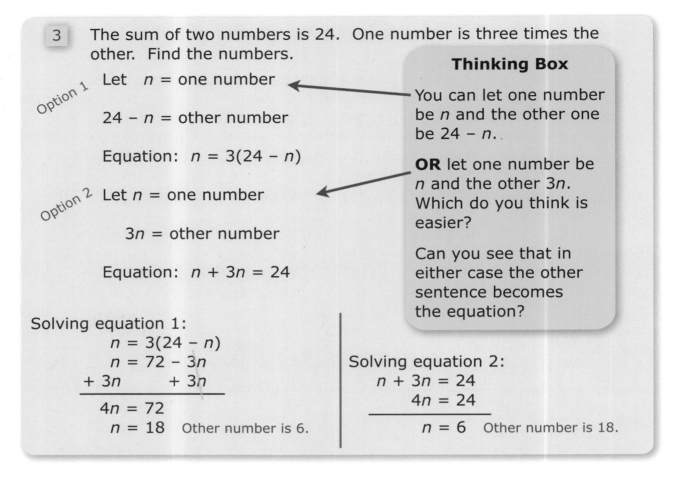

3 The sum of two numbers is 24. One number is three times the other. Find the numbers.

Option 1

Let n = one number

24 – n = other number

Equation: $n = 3(24 - n)$

Option 2   Let n = one number

$3n$ = other number

Equation: $n + 3n = 24$

Thinking Box

You can let one number be n and the other one be 24 – n.

OR let one number be n and the other $3n$. Which do you think is easier?

Can you see that in either case the other sentence becomes the equation?

Solving equation 1:
$$n = 3(24 - n)$$
$$n = 72 - 3n$$
$$+ 3n \qquad + 3n$$
$$\overline{}$$
$$4n = 72$$
$$n = 18 \quad \text{Other number is 6.}$$

Solving equation 2:
$$n + 3n = 24$$
$$4n = 24$$
$$\overline{}$$
$$n = 6 \quad \text{Other number is 18.}$$

Using a separate sheet of paper, solve these word problems.

1 Using the same calendar on page 67, Kimberly asked Andrea to add four days that form a square and only tell her the sum. Andrea said her sum was 100. Use algebra to find Andrea's days.

2 Six less than five times a number is 29. Find the missing number.

3 The sum of two numbers is 500. One of the numbers is three times the other. Find both numbers.

4 The quotient of a number divided by four yields the same number decreased by thirty-three. Find the number.

5 Twelve decreased by three times a number is equal to the original number increased by 4. Find the number.

6 Pick this month's calendar and use Kimberly's trick with a friend. Show your algebra.

Consecutive Integer Problems

Consecutive integer problems provide practice using algebra. You may not need to solve these types of problems in real life, but they truly demonstrate the power of using algebra instead of doing arithmetic in your head. The word **consecutive** means one after the other. The word **integer** means any number from this set: {... –3, –2, –1, 0, 1, 2, 3, ...} (see Chapter 1). You should not get any fractions or decimals for answers, so if you do, you will know right away that you made an error and can go back and check.

Suppose that you were asked for three consecutive integers starting with 101. You would answer: 101, 102, 103. If you were asked for three consecutive odd integers starting with 19, you would answer 19, 21, 23. Notice that odd integers are two units apart. The same is true of even integers. If you were asked for four consecutive even integers starting with 54, you would answer 54, 56, 58, 60. To go from an odd to an odd or from an even to an even you have to add two units. If the starting integer is unknown (x) but we know it's odd, the next odd would be $x + 2$, the next odd $x + 4$, etc. Say $x = 13$, then $13 + 2 = 15$, $13 + 4 = 17$, $13 + 6 = 19$, etc. Remember the 2, 4, 6 you see on the number line below is the number of **spaces** or units needed to get to the odd number if you start with an odd or to the next even, if you started with an even.

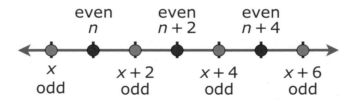

Let statements (these are the let statements you will use):

Consecutive Integers	Consecutive Even or Odd Integers
Let x = 1st consecutive integer	Let x = 1st consecutive even/odd integer
$x + 1$ = 2nd consecutive integer	$x + 2$ = 2nd consecutive even/odd integer
$x + 2$ = 3rd consecutive integer	$x + 4$ = 3rd consecutive even/odd integer
etc.	etc.

1. Find three consecutive integers whose sum is 267.

Let x = 1ˢᵗ consecutive integer
$x + 1$ = 2ⁿᵈ consecutive integer
$x + 2$ = 3ʳᵈ consecutive integer

Remember you can use any variable you want.

Equation: $x + x + 1 + x + 2 = 267$
$$3x + 3 = 267$$
$$x = 88$$

Solving the rest of the equation.

So, the first integer is 88, the second is 89, and the third is 90.
Check: $88 + 89 + 90 = 267$ √

2. Find four consecutive odd integers whose sum is 416.

Notice the let statement.

Let x = 1ˢᵗ consecutive odd integer
$x + 2$ = 2ⁿᵈ consecutive odd integer
$x + 4$ = 3ʳᵈ consecutive odd integer
$x + 6$ = 4ᵗʰ consecutive odd integer

Equation: $x + x + 2 + x + 4 + x + 6 = 416$
$$4x + 12 = 416$$
$$x = 101$$

Solving the rest of the equation.

So, the first odd integer is 101, the second odd integer is 103, the third odd integer is 105 and the fourth odd integer is 107.
Check: $101 + 103 + 105 + 107 = 416$ √

3. Find three consecutive integers such that three times the second integer results in –4 added to the sum of the first two integers.

Let x = 1ˢᵗ consecutive integer
$x + 1$ = 2ⁿᵈ consecutive integer
$x + 2$ = 3ʳᵈ consecutive integer

Notice that you must enclose the second in parentheses!

Sum of the first two integers.

Equation: $3(x + 1) = -4 + x + x + 1$
$$3x + 3 = -3 + 2x$$
$$\underline{-2x \qquad\qquad -2x}$$
$$x + 3 = -3$$
$$x = -6$$

Solving the rest of the equation.

Since you're adding each time to get your answers, remember to go to the right on the number line.

The first integer is –6. If you add one more you get –5. Add two more to –6 and you get –4.

4   Lisa's teacher said, "I'm thinking of three consecutive odd integers such that when you double the second one and subtract the third and add five, you get my age, which is 44."

Let x = 1st consecutive odd integer
$x + 2$ = 2nd consecutive odd integer
$x + 4$ = 3rd consecutive odd integer

Notice the need for parentheses.

Equation: $2(x + 2) - (x + 4) + 5 = 44$
$$2x + 4 - x - 4 + 5 = 44$$
$$x + 5 = 44$$
$$x = 39$$

Make sure you distribute correctly.

Answers: 39, 41, 43.
Check: $2 \cdot 41 - 43 + 5 = 44$
$$82 - 43 + 5 = 44 \checkmark$$

Remember the order of operations, go left to right.

Solve the following consecutive integer problems. Remember to show the correct let statement.

1   Find three consecutive integers whose sum is 0.

2   Find four consecutive integers whose sum is –38.

3   Find three consecutive even integers whose sum is 618.

4 Find two consecutive odd integers whose sum is 532.

5 Find three consecutive even integers such that six times the second results in five times the third.

6 Find three consecutive odd integers such that three times the third minus the second yields 32.

7 A scalene triangle whose perimeter is 72 inches has sides that are consecutive even integers. What is the length of the largest side?

8 Terri told Helen, "The combination to my locker is made up of three consecutive odd integers, and twice the first integer minus three times the third integer yields -35. You can open my locker if you can do algebra."

Coin Problems

Some word problems are full of information that is best organized using a chart. The chart is the let statement. Once the chart is filled out, writing the equation becomes very simple. Making a chart is a thinking skill that is not just applicable to these types of problems, but to many real life situations. When you need to solve a problem and you're given many facts and choices, your best strategy is to organize what you know and what you don't know by means of a chart or list.

In coin word problems you will create a chart with three columns. The first column is the number of coins. The second column is the value of the coin, and the third column is the amount of money you have in total. It helps to change the money into cents to avoid working with decimals (see Chapter 2). In the examples that follow the total value will be written in cents.

Let's think about how to generalize (use algebra) with money problems.

Number of Quarters	Value of Coin in Cents	Total Value in Cents
1	25	25
2	25	50
3	25	75
4	25	100
n	25	$25n$

Notice that each time we multiply the number of coins by the value of the coin to obtain the total value. So n number of coins times 25 cents is $25n$ cents.

Use a chart similar to the one above to answer the questions.

1. What is the value in cents of 1 dime? _____ 2 dimes? _____ 3 dimes? _____ 8 dimes? _____ n dimes? _____

2. What is the value in cents of 1 nickel? _____ 2 nickels? _____ 3 nickels? _____ 11 nickels? _____ n nickels? _____

3. What is the value in cents of 1 dollar? _____ 2 dollars? _____ 5 dollars? _____ 10 dollars? _____ n dollars? _____

Another concept to remember when working with money is that if you have a certain number of coins, say 120 dimes, and you give some of those coins (*n*) to your best friend, the correct way to write the number of coins you have left is **120 – *n***. The total you had is written first minus what you gave away. Always use a specific example with arithmetic to help you generalize how to write it in algebra. For example, if you have 120 dimes and you give away 20 dimes, you now have 120 – 20 or 100 dimes.

1   Maria's little brother has a piggy bank with only dimes and nickels. He has 5 <u>more</u> nickels than dimes. In total he has $1.75. How many of each coin does he have? ← There is your variable.*

The chart is your let statement.

	Number of Coins	Value of Each Coin (in cents)	Total Value (in cents)
dimes	*n*	10	10*n*
nickels	*n* + 5	5	5(*n* + 5)
total			175

These two rows add to your total money of 175 cents.

Notice the parentheses.

Equation: $10n + 5(n + 5) = 175$
$$10n + 5n + 25 = 175$$
$$15n + 25 = 175$$
$$\underline{-25 \quad\quad -25}$$
$$\frac{15n}{15} = \frac{150}{15}$$
$$n = 10$$

You cannot write $1.75 here since the entire chart is in cents. This is the same equation as .10*n* + .05(*n* + 5) = 1.75

The answer is 10 dimes and 15 nickels. To check: Does 10 dimes and 15 nickels add to $1.75? 10 dimes = $1.00 and 15 nickels = $0.75 so adding the two amounts totals $1.75. It checks! √

*You could have chosen nickels as the variable and then dimes would have been 5 less than nickels or *n* – 5. Pay attention to the key words like "more," "times," "exceeds," etc. Always make sure that you are using the units consistently throughout the equation. Lastly, make sure you always check your answers as coin problems are some of the easiest problems to check.

2   When Brian went to the bank, he deposited only nickels, quarters, and dimes into his savings account. The number of dimes exceeded the number of nickels by five, and the number of quarters was 16 less than the number of nickels. Find the number of each coin he deposited if his total deposit was $4.50.

	Number of Coins	Value of Each Coin (in cents)	Total Value (in cents)
nickels	n	5	5n
dimes	$n + 5$	10	$10(n + 5)$
quarters	$n - 16$	25	$25(n - 16)$
total			450

Equation: $5n + 10(n + 5) + 25(n - 16) = 450$

$$5n + 10n + 50 + 25n - 400 = 450$$
$$40n - 350 = 450$$
$$n = 20$$

Solving the rest of the equation.

Answers: 20 nickels, 25 dimes, 4 quarters

Check: 20 nickels = $1.00, 25 dimes = $2.50, 4 quarters = $1.00.
$1.00 + $2.50 + $1.00 = $4.50 √

3   Terra emptied her wallet and found 30 coins for a total of $4.30. Her only coins were nickels and quarters. How many of each coin did Terra have in her wallet?

	Number of Coins	Value of Each Coin (in cents)	Total Value (in cents)
nickels	n	5	$5n$
quarters	$30 - n$	25	$25(30 - n)$
total	30		430

Equation: $5n + 25(30 - n) = 430$

$$5n + 750 - 25n = 430$$
$$-20n + 750 = 430$$
$$n = 16$$

Solving the rest of the equation.

Answers: 16 nickels, 14 quarters

Practice

Answer the following questions. A chart has been provided for 1-4.

1 Show a check for example 3 (p. 75).

2 Patrick has three <u>times</u> as many dimes as he has nickels. In all he has $5.25 in only nickels and dimes. How many of each type of coin does he have?

Number of Coins	Value of Each Coin (in cents)	Total Value (in cents)

3 Hakim has a coin collection of only nickels, dimes, and quarters. He has twice as many nickels as quarters and two more dimes than quarters. In total he has $4.70. How many of each coin does he have?

Number of coins	Value of Each coin (in cents)	Total value (in cents)

4   Dan and Elena have been saving quarters and dimes for a long time. The day they decided to take the money to the bank they counted 100 coins. In total their deposit was $16.30. How many of each coin did they have? Make sure to title your chart.

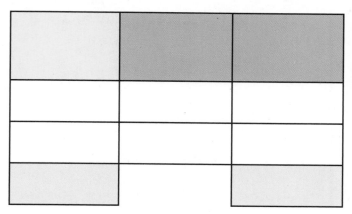

5   A bank teller dropped all the pennies she was counting on the floor. She knew she had 25 dimes and ten times as many pennies as nickels. Altogether her dimes, nickels, and pennies added up to $3.70. How many pennies did she drop? Make your own chart.

Age Problems

Word problems about peoples' ages can be confusing, but making a chart will help you. However, unlike coin problems it's not always obvious where to place the information and how to arrive at an equation. Here are some great strategies that will help you be successful with these types of word problems.

Age Word Problem Strategies

1 ▷ Read the problem carefully to decide which person should be labeled x (the variable).

2 ▷ Create a chart with the people on one side and the time periods on the other side.

3 ▷ Fill out the "Now" column based on the x if possible. If not possible, then fill out another column based on the x.

4 ▷ At this point, stop reading the problem and finish the chart based on your knowledge of how time works. Add the number of years for the future and subtract for past years.

5 ▷ Now, go back to the problem and read how the "blocks" on the chart are related according to what the problem says. That is your equation.

6 ▷ Solve the equation carefully.

7 ▷ Make sure your answer makes sense.

---

1 ▷ Three years from now José will be twice as old as Mike is now. The sum of their ages now is 21. How old is each boy now?

	Now	In Three Years
Mike	x	$x + 3$
José	$2x - 3$	$2x$

Steps 1-3: Read, create a chart, and fill in the information given.

Step 4: Complete the chart. Add three years to x and subtract 3 years from $2x$.

Equation: $x + 2x - 3 = 21$ ◀

$$3x - 3 = 21$$
$$x = 8 \quad \text{Solving the equation.}$$

Step 5: Use the other sentence to write the equation. The sum of their ages is 21.

Answers: Mike is 8 years old, José is 13 years old.

Try to remember that there are many ways to solve a word problem so be ready to justify your method and be open to listen to how others solved the same problem.

2 In five more years, Lucia's grandfather will be eight times as old as Lucia was two years ago. When you add their present ages the sum is 69 years. How old is each one now?

	Two Years Ago	**Now**	**In Five Years**
Lucia	$x-2$	x	$x+5$
Grandpa	$8(x-2)-5-2$	$8(x-2)-5$	$8(x-2)$

Steps 1-3: Read, create chart, fill in given information.

Step 4: Complete the chart. Add five years and subtract two years.

Equation: $x + 8(x - 2) - 5 = 69$
$x + 8x - 16 - 5 = 69$
$9x - 21 = 69$
$x = 10$

Step 5: Use another sentence relating the boxes of the chart to write the equation. Present ages add to a sum of 69 years.

Solving the equation.

Lucia is 10 years old, her grandfather is 59 years old

Answer the following questions using a chart. Charts for 1-5 are provided.

1 Sokhem is Chenda's older brother. In six more years Sokhem will be twice Chenda's age now. In six more years the sum of their ages then will be 60 years. How old is each now?

	Now	**In Six Years**
Chenda	x	
Sokhem		$2x$

Now follow step 4.

2 Cameron's dad is seven times as old as Cameron is now. One year ago he was nine times as old as Cameron was a year ago. Find Cameron's age now.

	One Year Ago	Now
Cameron	$x - 1$	x
His dad		$7x$

Finish the table first.

Use the second sentence to write your equation.

3 Mina's mother is four times as old Mina is now. Ten years ago Mina's mother was one more than three times Mina's age now. Find their ages now.

	Ten Years Ago	Now

4 Four years ago, Jane was the same age as Peter will be in three years. Right now, Peter is five years older than Alice, while Jane is twice Alice's age now. Find Peter's age four years ago.

	Four Years ago	Now	In Three Years
Jane			
Peter			
Alice	$x - 4$	x	

Finish the table first.

5   Steve is eight years older than his sister Sophie. Five years ago
     Steve was twice her age five years ago. Find their ages.

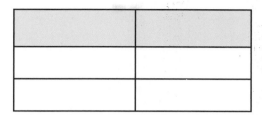

6   In four more years Miguel's grandmother will be five times as old
     as Miguel was three years ago. The sum of their ages now is 65.
     Find their ages now.

7   Ten years ago, Juanita's age was one-third the age she will be in
     6 years. Find Juanita's age now.

Word Problem Practice

Use a separate sheet of paper for these problems. Remember to show a let statement or a chart.

1. Lara entered a number on her calculator. She doubled it, then added 37. The result she got was 143. Use algebra to find her original number.

2. Find four consecutive integers whose sum is 110.

3. In a purse there are only dimes and quarters. There are two more dimes than quarters for a total of $4.40.

4. Find four consecutive odd integers such that four times the fourth minus the third yields 53.

5. JiMin said, "The difference in the ages of two people is 8 years. The older person is three times the age of the younger person. How old is each person?"

6. Find three consecutive odd integers whose sum is –57.

7. Avila has a bag with 30 coins. The bag only has nickels and quarters which total $7.10. Find how many nickels and quarters are in the bag.

8. In a triangle the angles are represented by $(10x +3)°$, $(10x + 10)°$, and $(11x + 12)°$. Find x and then find the measure of each angle.

9. In twenty-three years from now, Raul will be twice as old as he was two years ago. How old is Raul now?

10. One-third of a number less five equals twenty. Use algebra to find the number.

11. In a rectangle the length is three less than twice the width. If the perimeter of the rectangle is 84 inches, what is the length and width?

12. Jacob is two years older than Thomas, and Thomas is three years older than Maria. Find their ages if the sum of their ages now is 44.

13. Find three consecutive integers such that twice the third less the first is equal to 205.

14. Mario had $30 in dimes and quarters. If he has twenty more dimes than quarters, how many of each coin does he have?

Algebra Problems From the History of Math

1 From the Rhind Papyrus – Problem 24
A quantity plus $\frac{1}{7}$ of it becomes 19. What is the quantity?

> Many of these problems were not solved by algebra, but by what is known as the rule of false position.
>
> So to solve: $x + \frac{x}{7} = 24$, assume any value for x, say $x = 7$, so is $7 + 1 = 24$? No, but $8 \cdot 3 = 24$ so, if we multiply our guess, $x = 7$, by 3, we get 21, which is the correct answer.

2 Use the rule of false position to solve this problem: $n + \frac{n}{5} = 48$.
Hint: Try letting $n = 10$.

3 From the Rhind Papyrus – Problem 33
The sum of a certain quantity together with two-thirds of it, plus half of it, plus one-seventh of it becomes 37. What is the quantity?
(Hint: Use the LCD to eliminate the fractions in your equation.)

4 At the Yale University Babylonian collection there is a problem that dates back to early Babylonian times. To solve it, you need to know that 1 mina = 60 shequels and 1 shequel = 180 se (these are ancient measures of weight). Here's the problem:

I found a stone but did not weigh it. I added $\frac{1}{7}$ of its weight to the original weight and then added $\frac{1}{11}$ of that new weight and got one mina. What was the original weight? Hint: Change 1 mina to 10,800 se.

What is your equation? (Hint: Use the LCD to make the equation easier.)

5   Emily found a beautiful stone. Her friend weighed it but did not tell her the weight. She only told her that if $\frac{1}{2}$ of its weight was added to the original weight and then $\frac{1}{3}$ of that new weight was added to that new weight the end result be 40 ounces. How many pounds was the original stone? Hint: A pound is 16 ounces.

6   Bhaskara (1114-1185 BCE), an Indian mathematician made many contributions to mathematics. Many of his word problems were stories written in verse. In his famous book *Lilavati*, which was written for his daughter, named Lilavati (means "beautiful"), are many word problems in verse such as this one:

A fifth part of a swarm of bees came to rest on the flower of Kadamba, a third on the flower of Silinda.
Three times the difference between these two numbers flew over a flower of Krutaja, and one bee alone remained in the air, attracted by the perfume of a jasmine in bloom.
Tell me, beautiful girl, how many bees were in the swarm?

Chapter 4

From Words to Algebra – **More Word Problems**

Percent and Ratio Problems

The following examples demonstrate the power of using algebra to solve problems with percents and ratio. In Chapter 3 we used algebra to solve geometric word problems that involved the ratio of sides and angles. This section offers you more examples and applications.

Percent (sometimes it is written as per cent) is the ratio of a number to 100. The word percent means divided by 100 or hundredths. Percentage is the answer we get when we find the percent of a number. However, when we ask what percent of 20 is 5, we are finding the **rate** (such as a tax rate).

1   What percent $\underline{of}$ 40 is 7? Always translate "what percent" as $\frac{n}{100}$.

You can set this up as $\frac{n}{100} \cdot 40 = 7$ and solve the equation. However, it's much easier to set it up as a proportion (two ratios that are equal). 7 is to 40 in the same way that n (or x) is to 100.

$\frac{7}{40} = \frac{n}{100}$, cross multiply, $40n = 700$ and $n = 17.5$ so the answer is 17.5%

2   24 is 30% $\underline{of}$ what number?

Notice that if you use a proportion the number or word that follows "of" is the denominator of one of the fractions.

Set it up as $\frac{30}{100} = \frac{24}{n}$,

cross multiply, $30n = 2,400$, divide each side by 30, so $n = 80$.

Remember that 30% is the same as writing $\frac{30}{100}$.

To check, does 30% of 80 = 24? Yes!

3   Find 8% of $24. When you know the rate, it's much easier to just multiply $(.08) \cdot 24$. The answer is $1.92.

Remember that 8% is 8 hundredths or .08.

You can use a proportion, too. $\frac{8}{100} = \frac{n}{24}$, cross multiply,

$100n = 192$, $n = 1.92$ or $1.92.

Consider using proportions for these type of percent problems, except when you know the rate, but whichever method you use, it's important you understand and master your method.

4   Bob took a taxi that charged $5 for the first mile and $2.50 for each additional mile.
   a Write an equation or make a chart to represent how many miles the taxi drove if Bob paid a total of $20.
   b How many miles did Bob travel in the taxi?
   c Bob gave the taxi driver an additional $4 tip. What percent of the fare was his tip?

Answers

   a Let x = number of miles <u>after</u> the first mile
      Equation: $5 + 2.50x$ = $20   or 2.50x$ = $15
   b x = 6, so 6 + 1 (the first mile) so Bob traveled 7 miles.
   c Set up a proportion. $\dfrac{\$4}{\$20} = \dfrac{x}{100}$ or $\dfrac{1}{5} = \dfrac{x}{100}$; 20%

Use algebra to solve these percent problems.

1   Larry bought a car for $26,000 and paid 8% sales tax. What is the total cost he paid including tax?

> Did you know you can find the total including tax in one step by multiplying $26,000 by 1.08? Why does this work?

2   Josefina bought a cell phone for $200 and she paid 8.5% in sales tax. What was the tax she paid?

> Remember to change a percent to a decimal, move the decimal point twice to the left.
> Mnemonic device:
> **P**ercent to **D**ecimal go **L**eft
> (**P**lease **D**on't **L**augh!)

3   José got $14, which is his 5% commission for selling comic books at a comic book store where he works on the weekends. What was the total price, without tax, of the comic books he sold?

> This is asking:
> $14 is 5% of what number?

4   Marissa bought a pair of jeans for $50. This was after a 20% discount. What was original price of the jeans?

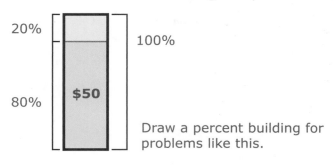

If the discount was 20%, then she paid 80%.

This asking: 80% of what number is $50?

Draw a percent building for problems like this.

5   Tamar's mom pays $800 a month for rent. Her income is $4,000 a month. What percent of her income does she spend on rent?

6   Joanna got 35 problems right out of 40 on her math test. What percent correct did she get?

7   What percent of this grid (all rectangles are the same size) is shaded red? _____ What percent is shaded yellow? _____ What percent of the grid is not blue? _____

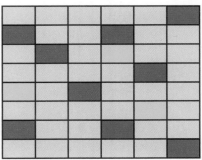

8   Adam paid $1.20 tax for a video game. He couldn't remember the cost of the video game, but he knew the sales tax was 5%. Find the cost of the video game.

Percent Increase and Decrease

To find the percent of increase or decrease, find the difference between the two amounts (subtract smaller from larger). Write that answer over the original amount and set it equal to $\frac{n}{100}$. If the amounts increased it will be percent increase and if amounts decreased then it's percent decrease.

1   The price of milk went up from $\underline{\$3.50}$ to $4.00. What is the percent increase?

difference between the two amounts   rounded to the nearest tenth

$\frac{.50}{3.50} = \frac{n}{100}$, cross multiply, $3.50n = 50$, $n = 14.3\%$

original amount

2   A blouse used to cost $35 and now it's on sale for $15. Find the percent of change.

difference between the two amounts   rounded to the nearest tenth

$\frac{20}{35} = \frac{n}{100}$, cross multiply, $35n = 2000$, $n = 57.1\%$ decrease

original amount

Since the price went down (discount), it's a percent of decrease.

Show your work in each of the following percent problems. Round to the nearest tenth.

1   Aisha bought a clock for $18 and later sold it to her friend for $12. What was the percent of discount (percent decrease)?

2   Mary Beth saw a dress for $36 and a week later the same dress was $40. What was the percent of markup (percent increase)?

3   Vladimir noticed that the laptop he wanted last month was selling for $1,500 and now it had gone up to $1,650. What was the percent increase?

Relative Error and Percent Error

Sometimes when you measure an object you might be off by a little bit. The closer we are to an actual measure the better, but no one is perfect and tools are also not perfect. However, to minimize our error we can find the relative error and percent error to know what is acceptable and what is not acceptable.

Relative error is the ratio of the **absolute value** of the difference of the measured or estimated amount less the actual value, divided by the **actual** value. When we change relative error to a percent, we call it **percent error**.

---

1   A carpet installer estimated a rectangular floor to be 8 ft by 10 ft. The actual floor is 8.5 ft by 10 ft. Find the relative error and the percent error.

Estimated area: 80 square feet   Actual area: 85 square feet

$$\frac{\left|85 - 80\right|}{85} = .059 \text{ rounded to the}$$
nearest thousandths

Remember to change a decimal to a percent, move the decimal point to the right two places.

Relative error = .059 and percent error = 5.9%

Mnemonic device: **D**ecimal to **P**ercent go **R**ight. (**D**on't **P**ick **R**oses!)

Find the relative error and the percent error in this problem.
Round your relative error to the nearest thousandth and your percent error to the nearest tenth.

1   You estimate that from your house to your best friend's house is 1.5 mi. The actual distance is 1.75 mi.

Sometimes you don't have actual measurements, so when you measure you need to need to be precise. A measurement should never be off by more than one half of the unit being used.

Percent Practice

Using a separate sheet of paper, solve these percent problems. Round your answer to the nearest tenth.

1. Find the tax Joe's dad paid when he bought a $240 lawnmower at a tax rate of 8%.

2. Joanna has the choice of buying a sofa bed for $1,500, or she can pay $75 a month for 2 years with no interest. What is the percent increase if she chooses the installment (monthly) plan?

3. In one month, the price of gas went up in a small town from $3.79 to $3.95. What was the percent of increase?

4. Joanna set up a proportion to solve the problem below. Did she set up the proportion correctly? If no, explain your thinking. What is the correct answer?

    4 is 40% of what number? $\dfrac{40}{100} = \dfrac{n}{4}$

5. Merritt bought a suit for $340. This price was after a 15% discount. Find the price of the suit before the discount.

6. In gym class the height of a student was estimated to be about 5'8". His actual height was 5'9". Find the relative error and the percent error. Hint: You might want to change the measurements to inches.

7. The cost of a birthday cake for 30 people is $31.80 including a 6% tax. What is the cost of the cake before the tax. Hint: The cost with tax is 106%. Draw a percent building to help you (see p. 87, #4).

8. Tom's uncle lends him $800 for the summer. At the end of the summer Tom needs to pay the money back plus 5% interest. How much does Tom owe his uncle?

9. Josef measured a picture frame and found it to be 47.5" × 72". Then he saw in the box that the actual measurements were 48" × 72". What is the relative error and the percent error?

10. Mr. Hendrickson insured his house for $285,000. This was 95% of its total value. What is the value of his house?

11. In a math test, there were 15 A's, 3 B's, 5 C's, 1 D, and 1 F. What percent of the class got A's and B's?

12. Draw a picture to show that you understand the difference between $\frac{1}{2}$% and 50%. Explain your drawing.

The Small Theater Problem

1   At a small theater, child tickets cost $3 and adult tickets cost $6. The amount of money collected was $54. We know 13 tickets were sold. How many of each type of ticket were sold? Finish the following table to find the answer.

Children		Adults	
#	Amount	#	Amount
1	$3	1	$6
2	$6	2	$12
3	$9	3	$18
4		4	
5		5	
6		6	
7		7	
8		8	
9		9	

a   What is your answer?

_____

b   Is making a table like this an efficient way to solve this type of problem? Explain your thinking.

_____

_____

_____

_____

c   If 100 tickets were sold for a total of $390, would continuing this table be the most efficient way to solve this problem? Why or why not? Explain your thinking.

_____

_____

_____

_____

Remember, the best strategy is the one you feel most comfortable with, but be ready to learn new strategies to make your work easier.

Mixture Problems

The Small Theater problem demonstrates the need for a different way of solving a problem when making a list would take too long. Any problem where amounts of different values are added together are called **mixture** problems and they are best solved by creating a chart and using algebra. Some mixture problems involve mixing types of food or different strength solutions.

Let's look at the Small Theater problem again, but let's use the numbers asked in question c.

1 At a small theater child tickets cost $3 and adult tickets cost $6. The amount of money collected was $390. We know 100 tickets were sold. How many of each type of ticket were sold?

	Number of Tickets	Cost per Ticket	Total Money
Children	n	$3	$3n$
Adults	$100 - n$	$6	$6(100 - n)$
Total	100		$390

Equation:
$$3n + 6(100 - n) = 390$$
$$3n + 600 - 6n = 390$$
$$-3n = -210 \quad \text{Solving the equation.}$$
$$n = 70$$

Notice the need for parentheses.

So there were 70 child tickets and 30 adult tickets sold.
Check: 70 @ $3 + 30 @ $6 = $210 + $180 = $390 √

2 A juice company needs 10% apple juice for its new drink. The lab only has 8% apple juice concentrate and 20% apple juice concentrate. How much should be mixed to obtain 36 gallons of a 10% solution?

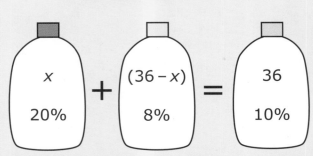

Making bottle pictures helps.

Equation:

Multiply by 100.

$$.20x + .08(36 - x) = .10(36)$$
$$20x + 8(36 - x) = 10(36)$$
$$20x + 288 - 8x = 360$$
$$12x = 72$$
$$x = 6 \quad \text{Solving the equation.}$$

Answer:
6 gallons of the 20% and 30 gallons of the 8% should be mixed.

3 The manager of a bulk food company wants to sell a mixture of peanuts and almonds. Peanuts usually sell for $4 per pound and almonds for $7 per pound. She wants her company to sell 100 lbs of both nuts and sell them for $5.56 per pound. How much of each nut would she need?

	Number of Pounds	Cost per Pound	Total Money
peanuts	n	$4	$4n$
almonds	$100 - n$	$7	$7(100 - n)$
Total	100		$5.56

Equation: $4n + 7(100 - n) = 100(5.56)$
$4n + 700 - 7n = 556$
$-3n + 700 = 556$ Solving the equation.
$-3n = -144$
$n = 48$

Answer: 48 lbs of peanuts, 52 lbs of almonds

Some mixture problems add water to a solution to dilute it. Water has 0% concentration of whatever solution it is being added to. Some problems that deal with chemistry add pure acid. Any solution that is pure, such as pure acid, is considered 100% concentrate. Use a chart or make drawings to help you organize your information.

4 Five gallons of an 80% orange juice drink was mixed with 5 gallons of water. What is the percent of orange juice in the new drink?

WATER

| 5g | WATER 5g | 10g |
| 80% | 0% | x% |

$+$ $=$

Equation: $5(.8) + 5(0) = 10x$
$4 + 0 = 10x$
Solving the equation. $4 = 10x$
$x = .4$ or 40%

Answer: The percent of orange juice is now 40%.

Make sure your answer makes sense. If a solution is being diluted then the concentration has to be less than what you started with.

Mixture Practice

Use a chart or pictures to solve the following mixture problems. Charts or pictures are provided for 1-4. Make sure your answer makes sense.

1　Eight liters of a 25% blue coloring solution are added to several liters of a 70% blue coloring solution and the result is a 40% solution. Use these bottles to help you find how much of the 70% solution was added.

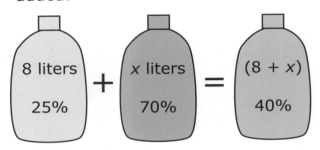

2　Tickets to a show cost $2.50 for children and $5.00 for adults. The person at the ticket counter knows he's sold 548 tickets and made $2,460, but he cannot remember how many child tickets were sold. Find how many child tickets were sold. Finish this chart to help you.

	Number of Tickets	Cost per Ticket	Total Money
Children	n		
Adults	548 – n		
Total	548		

3 How many liters of a 10% saline solution should be added to 80 liters of a 35% saline solution to obtain a mixture that is 30% saline solution? Use these flasks to help you.

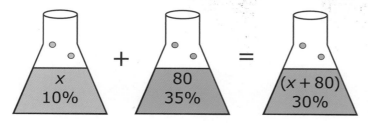

4 How many pounds of dark chocolate worth $14 a pound must be mixed with 12 pounds of milk chocolate worth $6 a pound to produce a mixture of both chocolates worth $10 a pound? Finish this chart to help you.

	Number of Pounds	Cost per lb	Total Money
dark		$14	
milk	12	$6	
Total			

5 In a chemistry experiment, pure acid is to be added to a 20% acid solution to obtain 50 liters of a 70% solution. How many liters of each should be used? Make your own chart or drawing.
Hint: 100% = 1.

More Practice

Using a separate sheet of paper, solve these mixture problems. Make your own chart or drawing.

1. At Ithaca Bakery, a pound of regular coffee sells for $10 and a pound of decaffeinated coffee sells for $14. How much of each type of coffee should be mixed to create 40 pounds of a mixture that would sell for $12.50?

2. At a local store, orange jelly beans sell for $7 a pound and red jelly beans sell for $3.50 a pound. How many pounds of the orange jelly beans should be added to 10 pounds of the red jelly beans to sell a mixture of both for $5 a pound?

3. An experiment calls for 30% of a saline solution, but the lab has only 40% and 10% saline solutions available. How much of each should be mixed to obtain 15 liters of a 30% solution?

4. Ten quarts of 100% pure cherry juice are added to 90 quarts of a fruit juice that only contains 20% pure cherry juice. What is the percent concentration of pure cherry juice in the new mixture?

5. How many pounds of a candy that is 50% chocolate should be mixed with 10 pounds of candy that is 20% chocolate to make a candy that is 25% chocolate?

6. An after-shave company wants to know how many ounces of pure water must be added to 50 ounces of a 40% solution of alcohol to arrive at a 10% alcohol solution. Find the number of ounces of pure water.

7. How many grams of 45% olive oil must be mixed with 6 grams of pure olive oil to obtain a salad dressing with 78% olive oil?

8. Three cubic meters of soil that contains 20% sand was mixed with 7 cubic meters of soil containing 40% sand. What is the concentration of sand in the new mixture?

9. How many quarts of a 30% sugar solution should be mixed with 8 quarts of a 50% sugar solution to obtain a 40% solution?

10. Write your own mixture problem. You can use problem 9 to help you.

Motion Problems

Motion or distance word problems can be challenging, but once you understand how to diagram what is happening and can put the information on a chart, you will rank as one of the best problem solvers around! These problems may have an intimidating reputation, but only because they are often taught without strategies. It's impossible to solve a problem that you can't visualize, so even if you're not the best artist, making a drawing really helps.

The Far Side by *Gary Larson* 7/1
©1990 by Universal Press Syndicate

Math phobic's nightmare

The most important concept you need to know for these problems is that how far you go (**distance**), whether you walk or are in a car or plane, is the result of how fast (**rate** of speed) and how long (**time**) you travel. That is the meaning of this formula:

$$\textbf{distance} = \textbf{rate} \cdot \textbf{time}$$
$$d = r \cdot t$$

Distance Problems

Larry's car is going at a rate of 30 mph (miles per hour). Study this chart to understand how to determine the distance he travels.

Larry's speedometer

Rate (r) · Time (t) = Distance (d)
30 mph · 1 hour   =   30 miles
30 mph · 2 hours   =   60 miles
30 mph · 3 hours   =   90 miles
30 mph · 4 hours   =   120 miles
30 mph · 6.5 hours =   195 miles

Use the distance formula to answer these questions.

1 Later Larry picked up his speed to 40 mph. How far can he go in

   a 2 hours? _____,   b 4.5 hours? _____,   c 15 minutes? _____

2 If he's traveling at the rate of 40 mph and travels 120 miles, how many hours did he drive? _____

3 What is his average speed if he travels 300 miles in 5 hours? _____

4 It's approximately 670 miles From Atlanta, GA, to Miami, FL. If Laura drove at an average speed of 67 mph, how long would it take her to get there? _____

5 The distance from Los Angeles, CA, to Portland, OR, is approximately 665 miles. Michael wants to get there in approximately 9.5 hours. What would his average speed have to be? _____

6 It took Rosa 6.5 hours to travel from Albuquerque, NM, to Phoenix, AZ, going at an average rate of 65 mph. What is the approximate distance between these two cities? _____

7 It took Dave 14 hours to fly from New York City to Johannesburg, South Africa. The distance traveled was 7,975 miles. What was the approximate speed of the jet? _____ Round to the nearest tenth of a mile.

8 Terri traveled from Ithaca, NY, to Philadelphia, PA, to visit her grandson Paulo. Her trip took her 4.5 hours by car and she averaged about 60 mph. How far is Ithaca from Philadelphia? _____

Toward and Away Problems

1   Dani and Netta leave school at the same time and travel in opposite directions. Netta walks at the rate of 2 mph and Dani walks at the rate of 2.5 mph. After how much time would they be 9 miles apart if they kept walking at those rates?

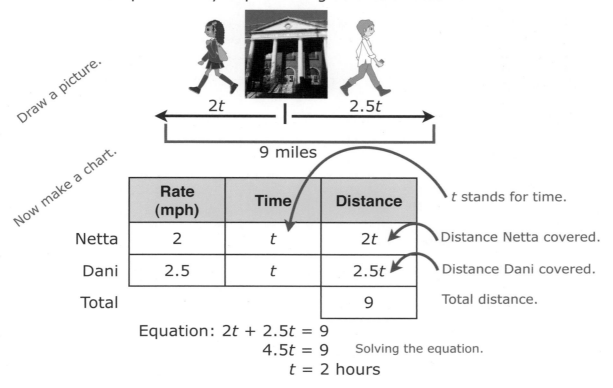

Draw a picture.

Now make a chart.

	Rate (mph)	Time	Distance
Netta	2	t	$2t$
Dani	2.5	t	$2.5t$
Total			9

t stands for time.

Distance Netta covered.

Distance Dani covered.

Total distance.

Equation: $2t + 2.5t = 9$

$4.5t = 9$ Solving the equation.

$t = 2$ hours

2   Franny and Kate are 225 miles apart and are driving toward each other. Franny is going 40 mph and Kate is going 50 mph. If both leave at the same time, how long does it take for them to meet?

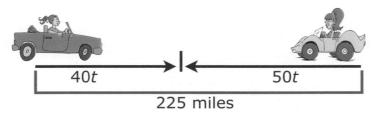

Equation: $40t + 50t = 225$

$90t = 225$

$t = 2.5$ hours

	Rate (mph)	Time	Distance
Franny	40	t	$40t$
Kate	50	t	$50t$
Total			225

Total distance.

Motion Problems

Solve the following motion problems. Remember to make a drawing and then a chart.

1   Two trains are on the same track and heading towards each other. Latawnya, the city's engineer, knows that train A is traveling at 80 mph and train B at 60 mph. If the trains are 840 miles apart, how long does Latawnya have to fix the problem before they crash?

2   Viktor is driving at 40 mph and Juan is driving at 50 mph. If they both leave the same place and go in opposite directions, how long before they are 630 miles apart?

3   An airplane leaves Miami, Florida, at the same time that another airplane leaves Santiago, Chile. The planes are heading toward each other at the rates of 625 mph and 575 mph respectively. If the two cities are 4,200 miles apart, how long will it take until the planes pass each other?

4   Two buses leave the same location at 2 p.m. going in opposite directions and making no stops. The yellow bus is going west at 32 mph and the red bus is going east at 48 mph. At what time on the clock will they be 160 miles apart?

5   Sadie and Julia leave camp at the same time going in opposite directions. Sadie drives at a rate of 55 mph. After 3 hours they each arrive home. If their homes are 345 miles apart, find Julia's rate.

6   A girl drove her bike at the rate of 10 mph and then after a flat tire she walked at the rate of 2 mph. The entire trip took 2 hours for a total of 16 miles. How long did she walk, and how long did she bike?

	Rate (mph)	Time	Distance
Biking	10	t	
Walking	2	$(2 - t)$	
Total		2 hours	16 miles

Chase Problems

Again, the best way to solve these problems is to make a drawing so you visualize what is happening in the problem and then proceed to make a chart.

1   Mrs. Perl left school at 7 a.m. for an out-of-town meeting and she's traveling at 40 mph. Two hours later, her husband realizes that she left some important papers and he starts to overtake her. He is traveling 60 mph. At what time of the day does he reach his wife?

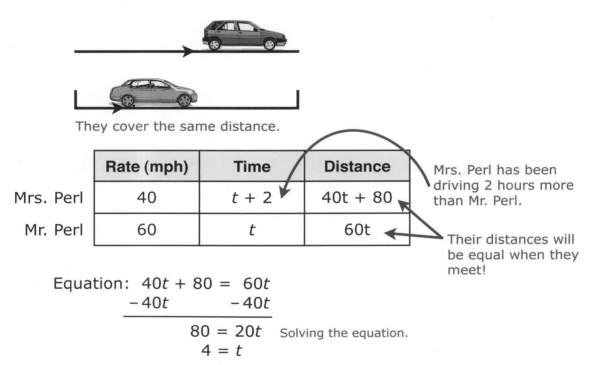

They cover the same distance.

	Rate (mph)	Time	Distance
Mrs. Perl	40	$t + 2$	40t + 80
Mr. Perl	60	t	60t

Mrs. Perl has been driving 2 hours more than Mr. Perl.

Their distances will be equal when they meet!

Equation: $40t + 80 = 60t$
$$-40t \qquad -40t$$
$$80 = 20t \quad \text{Solving the equation.}$$
$$4 = t$$

So Mr. Perl spent 4 hours on the road and his wife 6 hours. Since she left at 7 a.m., they met at 1 p.m. Do not forget to make a drawing.

Sometimes vehicles (or people) are following each other but one gets ahead of the other as in the next example.

2   Two runners are running a marathon. Runner A runs twice as fast as runner B. In 2 hours they are 12 miles apart. Find the rate of each runner.

B   A

Can you see that in **2** hours the distance runner B travels plus 12 miles equals the distance Runner A travels?

B's distance | 12 miles

A's distance

	Rate (mph)	Time	Distance
Runner A	$2r$	2	$4r$
Runner B	r	2	$2r$

Equation: $2r + 12 = 4r$

$$\underline{-2r \qquad\qquad -2r}$$

$$12 = 2r \qquad \text{Solving the equation.}$$

$$6 = r$$

So, Runner B runs at 6 mph while Runner A runs at 12 mph.

Solve the following motion problems. Remember to make a drawing and a chart.

1. A train left Ithaca, N.Y., going toward New York City traveling 70 mph. Three hours later, a train left the same location in Ithaca on parallel tracks also going towards New York City traveling 100 mph. When did the faster train overtake the slower train?

Rate (mph)	Time	Distance

2   At 5 p.m. a plane left an airport and flew north at 300 mph. At 5:30 another plane left the same airport, following the same course and going 350 mph. After how much time did the second plane pass the first plane? What was the time on the clock? Assume they are in the same time zone.

3   A bus and a train start for the same destination at the same time. The highway runs along the railroad track. The bus averages 31 mph and the train 39 mph. In how many hours will they be 24 miles apart?

4   A doctor is already 213 miles on her way, traveling by train, to a region in South Africa when her nurse practioner realizes she left a box of vaccines behind. The nurse practioner jumps on a plane going 320 mph. How fast is the doctor going if the plane overtakes the train in three-quarters of an hour?

Motion Match

Write the letter of the quantity that is equal.

_____ (1) 120 mph

_____ (2) Two women start in the same place and go in opposite directions. One travels 45 mph and the other 60 mph. How far are they after t hours?

_____ (3) Number of miles covered in three-quarters of an hour by a helicopter going 140 mph.

_____ (4) Jo drives at a rate of r mph and Lu drives 40 less than twice Jo's rate. Write an expression for Lu's rate.

_____ (5) Tamar's driving rate if she traveled 210 miles in 3.5 hours.

_____ (6) Rate traveled by Ross if he drives twenty miles per hour less than his son Joe, who drives ar a rate of r mph.

_____ (7) Time traveled if distance covered was 200 miles at 60 mph.

_____ (8) Time traveled if distance covered was 200 miles at 40 mph.

(a) 5 hours

(b) $r - 20$

(c) $60t$

(d) 3 hours and 20 minutes

(e) 105 miles

(f) $2r - 40$

(g) 2 miles per minute

(h) 60 mph

(i) $105t$

More Practice

Using a separate sheet of paper, solve the following motion problems. Remember to make a drawing and a chart.

1   The average rate of a car is 10 miles more per hour than that of a bus. In 5 hours the bus can travel the same distance as the the car can travel in 4 hours. What is the rate of each?

2   A truck traveled at an average speed of 60 mph to pick up a load of rocks. With the truck fully loaded, the average speed was 40 mph. The entire trip was 400 miles. Find the average speed* of the truck for the whole trip. Use the chart to help.

*You cannot just average the two rates because the time it took each way was different.

	Rate (mph)	Time	Distance
Going	60	200 ÷ 60	200
Returning	40	200 ÷ 40	200
Total			400

Now, add total time and use it to find the average rate.

3   An airplane traveling 500 mph leaves Baltimore 13.5 hours after a cruise ship has sailed. If the plane overtakes the ship in 1.5 hours, find the rate of the cruise ship.

4   Nadine's trip to Toronto took 5 hours and the trip back took 4 hours. She averaged 50 km/h on the way there. What was her average speed on the way back?

5   Two trains are 500 miles apart. They start towards each other at the same time. Train A is going 20 miles per hour faster than Train B. They meet in 4 hours. Find the rate of each train.

Work Problems

"Work" word problems are word problems where you are given the rate that each person (or machine) can do a job, and then asked how much sooner the job could be done if more than one person (or machine) worked together. Because these problems often appear in standardized tests you will find many sources which show different methods as to how to solve these types of problems. The following method will save you time, but it's important that you understand why this method works.

If Jim can paint a room in 3 hours, how much of the room can he paint in one hour? In one hour Jim can only complete $\frac{1}{3}$ of the room. By the same token, if Jim can only paint $\frac{1}{5}$ of the dining room in one hour, how long would he need to complete the painting of the dining room? It should be clear that in 5 hours the dining room would be finished. Assume in all these problems that the person is working at the given rate consistently and without taking breaks.

Finish the following list to help you understand how someone's rate of work affects the amount of time needed to complete that work.

Suppose that Lisa can plant a garden in 5 hours.

Hours Working	Fraction of the Garden Planted
1 hour	$\frac{1}{5}$
2 hours	_____
3 hours	_____
4 hours	_____
5 hours	_____

It should be clear that every hour another $\frac{1}{5}$ of the garden gets done. And that in 5 hours, 1 garden of that same size has been planted. If she worked 10 hours, then 2 gardens of that same size could get planted. Certainly, the job would go faster if Lisa had a helper or two!

The time spent working (*t*) multiplied by the rate (*r*) results in the amount of the job that is completed. When *t* is the total time needed to complete the job then *t* times the rate equals **1** (one complete job).

1   Lisa can plant a garden in 5 hours and her son Stephen can plant the same garden in 3 hours. How long would it take both of them to plant the garden if they worked together?

	Rate per Hour	Hours Working	Amount of Job Finished
Lisa	$\frac{1}{5}$	t	$\frac{1}{5}t$
Stephen	$\frac{1}{3}$	t	$\frac{1}{3}t$
Total job			1

Equation: $\frac{1}{5}t + \frac{1}{3}t = 1$

Multiply through by 15 (LCD).

$$3t + 5t = 15$$
$$\frac{8t}{8} = \frac{15}{8}$$
$$t = 1\frac{7}{8} \text{ hr}$$

So working together, Lisa and Stephen finished the garden in 1 hour and 52.5 minutes. (Take $\frac{7}{8}$ of 60 minutes to get 52.5 minutes.)

2   Pump A can fill a pool in 3 hours. Pump B can fill the same pool in 8 hours, and pump C can fill the same pool in 6 hours. How long would it take to fill the pool if all pumps are used at the same time?

	Rate per Hour	Hours Pumping Water	Amount of Job Finished
Pump A	$\frac{1}{3}$	t	$\frac{1}{3}t$
Pump B	$\frac{1}{8}$	t	$\frac{1}{8}t$
Pump C	$\frac{1}{6}$	t	$\frac{1}{6}t$
Total			1

Equation: $\frac{1}{3}t + \frac{1}{8}t + \frac{1}{6}t = 1$

Multiply through by 24 (LCD).

$$8t + 3t + 4t = 24$$
$$\frac{15t}{15} = \frac{24}{15}$$
$$t = 1\frac{3}{5}$$

So the pool can be filled in 1 hour and 36 minutes.

(Take $\frac{6}{10}$ or $\frac{3}{5}$ of 60 to get 36 minutes.)

Work Problems

Using a separate sheet of paper, solve the following work problems.

1 Mara needs to make some decorations for the school dance. She can cut a box of paper into snowflakes in 12 minutes, and Laura can do the same box in 15 minutes. How long would it take them if they work together on the same box?

Rate per Minute	Minutes Working	Amount of Job Finished
	t	
	t	
		1

2 Jackie can mow her yard in 2 hours and her dad can do it in one hour. How much time would it take them to mow the yard if they work together with two exact mowers? Hint: Change their times into minutes.

3 A pipe can fill a city's water tank in 5 days while a second pipe can fill the same water tank in 8 days. There is a third pipe which could be used in emergencies and this last one can fill the tank in 6 days. How many days would it take if they could all be used at the same time? Round your answer to the nearest unit.

Tina and Jane's Problem

There are more complicated work problems that involve algebra steps we haven't covered so far in this book. The following problem illustrates this. Use the choices below to plug in and find the correct answer.

Tina works half as fast as Jane. Working together they can finish a job in 8 hours. What is the rate of each girl?

Suppose that Jane can complete her job in 6 hours. Each hour she completes $\frac{1}{6}$ of the job. If Tina works half as fast then she can complete the same job in _____ hours, so in one hour she completes _____ of the job.

Since we don't know their rates, we can say that Jane's rate per hour is $\frac{1}{x}$ then Tina's rate must be $\frac{1}{2x}$.

Together in 8 hours they complete one job. This is the equation:

$$8 \cdot \frac{1}{x} + 8 \cdot \frac{1}{2x} = 1$$

Which of the following is the correct answer? Plug in each choice to check. We will learn how to solve these types of equations later on.

  a $x = 2$
  b $x = 12$
  c $x = 6$
  d $x = 8$

What is Jane's rate per hour? What is Tina's rate per hour? Explain your thinking.

_____

_____

_____

Chapter 5

Inequalities, Compound Inequalities, and Absolute Value

In Chapter 3 you learned how to translate words into algebraic equations. In this chapter you will learn how to translate and solve word problems with inequalities. You will also learn how to solve absolute value equations and inequalities. Remember that inequalities are sentences with $>$, $\geq$, $<$, $\leq$ or $\neq$. When you translate inequalities, the verb (i.e. "is") must be immediately in front of the words "greater than" or "greater than or equal" or to the words "less than" or "less than or equal."

Translating Tips

n **is less than** m is the inequality $n < m$
(the three words "is less than" must be together!)

n less m is the expression $n - m$

n less than m is the expression $m - n$

----

a **is greater than** b is the inequality $a > b$

a more than b is the expression $a + b$

The words **"at least"** mean greater than or equal to ($\geq$).

The words **"at most"** mean less than or equal to ($\leq$).

Practice translating these inequalities. Use the variables indicated.

1   Maria's age (m) is less than Julia's age (j). _____

2   To get into the Superman Ride of Steel at the amusement park, your height (h) must be at least 54 inches. _____

3   The cost (c) of the shirt is at most \$16. _____

4   -3^2 does not equal 9. _____

5   The profit (p) for a company must be at least \$22,000 a year. _____

Understanding How To Solve Inequalities

Inequalities are solved in a similar way as equations except for a few cases. To understand these cases, let's take a true statement, 20 > 10, as an example.

Case 1 Can we add the same number to each side and preserve the truth of the inequality?

$$\begin{array}{r} 20 > 10 \\ +5 \quad +5 \\ \hline 25 > 15 \end{array}$$

Yes, since 25 > 15 is still a true statement, we know addition preserves the truth of the inequality.

Case 2 Can we subtract (which is the same as adding a negative) to each side and preserve the truth of the inequality?

$$\begin{array}{r} 20 > 10 \\ -4 \quad -4 \\ \hline 16 > 6 \end{array}$$

Yes, subtracting (or adding a negative) preserves the truth of the inequality.

Case 3 Can we multiply each side by a positive number and preserve the truth of the inequality? Answer and explain your thinking.

$$\begin{array}{r} 20 > 10 \\ \cdot 5 \quad \cdot 5 \\ \hline \end{array}$$

_____

_____

Case 4 Can we multiply each side by a negative number and preserve the truth of the inequality? Answer and explain your thinking.

$$\begin{array}{r} 20 > 10 \\ \cdot (-3) \quad \cdot (-3) \\ \hline \end{array}$$

_____

_____

Case 5   Can we divide each side by a positive number and preserve the truth of the inequality? Divide by a positive number. Answer the question and explain your thinking.

20 > 10   _____

_____

Case 6   Can we divide each side by a negative number and preserve the truth of the inequality? Divide by a negative number. Answer the question and explain your thinking.

20 > 10   _____

_____

Explain what you discover. _____

_____

_____

$$>$$

$$\geq$$

Inequalities are solved just like equations except for cases 4 and 6. When solving an inequality, you must **reverse** the inequality symbol every time you multiply or divide by a negative number.

$$<$$

$$\leq$$

1   Solve the following inequality.

$-3(x + 5) > 2(x + 10)$
$-3x - 15 > 2x + 20$
$\underline{-2x \qquad\qquad -2x}$ Subtracting a negative term does not affect the inequality symbol.

$-5x - 15 > 20$
$\underline{\quad +15 \qquad +15}$

$\dfrac{-5x}{-5} > \dfrac{35}{-5}$ ←   Dividing by a negative reverses the inequality symbol.

$x \;\; <\; -7$

2 Solve the following inequality and graph it over the set of real numbers.

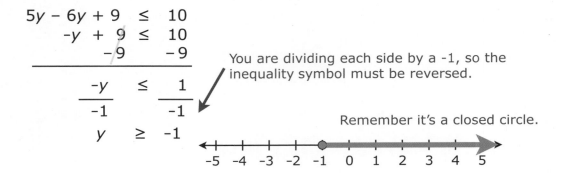

$$5y - 6y + 9 \leq 10$$
$$-y + 9 \leq 10$$
$$\underline{-9 \quad -9}$$
$$\frac{-y}{-1} \leq \frac{1}{-1}$$
$$y \geq -1$$

You are dividing each side by a -1, so the inequality symbol must be reversed.

Remember it's a closed circle.

Important note: If you solve an inequality and you end up with this type of statement, -5 > x, it's best that you write it as x < -5 to make it easier to graph. Reversing the inequality symbol here has nothing to do with multiplying and dividing by a negative—it has to do with the actual meaning of the inequality. If 5 > 4 then 4 < 5. Sometimes it's easy to make graphing mistakes if your variable is not on the left side.

3 Solve the following inequality and graph it over the set of real numbers.

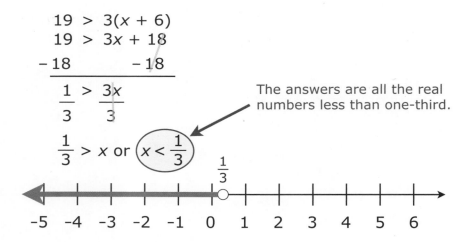

$$19 > 3(x + 6)$$
$$19 > 3x + 18$$
$$\underline{-18 \qquad -18}$$
$$\frac{1}{3} > \frac{3x}{3}$$
$$\frac{1}{3} > x \text{ or } \boxed{x < \frac{1}{3}}$$

The answers are all the real numbers less than one-third.

You should always pick an answer in your solution set and check it in the original inequality to make sure you have done the problem correctly. For example, in the above inequality we can check "0" which is in the shaded area to see if it works.

Is 19 > 3(0 + 6)? Is 19 > 3(6)? Yes! So we know that our arrow is pointing in the right direction.

Inequality Practice

Solve the following inequalities. Remember to reverse the inequality symbol <u>every time</u> you multiply or divide by a <u>negative number</u>. Graph only the odd number problems.

1   $-r > -3$

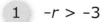

2   $-6 > x - 5$

3   $-(x + 3) \leq -1$

4   $-2(y - 5) \geq y - 11$

5   $-3(5 - x) > -2x$

6 $-\dfrac{4}{3}w + 3 < 11$

7 $8y + 5 > 7(y + 1)$

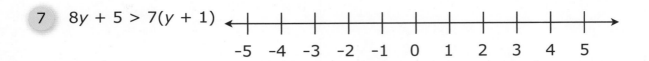

-5 -4 -3 -2 -1 0 1 2 3 4 5

Answer the following questions.

8   Assume that you can only use the set $\{-2, -1, 0, 1, 2\}$ for the values of w. We call this set our domain. So far our domain has been the set of real numbers. If $w \in \{-2, -1, 0, 1, 2\}$ and those are the only values you can substitute for w, what is the solution set for the inequality below? Explain your thinking.

$-2w > 2$

    a $\{0, 1, 2\}$ _____

    b $\{-2, -1\}$ _____

    c $\{-2\}$

    d $\{-2, -1, 2\}$ _____

9   If $a > b$ and both a and b are negative numbers, and if x is also a negative number, then what is the relationship between ax and bx? Explain your thinking. Hint: Use some values for the variables.

    a $ax > bx$
                   _____

    b $ax = bx$

    c $ax < bx$
                   _____

    d   cannot tell
                   _____

10   What are the three largest consecutive <u>integers</u> that make this inequality a true statement?

$-2x + 5 > 11$

_____

Solving Inequality Word Problems

Solving word problems with inequalities is similar to solving word problems with equations in that you must pay close attention to the key words listed on the first page of this chapter. Here are two examples of similar sounding problems. One is an equation and one is an inequality.

| -20w is one less than twice w. | -20w is less than twice w. |

The sentence inside the blue rectangle is an equation. It translates to $-20w = 2w - 1$. However, the sentence in the yellow rectangle is an inequality. It translates to $-20w < 2w$. Notice in the yellow rectangle that "is less than," all three words, are side by side. In the sentence in the blue rectangle, "is" is separated from "less than" by the word "one." So "is" in the blue rectangle is the equal sign.

Look at these examples of word problems involving inequalities.

1   Find the two largest consecutive even integers whose sum is less than 52.

Let n = 1st consecutive even integer
$n + 2$ = 2nd consecutive even integer

$$
\begin{aligned}
\text{Equation: } n + n + 2 &< 52 \\
2n + 2 &< 52 \\
-2 \quad -2& \\
\hline
\frac{2n}{2} &< \frac{50}{2} \\
n &< 25
\end{aligned}
$$

Since the first integer that is less than 25 is the integer 24, then the answers are 24 and 26. Their sum is less than 52.

In the next activity, be careful with the words "at least" and "at most." Refer back to the first page of this chapter if you need help. A great thinking strategy when you have trouble with a problem is to use easier numbers or think of an example that you are familiar with. For example, what does it mean to be at least 14 years old? What does it mean to be at most twenty years old?

Word Problems

Solve the following problems.

1   Kendra has $1,000 in a savings account at the beginning of the school
    year. She wants to withdraw $25 each week to help her mother with
    car expenses and still have $200 left to go on a trip. How many
    weeks can Kendra withdraw $25 per week and still have $200 left?
    Write an inequality to represent this situation. Solve your inequality.

2   Marco wants to take a taxi to visit his friend Todd. A taxi charges a
    flat rate of $1.75 plus $.65 per mile. Marco has no more than $12
    to spend on the taxi, including tip, and Todd is 14 miles from where
    Marco is located. Write and solve an inequality to determine if Marco
    has enough money to take a taxi. As long as he can afford the trip,
    he will use whatever he has left for a tip. Don't worry about the trip
    back since Marco's parents will pick him up.

3   If eight less than twice a real number is less than one more than the
    number, what can the number be? Solve by using an inequality and
    then graph your solution.

4   The sum of two consecutive odd integers must be more than -200.
    Find the least two possible values for the integers.

5   The base of a regular pentagon statue has a perimeter that must
    be less than 125 meters. Find the greatest possible whole number
    dimension for one side.

6   Carmen is designing a sandbox. The dimensions are whole
    numbers. The length is three times the width, but the perimeter
    must be at most 72 feet. What are <u>all</u> the possible dimensions of
    Carmen's sandbox?

Solving Compound Inequalities

A **compound inequality** is a statement that contains two inequalities at the same time (Chapter 1, p. 10). A compound inequality can be an **AND statement** such as $-5 < x \le 10$ which means the values of x must be less than or equal to 10 AND at the same time greater than -5. In other words, all the real numbers that are between -5 and 10 not including -5, but including 10. You can also have a compound inequality that is an **OR statement**. These are written separately, for example, $y < 0$ or $y > 3$. So the answer meets one of the inequalities but not necessarily the other one.

1   Solve and graph this compound inequality.

$$-1 < w + 8 < 12$$

$$
\begin{array}{c|c}
-1 < w + 8 & w + 8 < 12 \\
\underline{-8 \qquad -8} & \underline{-8 \quad -8} \\
-9 < w & w \quad < 4
\end{array}
$$ Solve each inequality separately.

or

$w > -9$

So, $w > -9$ AND $w < 4$, which can also be written as $-9 < w < 4$.

Now, as long as there are no variables except in the middle of the compound inequality, it's easier to solve this AND inequality in this manner.

$$
\begin{array}{c}
-1 < w + 8 < 12 \\
\underline{-8 \qquad -8 \quad -8} \\
-9 < \quad w \quad < 4
\end{array}
$$

Remember, this reads: "-9 is less than w AND w is less than 4.

2   Solve and graph this compound inequality.

$$-x + 5 \geq -1 \quad OR \quad x - 6 > 1$$
$$\underline{\quad -5 \quad -5 \quad} \qquad \underline{\quad +6 \quad +6 \quad}$$
$$-x \quad \geq -6 \qquad x \quad > 7$$
$$x \quad \leq 6$$

Notice the inequality
symbol reversed.

Again, solve each inequality separately. Notice it's an OR compound inequality.

Can a real number be less than or equal to 6 AND at the same time be greater than 7? That is the reason this is an OR statement.

So, $x \leq 6$ OR $x > 7$.

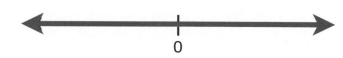

3   Solve the following compound inequality.

$$w - 3 < 1 \quad OR \quad w + 3 > -3$$
$$\underline{\quad +3 \quad +3 \quad} \qquad \underline{\quad -3 \quad -3 \quad}$$
$$w \quad < 4 \qquad w \quad > -6$$

So, $w < 4$ OR $w > -6$.

Can you see that because it's an OR compound inequality, any real number makes at least one of these inequalities a true statement? So the solution is the set of real numbers.

Remember that an AND statement must satisfy BOTH inequalities at the same time. However, an OR statement only has to satisfy one of the inequalities and not necessarily the other one, although it could satisfy both. For example, in the example above, the number 2 satisfies both statements since 2 is less than 4 and greater than -6. The number -10 satisfies the inequality $w < 4$ since -10 is less than 4, but it does not satisfy the inequality $w > -6$. The number -10 is still part of the solution since the compound inequality is an <u>OR</u> statement. When in doubt always check a few numbers to support your answer.

Practice

Solve and graph the following compound inequalities.

1 $8 > -2w > -2$

2 $-8 \leq 3y + 1 \leq 16$

3 $25 > 5x + 10 \geq -10$

4 $6y - 6 > 30$ or $-y > 5$

5 $4x + 2 < 6$ and $.5x > 5$

Thinking Again About Inequalities

It's easy to overlook how often we use inequalities and compound inequalities in the real world. Look at the examples below.

> The speed limit on Route 81 is at least 40 mph but not more than 65 mph.
>
> Ms. Kaplan does not want to spend more than $135 on her cable/Internet bill.
>
> The maximum weight allowed on the Trumansburg Bridge is 3,000 lbs.
>
> Jonah's iPhone has a data limit of 300 MB.

Find five real-world examples of inequalities. Write a sentence stating the inequality and then translate it in symbolic form. Include at least one compound inequality. You can search the Internet for examples.

1 _____

_____

2 _____

_____

3 _____

_____

4 _____

_____

5 _____

_____

Solving Absolute Value Equations

An equation or an inequality with an **absolute value** symbol ($|\ |$) must be solved differently than the equations or inequalities you've done before. To understand the steps needed, let's review what is meant by absolute value. The absolute value of a number is the distance a number is away from 0, and the answer is always positive.

When solving an absolute value equation or inequality, you must consider two cases. When we see $|x| = 8$, we must consider that x inside the absolute value symbol can be 8 or –8 since the absolute value of either one is positive 8.

Solve for the variable.

1. $|w + 12| = 20$ You need to consider two cases.
     Either $(w + 12) = 20$ or $-(w + 12) = 20$.

Case 1	Case 2
$w + 12 = 20$	$-(w + 12) = 20$
$\underline{-12\quad -12}$	$-w - 12 = 20$
$w = 8$	$\underline{+12\quad +12}$
	$-w = 32$
	$w = -32$

Be careful when distributing the negative.

So the answers are $w = 8$ or $w = -32$.   The check is very important!

$|w + 12| = 20$	$|w + 12| = 20$
$|8 + 12| = 20?$	$|-32 + 12| = 20?$

Yes! The absolute value of 20 does equal 20 and the absolute value of –20 does equal 20.

Note: Case 1 and Case 2 can also be written like this: Both sides have been divided by –1.

   Case 1: $w + 12 = 20$ or Case 2: $w + 12 = -20$.

However, writing it this way may make it seem like an absolute value can equal a negative number. It's actually saying that the expression inside the absolute value is 20 or –20. Following the method in Example 1 will make it easier later to solve inequalities with absolute value.

Practice

1. Solve these two absolute value equations. Explain why these two equations are different.

   a $|w| + 5 = 6$ b $|w + 5| = 6$

   _____

   _____

   _____

   _____

2. Check both equations above.

3. Solve $2|y| + 3 = 4y - 5$. I've set the two cases for you below.

   Case 1: $2y + 3 = 4y - 5$ | Case 2: $2(-y) + 3 = 4y - 5$

4. Explain why this equation has NO solution. $|x + 8| = -3$

   _____

   _____

5) $|3x + 9| = 0$

6) $|2w| + 6 = 3w - 1$

7) $w + 5 = |w| + 5$

8) $6|x - 2| = -4$

9) $|2x + 6| = 3$

Absolute Value Inequalities

To solve and graph an absolute value inequality, make sure to use two cases. Here's one example.

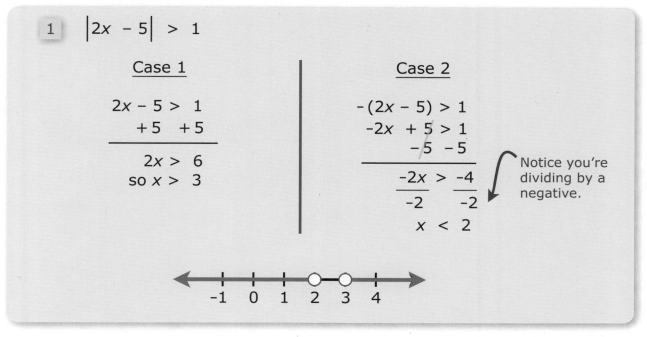

1    $|2x - 5| > 1$

Case 1		Case 2

Case 1

$2x - 5 > 1$
$ + 5 \quad + 5$
$\overline{}$
$2x > 6$
so $x > 3$

Case 2

$-(2x - 5) > 1$
$-2x + 5 > 1$
$ -5 \quad -5$
$\overline{}$
$\dfrac{-2x}{-2} \quad \dfrac{-4}{-2}$
$x < 2$

Notice you're dividing by a negative.

Solve and graph these absolute value inequalities. Make sure you read each problem first before you start.

1    $|x + 3| - 4 \leq 0$

2    $3|y + 5| > 3$

3 $|m - 5| < -2$

4 $|3x + 8| \geq 0$

5 $|2x| - 5 < 3$

6 $|3x - 2| \geq 10$

Challenge

Use your reasoning skills to solve this compound absolute value inequality. Graph the solution. Hint: Find where the intersections occur.

$$6 \ < \ |x + 1| \ \leq \ 8$$

Chapter Review

Write the letter of the yellow card that matches the blue card. The cards can also be traced on another sheet of paper and cut out.

1 _____	a
Twice the sum of *w* plus 5 is less than 150.	$125 < x < 150$

2 _____	b
Kat has 3 pets. Together Kat and Steve have at most 15 pets.	$\dfrac{x}{3} \leq 15$

3 _____	c
The quotient of a number and 3 is not greater than 15.	$x - 5 \geq 150$

4 _____	d
Three times Laura's salary is greater than $15 an hour.	$2x + 5 < 150$

5 _____	e
Twice Wilbur's salary plus $5 is less than $150.	$2(w + 5) < 150$

6 _____

The difference of 5 less than a number is at least 150.

f

$$|x + 10| \geq 150$$

7 _____

Larry said his weight is more than 125 lbs but no more than 150 lbs.

g

$$3x > 15$$

8 _____

The distance Mary traveled going south plus 10 miles going west was at least 150 miles.

h

$$3 + x \leq 15$$

9 _____

The down payment for the sofa will be from $125 to $150 inclusive.

i

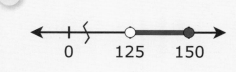

10 _____

Terri said her bowling score is always between 125 and 150.

j

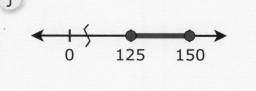

The term **absolute value** has been in use since the 19th century. The notation | | was invented by Karl Weierstrass, a famous German mathematician (1815-1897) who also is known for his study of functions. We will study functions at a later chapter.

Chapter 6

Polynomials

In this chapter we will learn how to work and master polynomials, the very tools of algebra. What is a polynomial? "Poly" means many and "nomial" refers to numbers. A **polynomial** is an **expression** with numbers and variables, or it can even be a number (constant) alone. So far you've worked with polynomials when they were inside equations. But in this chapter you will learn the rules to operating with variable terms. The stronger you become at working with polynomials the stronger an algebra student you will become.

A polynomial has terms that are raised to **whole number exponents**. If a variable is raised to a negative power, or you see a term with the square root of a variable, or a variable in the denominator then the expression is <u>not</u> a polynomial. Here are some examples to study.

Polynomials	NOT Polynomials
-5	$\dfrac{5}{w}$
$2x^3 - 8x + 7$	$2x^{-3} - 2x$
$18 + ab$	$5\sqrt{x}$
$\dfrac{34w^4}{3}$	
$5a^3 + 2ab - c + 4$	$10w^{1/3}$

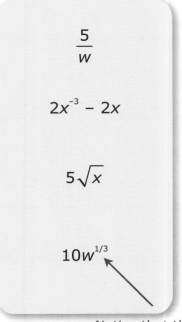

Notice that the exponent on the variable is not a whole number.

A polynomial is classified by the number of **terms** it contains. Monomials ("mono" means one) have one term (or group). Binomials ("bi" means two) have two terms and trinomials ("tri" means three) have three terms. A **term** is a group that is separated by addition and subtraction. By the way, any polynomial with more than three terms is just called a polynomial.

Below are examples to study so you can understand the definition of a **term** and how to classify polynomials.

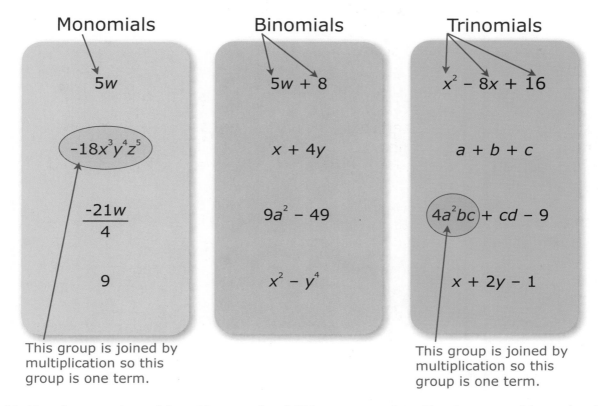

Monomials	Binomials	Trinomials
$5w$	$5w + 8$	$x^2 - 8x + 16$
$-18x^3y^4z^5$	$x + 4y$	$a + b + c$
$\dfrac{-21w}{4}$	$9a^2 - 49$	$4a^2bc + cd - 9$
9	$x^2 - y^4$	$x + 2y - 1$

This group is joined by multiplication so this group is one term.

This group is joined by multiplication so this group is one term.

Notice how only subtraction and addition separates the terms. Also, don't forget that the **coefficient** is the number in front of the variable.

Polynomials and their terms are often classified by their degree. The degree of a term is the sum of the <u>exponents</u> of the variables. For example, the term $-18x^3y^4z^5$ has a degree of 12. Add the exponents: 3 from the x, 4 from the y, and 5 from the z. The term $5w$ has a degree of 1. Do not add the coefficients.

To find the degree of a polynomial, find the degree of each term, then select the degree that is the largest. The degree of a polynomial is the same as the degree of its largest-degree term. For example, in the polynomial $4w^3y^2z - 10wz + 3$, the first term $4w^3y^2z^1$ has a degree of 6. Add the exponents: 3 from the w, 2 from the y, and 1 from the z. The second term, $-10w^1z^1$, has a degree of 2, 1 from the w and 1 from the z. The last term of 3 has a degree of 0 since there is no variable. So the degree of the polynomial is 6. It gets its degree from the <u>largest sum</u>. You do <u>not</u> add all the exponents throughout the polynomial.

The purpose of finding the degree will be useful only later when we use polynomial equations to graph. The degree will tell us if the figure is a line or a circle, etc. More on this when we study <u>functions</u>.

Determine if the polynomial is a monomial, a binomial, a trinomial, or just a polynomial and state its degree. Study the examples below to help you first.

1 $\underbrace{8P^3Q^2}_{\text{degree 5}} + \underbrace{9P^2Q}_{\text{degree 3}} - \underbrace{3}_{\text{degree 0}}$

> This is a trinomial because it has three terms. The degree of the polynomial is 5. The first term has a degree of 5 (add the exponents), the second term has a degree of 3, and the last term has a degree of 0 since there is no variable. Taking the term that has the largest sum gives you the degree of the polynomial.

2 $\underbrace{2x^2}_{\text{degree 2}} - \underbrace{5x^4y^8}_{\text{degree 12}}$

> This is a binomial because it has two terms. The degree of the polynomial is 12 (the sum of the exponents of the second term is higher than the degree of the first term which is 2, so the polynomial gets the degree of the term that has the largest sum).

State the type of polynomial and its degree.

		Type	Degree
1	$5x + 2$	_____	_____
2	$3x^5 - 6x^4 + x$	_____	_____
3	-24	_____	_____
4	$a + b - c + d$	_____	_____
5	$-30t^8 - 18t^4w$	_____	_____
6	$-5x^8y^3 + 2yz + y^6$	_____	_____
7	$2ab^3 + 4ab + b - 3$	_____	_____
8	$2x^3y^2z$	_____	_____

Sometimes it's very helpful to read and write polynomials by arranging the terms in **standard form**. This means arranging the terms with the highest degree first going down to the term with the lowest degree.

1   Write this polynomial in standard form.

$-8 + 2x^2 - 3x^4 + 9x$

Answer: $-3x^4 + 2x^2 + 9x - 8$

2   $2x^2y + x^3 + 10 - 4xy^2$

Since x is first before y in the alphabet, start with the highest degree term and let the x's decrease as shown here.

Answer: $x^3 + 2x^2y - 4xy^2 + 10$

Write the following polynomials in standard form.

1   $5x + 7x^3$ _____

2   $7a^3 - a^4 + 1$ _____

3   $6 + 2w^2 + w^3 - 11w$ _____

4   $7ab^3 + 2a^3b^2 + 9 - 4b$ _____

5   $-3c + 2a - a^2$ _____

6   $-40 - y^2 + y$ _____

7   $-10M + 11M^2 + 18$ _____

Remember, when you work with polynomials your answer is not wrong if your answer is in a different order, as long as all the terms are correct. It's just easier to communicate your answer if you write it in standard form.

Addition of Polynomials

Understanding Like Terms

In order to add and subtract polynomials, you can only combine (or put together) like terms. Like terms are any terms that have <u>identical endings</u>. While the coefficients can differ, the rest of the term must be exactly the same. Variables and their exponents must match. Examples are below.

Given Term	Like Terms			Not Like Term
$5x^3$	$-8x^3$	$89x^3$	$4x^3$	$5x^4$
$8ab$	$-15ab$	ab	$4ab$	$-10b$
$7B$	B	$-200B$	$15B$	$-200b$
$10yw$	$8wy$	$-90yw$	$\frac{2}{3}yw$	$10y$
$-30a^2b^3c$	a^2b^3c	$11a^2b^3c$	$.5a^2b^3c$	$8a^2b^3c^2$
84	-9	11	$\frac{1}{4}$	$84b$

This term is a constant and constants can be combined with other constants.

This 84 is a coefficient and not a constant.

Notice that in the case of $7B$, all similar terms should also have caps. A small "b" is a different variable than a big "B." Also, remember yw is the same as wy. Again, to combine terms, you must only combine terms that have the <u>exact</u> same ending, as we will see in these examples.

Add the following polynomials. Write your answer in standard form.

1 $(3x^2 + 8x - 6) + (10 + 9x - 5x^2)$ Please notice that when we add terms the ending remains the same. Always watch your signs.

Answer: $-2x^2 + 17x + 4$

2. $(9a^2b + 18ab^2 - 3c) + (-9a^2b + ab^2 - 10c)$

     Answer: $0a^2b + 19ab^2 - 13c$

            or $19ab^2 - 13c$

3. $(2xy + 3) + (-4x + 4) + (-9xy + x - 5)$

     Answer: $-3x - 7xy + 2$ It helps to cross out the terms as you combine them.

Circle which terms are like terms.

1. $9x, \quad -10xy, \quad 9y, \quad -10x$

2. $3ab^2, \quad -45ab^2, \quad .05a^2b, \quad 20ab$

3. $2wt, \quad 5w, \quad 24t, \quad -5tw$

4. $-199v^3, \quad vt^3, \quad v^3, \quad v^3t^3$

Write a term that is a like term to the given term below:

5. $-8w^4$ _____

6. $10abc$ _____

7. $\frac{1}{5}g^5$ _____

8. x^3y^3z _____

9.   Explain why these are not like terms. $-5x^5y^6z^4$ and $-5x^5y^6z^3$.

_____

_____

10.   If $x = 3$, show that adding $2x + 3x^2$ IS NOT $5x^3$. What does this illustrate? Explain your thinking.

_____

_____

11 If $x = 3$, show that adding $2x^2 + 3x^2$ IS the same as $5x^2$. What does this illustrate? Explain your thinking.

_____

_____

> Please remember that algebra is generalized arithmetic. When you have a doubt about what to do in an algebra problem, try a simple arithmetic problem that illustrates the same concept.

Add the following polynomials. Write your answer in standard form.

12 $(15c^2 + 2c - 56) + (-14c^2 + c - 2)$

13 $(-2abc + 2) + (-6abc + 4) + (-abc - 8)$

14 $(8a^2 - 2a - 6) + (-9a^2 - 5a + 4)$

15 $(70 + 2ab - a) + (a + 5ab - 70)$

16 $(18x + 24) + (-19x - 1) + (2x^2 - x + 2)$

17 $(w + 2) + (2w - 9) + (6 + w)$

18
$$\begin{array}{r} 2r + 5 \\ + \; -5r - 10 \\ \hline 8r - 2 \end{array}$$

Notice that a problem can be written vertically as well as horizontally.

Find the missing polynomial.

19 $(4v^3 + 2v + 8)$ + (_____) = $(5v^3 - 5v + 2)$

20 $(5ab^2 + 2ab + 4) + ($_____$)$ = $(-6ab^2 + 2c + 1)$

Understanding Like Terms

Now that you know the rules of combining like terms, the following is a geometric interpretation to help you visualize why you can only combine terms that have the same ending.

This square has an area of x^2 square units since the distance on each side is x. Remember, to find its area, multiply base times height.

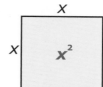

This rectangle has an area of x square units since the length is x and the width is 1.

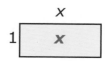

And this square has an area of **1** square unit since it's 1 unit on each side.

When we add $(2x^2 + 3x + 4) + (x^2 + 2x + 3)$

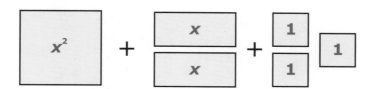

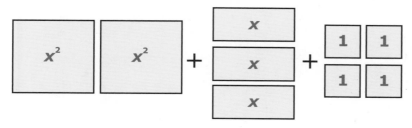

Can you see that you get $3x^2 + 5x + 7$? If you have a negative quantity, you can use a different color to represent the negative quantity. On the next page, there are some tiles that can be traced onto a sheet of paper to cut out. The magenta ones indicate negative quantities. Try to create your own problems using the tiles provided.

Tile Addition

Use the tiles below to show the sum of $(x^2 + 2x - 4) + (2x^2 - 4x + 5)$.
You can paste your result below or on a separate sheet of paper.

x^2	x^2	x^2	$-x^2$
x	x	x	$-x$
x	x	$-x$	$-x$
x	x	$-x$	$-x$

1	1	1	1	1	1	-1	-1	-1	-1
1	1	1	1	1	1	-1	-1	-1	-1

Subtraction of Polynomials

If you remember from Chapter 1, subtraction is the same as adding the additive inverse. You also need to remember the key words <u>from</u>, <u>less</u>, and <u>less than</u>. Just as in addition, you can only combine like terms.

1 $(5x - 3) - (2x + 5)$ The subtraction sign is in the middle. You must change the signs of every term that follows that subtraction sign.

Rewrite: $5x - 3 + (-2x - 5)$

Answer: $3x - 8$

---

2   Take $(-3ab - b + 2)$ from $(-2ab + 2b - 5)$.

Rewrite: $(-2ab + 2b - 5) - (-3ab - b + 2)$

$(-2ab + 2b - 5) + (3ab + b - 2)$

Remember that the words <u>from</u> and <u>less than</u> reverse the order.

Answer: $ab + 3b - 7$

---

3   What is $(-15 + 2b^2)$ less than $(8b^2 + b - 4)$?

Rewrite: $(8b^2 + b - 4) - (-15 + 2b^2)$

$(8b^2 + b - 4) + (15 - 2b^2)$

Answer: $6b^2 + b + 11$

One suggestion to help with distributing the subtraction sign is to put a **1** (so you have -1) in front of what you're about to subtract.

4 $(8a^2b + 2c - 4) - (-12a^2b - 4c + 6)$

Rewrite $(8a^2b + 2c - 4) - \mathbf{1}(-12a^2b - 4c + 6)$

Distribute: $8a^2b + 2c - 4 + 12a^2b + 4c - 6$

Answer: $20a^2b + 6c - 10$

Practice

Simplify. Write your answer in standard form.

1 $(34P + 5) - (-4P - 8)$

2 $(2x^2 + 5x - 3) - (4x^2 - 6x + 4)$

3 $(-2ab + a - 4) - (9 + 2a - 2ab)$

4 $(4w + 4) - (4w + 4)$

5   From $(-5B + 3)$ subtract $(-2B - 5)$

6   Take $(6x^3 + 3)$ from $(7x^3 + 2x - 8)$

7 $(9A + 4)$ less $(4A - 18)$

8 $(9A + 4)$ less than $(4A - 18)$

9   Subtract $(4a^4 + 2a^3 - 1)$ from $(3 + 3a^3 + a^4)$

10   Simplify $(-9x + 5) - (8x - 6) + (9x + 1)$

11   Simplify $(8y + 2x + 2xy + 1) + (3xy + 1) - (-8y - 3xy + 2)$

12   What is WRONG in this problem? Explain your thinking. What is the correct answer?

$(12a^3 + b) - (3a - b)$ results in $9a^2 + 2b^2$

_____

_____

Exponents in Monomials

To be an expert at multiplication of polynomials it's important to review how to work with exponents. As you know, when a base is raised to a power, say 4^3, it means that the base (4) is being multiplied by itself three times, (4)(4)(4) which equals 64.

In the expression $5x^3$, only the x is being taken to the third power, meaning $(5)(x)(x)(x)$. In $5x^3$, the coefficient 5 is not being taken to the third power. However, if you see $(5x)^3$, then this means $(5x)(5x)(5x)$, which is the answer $125x^3$.

When you multiply monomials, for example, $(4x^3)(-5x^4)$, you multiply the coefficients and then record how many x's you are multiplying. $(4x^3)(-5x^4)$ means $(4)(x)(x)(x)(-5)(x)(x)(x)(x)$. You have 7 factors of x. So the answer is $-20x^7$. YES, you can multiply unlike terms. You are just counting the number of factors of each same variable.

Multiplication of Monomials

Multiply the coefficients. For each base variable, **add** the exponents of the same base.

1. Multiply $(3a^2b)(-3a^4b^4)$

   Multiply the coefficients, -9. Remember you are not adding.
   You have 6 factors of a and 5 factors of b.
   Answer: $-9a^6b^5$

2. Find the product $(-3abc^4)(2ac^5)$

   Answer: $-6a^2bc^9$

3. Multiply $(-w)(-3w^7)$ Remember that $-w$ means $-1w$.

   Answer: $3w^8$

4. Simplify $(-6p)^3$
   $(-6p)(-6p)(-6p)$ Remember to write this out.
   Answer: $-216p^3$

Practice

Practice following the rules for multiplying monomials.

1. $(9w^4)(-4w^6)$

2. $(-2a)(2a)$

3. $(-7x)(-7x^5)$

4. $(6g^3)(8g^3)(2g)$

5. $(-y^5)(-y^6)$

6. $\left(\frac{3}{4}w^7\right)(4w^{10})$

7. $\left(-\frac{1}{2}a\right)\left(-\frac{2}{3}a^4\right)$

8. $(10t^5)(-19t^5)(-t)$

9. $(11ab^3c^6)(-11ab^4c)$

10. $(-8d)(-8f)(-2d^6)$

11. $(-10r)(10r^4)(10r^6)$

12. $(15y^5z^3)(-.2y^7z)$

13. $(4ef^6)(\underline{\hspace{1cm}}) = -16ef^8$

14. $(\underline{\hspace{1cm}})\left(-\frac{2}{5}w^4\right) = 8w^9$

Write the following problems out. See if you can find your own shortcut for doing these problems.

15. $(-3a)^3$ = _____   = _____

16. $(-4w^2)^4$ = _____   = _____

17. $(5c^3d)^3$ = _____   = _____

18. $(-10g^5t^8)^4$ = _____   = _____

When a monomial is taken to a power, follow this rule.

Take the **coefficient** to that power and then multiply the exponent of each variable by the outside exponent.

$$(-10g^5t^8)^4 = (-10)^4(g^{5 \cdot 4})(t^{8 \cdot 4}) = 10{,}000g^{20}t^{32}$$

The following problems are a little harder. Again, when in doubt, write out the expressions and take your time. Math doesn't have to be rushed!

1. $(3a^3b^2)^2(-2ab)$

2. $(-5c)(-5c^4)^2$

3. $(4a)^2(-4a^2)^2$

4. $(-w)^3(2w^4)(w)$

5. $(-6e^4)^2(-2e)^2$

6. $\left(\frac{1}{2}a^5b^3\right)^2(-2a)^2(3ab)$

7. $(.5x^2)^2(.001x^3)(10x)$

8. Francois thought that $(-1)^{19}$ equaled -19 and Luis thought that it equaled -1. Who is right? Explain your thinking.

_____

_____

Multiplication of a Polynomial by a Monomial

To multiply a monomial by a polynomial, use the **distributive property** and apply the rules you just learned.

1   Multiply $-4x(2x - 3y)$ This is a monomial multiplying a binomial.

Answer : $-8x^2 + 12xy$

2   Multiply $8a^2b(2ab^2 - 5a + 1)$ This is a monomial multiplying a trinomial. Don't forget to multiply by the last term, too.

Answer: $16a^3b^3 - 40a^3b + 8a^2b$

3   Multiply $(5 + 2y - w + w^2)(-3aw)$ You can write the monomial in front, or you can distribute as it is written.

Answer: $-15aw - 6ayw + 3aw^2 - 3aw^3$

Answer the following questions.

1   Why is $-6ayw$ the same as $-6awy$? Explain your thinking.

_____

_____

2   One of your friends had to multiply $(2x)(3x)(5x^2)$ and got this answer $6x^2 + 10x^3$. Can you explain what she/he did wrong? What is the correct answer?

_____

_____

_____

3   Is there an easier way to do this problem: $5w(6y + y)$?

_____

_____

More Practice

Using a separate sheet of paper if needed, find each product. Remember to be careful with your signs.

1 $11(m - 7)$

2 $8y(-2y^2 + y - 10)$

3 $-9a(2a^2 - 6a + 1)$

4 $2ab(3a - 2b - c)$

5 $-w(3w^6 - 2w^5 + 2w^4 - 1)$

6 $18y^5(-2y^4 - 10y + 3)$

7 $abc(a^2b^3c^5 + a^6b - c^8)$

8 $(2x^3 + 3a - 1)(-2ax)$

9 $(-p^5 - p^4 + p^3 - p^2 - p)(-15p)$

10 $\frac{1}{2}a^4\left(4a^3 - 8a^2 - \frac{2}{3}a\right)$

Simplify when possible.

11 $(4a^2b)(2ab)(-2b)$

12 $(4a^2b)(2ab - 2b)$

13 $(-7a)^2(-7a^2)$

14 $(acd)^2(acd^2)$

15 $(90t - 2)(-t)$

16 $(90t - 2)(-t)^2$

17 $2ab(3a^2b + 1) - 7ab$

18 $9w^3z(-9wz + 1) + 10w^4z^2 + w^3z$

Multiplication of Binomials

Binomial multiplication is one of the most important skills in algebra. To multiply binomials follow these examples.

1 $(y + 3)(y + 4)$

This is the same as $y(y + 4) + 3(y + 4)$. You can write it like this and do the work, but I encourage you to do the following and use arrows!

Multiply the first term of the first binomial times the first term of the second binomial, then multiply the first term of the first binomial times the second term of the second binomial. Then multiply the second term of the first binomial times the first term of the second binomial and then multiply the second term of the first binomial times the second term of the second binomial. Lastly, always check if you can simplify your result.

$(y + 3)(y + 4)$

$y^2 + 4y + 3y + 12$ Remember $y \cdot 4$ is better written as $4y$.

$y^2 + 7y + 12$ After multiplying, you need to look for like terms in case you can simplify your answer.

2 $(x + 5)(x - 9)$

$x^2 - 9x + 5x - 45$ Be careful with the signs!

$x^2 - 4x - 45$

3 $(c + 8)(c - 8)$

$c^2 - 8c + 8c - 64$ Notice how the middle terms cancel each other.

$c^2 - 64$ Think: What types of binomials end up with middle terms canceling?

4 $(x + y)^2$ This means $(x + y)(x + y)$. Make sure to write it out!
$(x + y)(x + y)$

$x^2 + xy + yx + y^2$ Remember that yx is the same as xy. Multiplication is commutative.

$x^2 + 2xy + y^2$

Practice

Practice multiplying these binomials following the examples. Please do first times first, first times second, second times first, and second times second! If you hear someone telling you to do FOIL, tell them to wait.

1. $(a + 5)(a + 4)$

2. $(a + 5)(a - 4)$

3. $(a - 5)(a + 4)$

4. $(c + 8)(c + 2)$

5. $(y + 9)(y - 10)$

6. $(r - 1)(r + 7)$

7. $(w - 5)(w - 7)$

8. $(c - 2)(c - 6)$

9. $(y - 11)(y - 11)$

10. $(v - 8)(v - 8)$

11. $(g - 6)(g + 6)$

12. $(p + 12)(p - 12)$

13. $(x + 9)(x - 9)$

14. $(y + 13)(y - 13)$

15. $(a + b)(a - b)$

16. $(7 + w)(2 + w)$

17. $(c + d)(e + f)$

18. $(c + d)(e - f)$

19. $(x + 7)^2$

20. $(x - 10)^2$

Using FOIL

What is FOIL anyway? FOIL is a shortcut for multiplying binomials in your head. FOIL stands for F – multiply the first term times the first term, the L – multiply the last term times the last term. Then the O and the I stand for add the Outer terms and Inner terms after you multiply them.

1   $(x + 3)(x – 11)$

x^2 -33   (first times first and last times last)

outer terms

$(x + 3)(x – 11)$

inner terms

Now, in your head, multiply outers and inners and combine them. So -11x (outer terms) is combined with 3x (inner terms) which gives you -8x.

Answer: $x^2 – 8x – 33$

Use FOIL to quickly do these problems in your head.

1   $(x + 6)(x + 7)$

2   $(y + 5)(y + 8)$

3   $(v + 1)(v – 9)$

4   $(w – 7)(w + 8)$

5   $(a + 4)(a – 6)$

6   $(w + 9)(w – 8)$

7   $(y + 10)(y – 11)$

8   $(x – 6)(x – 6)$

9   $(x – 1)(x – 10)$

10   $(b – 7)(b – 8)$

11   $(c – 5)(c + 5)$

12   $(y – 3)(y + 3)$

13   $(e + f)(e – f)$

14   $\left(w + \frac{1}{2}\right)\left(w + \frac{1}{2}\right)$

15   $(3 + w)(3 + w)$

16   $(r + 18)(r + 3)$

17   $(d – 12)(d – 3)$

18   $(a – b)(a – b)$

19   $(r – 1)(r + 99)$

20   $(4 – x)(4 + x)$

Using a separate sheet of paper, answer the following questions.

21   Why is $16 – x^2$ different than $x^2 – 16$? Explain your thinking.

22   For this problem, $(x + 5)(x + 5)$, a student wrote the answer as $x^2 + 25$. Show by letting $x = 3$, that $x^2 + 25$ is the incorrect answer. What is the correct answer?

While "FOIL" is a handy shortcut for easy binomials, the following problems are best solved by multiplying every term out as we did before. Study the following examples. You will now learn how to multiply binomials times any kind of polynomial.

1 $8(c + 4)(c - 1)$

Here, you can multiply the 8 times the $(c + 4)$ and then proceed, OR you can multiply $(c + 4)(c - 1)$ and then that answer times 8. The first method is recommended so that you don't forget to multiply your answer by 8 at the end, which is a common mistake.

$8(c + 4)(c - 1)$
$(8c + 32)(c - 1)$
$8c^2 - 8c + 32c - 32$

$8c^2 + 24c - 32$

It's very important to note that the problem is NOT $8[(c + 4) + (c - 1)]$ so the 8 only multiplies either one of the binomials but not both! For example, if you had to multiply $7 \cdot 5 \cdot 2$, you can multiply the 7 times the 5, get 35 and then times 2 which is 70, OR you can multiply the 5 times the 2 which is 10 and then 7 times 10 which is 70 again. It's incorrect to multiply the 7 times the 5 and then the 7 times the 2. Just remember $7 \cdot 5 \cdot 2$ is NOT the same as $7 \cdot (5 + 2)$. Please remember algebra is generalized arithmetic. You can always substitute numbers to make sure the laws of arithmetic are applied correctly.

2 $(y + 5)(y^2 + 2y - 3)$

Multiply the first term in the binomial by each term in the trinomial. Then multiply the second term in the binomial by each term in the trinomial and don't forget to simplify.

$y^3 + 2y^2 - 3y + 5y^2 + 10y - 15$

$y^3 + 7y^2 + 7y - 15$ Write your answer in standard form.

3 $(a + b)^3$

Write this out as $(a + b)(a + b)(a + b)$.

$(a^2 + 2ab + b^2)(a + b)$ This is what you get after you multiply the first two binomials. Then do as in example 2.

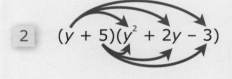

$a^3 + a^2b + 2a^2b + 2ab^2 + b^2a + b^3$ Same as ab^2.

$a^3 + 3a^2b + 3ab^2 + b^3$

> **4** $6a(a + 2)(a - 5)$
>
> $(6a^2 + 12a)(a - 5)$ Remember to multiply the $6a$ times the first binomial.
>
> $6a^3 - 30a^2 + 12a^2 - 60a$
>
> $6a^3 - 18a^2 - 60a$ Remember to simplify your answer and write it in standard form.

Using a separate sheet of paper, multiply the following polynomials. Make sure to simplify.

1 $(a - 13)(a + 13)$ **11** $(a + b)^3$

2 $(v + 6)^2$ **12** $(a + b)(b + c)(c + d)$

3 $(a - 4)^2$ **13** $(2w + 1)(r + 3w)(b - y)$

4 $12(a - 11)(a + 11)$ **14** $x^3(x - 3)(x + 3)$

5 $(x + 3)(x^2 + 3x - 1)$ **15** $\left(\frac{3}{4} + x\right)\left(\frac{3}{4} - x\right)$

6 $5(r + 2)(r^2 + 3r + 4)$

7 $(5x^3)(x - 5)^2$ In problem #7, make sure you square the binomial first.

8 $(t - 6)(t^2 - 2t - 5)$

9 $(c + 4)(c - 5)(c - 2)$

10 $(x + y)(x^2 + 2xy + y^2)$

Each of these answers contains a common error made by a student. Find the error and correct the answer.

16 $(20 + w)(20 - w)$ _____

    Student answered: _____
      $w^2 - 400$

                                   _____

17 $(a + 7b)(a + 7b)$ _____

    Student answered: _____
    $a^2 + 14a^2b^2 + 49b^2$

                                   _____

Special Products

When multiplying polynomials, the following special products are important to remember. However, when in doubt about these, take your time and multiply as you have been shown.

Difference of Two Squares

memorize

$$(a + b)(a - b) = a^2 - b^2$$

Squaring Binomials

$$(a + b)^2 = a^2 + 2ab + b^2$$

$$(a - b)^2 = a^2 - 2ab + b^2$$

memorize

Cubing Binomials

$$(a + b)^3 = a^3 + 3a^2b + 3ab^2 + b^3$$

$$(a - b)^3 = a^3 - 3a^2b + 3ab^2 - b^3$$

memorize

Using a separate sheet of paper, follow the special product formulas above to quickly do these problems.

1. $(r + 5)(r - 5)$

2. $(x + 15)(x - 15)$

3. $(p + 25)(p - 25)$

4. $(x + y)(x - y)$

5. $(w - 9)(w + 9)$

6. $(1 + 3w)(1 - 3w)$

7. $(a + r)^2$

8. $(k + 14)^2$

9. $(a + 12)^2$

10. $(x + 1)^2$

11. $(a + 3)^2$

12. $(2a + b)^2$

13. $(2a - b)^2$

14. $(1 - 3x)^2$

15. $(x + y)^3$

16. $(x - y)^3$

17. $(x + 2)^3$

18. $(x - 3)^3$

Polynomial Gardens

Below is a geometric representation of how a rectangle with sides $(x + 3)$ and $(x + 2)$ yields an area of $x^2 + 5x + 6$. Study the rectangle below. This is called creating a "polynomial garden." You can decorate it with trees and flowers if you want for fun.

$$(x + 3)(x + 2)$$

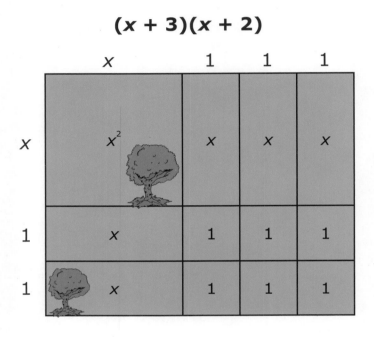

Using the tiles on the next page, make a polynomial garden to represent the answer to any of these products. These are some you can choose or try your own.

1    $(x + 2)(x + 1)$

2    $(x - 2)(x + 2)$

3    $(2x + 1)(x + 2)$

Tiles

Trace these tiles onto a sheet of paper to cut out.

x^2	x^2	x^2	$-x^2$
x	x	x	$-x$
x	x	x	$-x$
x	x	x	$-x$

1	1	1	1	1	1	1	-1	-1	-1
1	1	1	1	1	1	1	-1	-1	-1

1	1	1	1	1	1	1
1	1	1	1	1	1	1

Division of Monomials

As you know already, division is the inverse operation of multiplication. Take a look at these examples to help you understand how to divide monomials.

1   Divide: $\dfrac{50a^5}{-10a^2}$

     This means: $\dfrac{50 \cdot a \cdot a \cdot a \cdot a \cdot a}{-10 \cdot a \cdot a}$

Divide the coefficients. Notice that two pairs of a's cancelled (any number divided by itself is one) leaving you with an answer of $-5a^3$.

Division of Monomials

Divide the coefficients. For each base, **subtract** the exponents of the same base.

---

2   Find the quotient: $\dfrac{-30n^3t^6}{-60n^3t^5}$

Divide the coefficients and you get $\dfrac{1}{2}$ or .5. The n's cancel, and five of the t's cancel, leaving a t in the numerator.

The answer is $\dfrac{1}{2}t$ or .5t.

Notice that $\dfrac{n^3}{n^3}$ is the same as n^0; therefore n^0 is 1.

Any number to the zero power is 1.

Practice

Using a separate sheet of paper, practice dividing monomials. Assume no variables in the denominators are zero.

1) $\dfrac{-4w^3}{2w}$

2) $\dfrac{2r^5}{2r^5}$

3) $\dfrac{-8abc^4}{-2ac}$

4) $\dfrac{10t^6}{-20t^4}$

5) $\dfrac{51c^4d^5e}{3c^4d^2}$

6) $\dfrac{3n^4y^6}{51ny}$

7) $\dfrac{(-4a^3b)^2}{-4a^3b}$

8) $\dfrac{9^2h^3y}{-9h^3}$

9) $\dfrac{-3^2h^5}{-27h}$

10) $\dfrac{(5gh)^3}{(5gh)^3}$

11) $50abc \div -50$

12) $\dfrac{ac^5}{-2ac^5}$

13) $\dfrac{-900xy^5}{-9,000y}$

14) $\dfrac{57wxz}{-3wz}$

15) $\dfrac{-3wxz}{57wz}$

16) $8x^5 \div -16x^4$

17) $-16x^5 \div 48x^5$

18) $\dfrac{(-6)^2p^3rs^6}{-4p^3rs^3}$

19) $-5^2ab^5 \div -5ab^5$

20) $\dfrac{-7h^{12}}{-700h^6}$

Understanding Negative Exponents

To understand negative exponents, let's start with what you know first. Look at the charts below and then try to determine the next answer on the table. Think about what **operation** is taking place as the exponents decrease.

Base Is 10

$10^5 = 10·10·10·10·10 = 100,000$

$10^4 = 10·10·10·10 = 10,000$

$10^3 = 10·10·10 = 1,000$

$10^2 = 10·10 = 100$

$10^1 = 10$

$10^0 = 1$

$10^{-1} = $ _____

$10^{-2} = $ _____

Base Is 2

$2^5 = 2·2·2·2·2 = 32$

$2^4 = 2·2·2·2 = 16$

$2^3 = 2·2·2 = 8$

$2^2 = 2·2 = 4$

$2^1 = 2$

$2^0 = 1$

$2^{-1} = $ _____

$2^{-2} = $ _____

Can you see that as the exponent decreases, the amount as you move from one line to the next down the column is being divided by the base? So 10^{-1} is 1 divided by 10 or $\frac{1}{10}$, and 2^{-1} is 1 divided by 2 or $\frac{1}{2}$. Once again, dividing the previous amount by the base, 10^{-2} is $\frac{1}{100}$, and 2^{-2} is $\frac{1}{4}$. While you can write these answers as decimals, I've kept them as fractions so you can see that a negative exponent implies a **reciprocal**.

1   Divide $\frac{w^5}{w^6}$

$(w \neq 0)$

You can write it as w^{-1} or $\frac{1}{w}$.

2   Find the quotient. $\dfrac{-60m^4}{6m^7}$ $(m \neq 0)$

The answer is $-10m^{-3}$ or $\dfrac{-10}{m^3}$

---

3   Rewrite this quotient with positive exponents. $\dfrac{m^{-5}n^{-2}}{m^{-6}n}$
$m \neq 0, n \neq 0.$

You can do this problem two ways. First, you can use the division rules so that $m^{-5-(-6)}$ is m^1 or m. Then $n^{(-2-1)}$ is n^{-3} or $\dfrac{1}{n^3}$.

The answer is $\dfrac{m}{n^3}$.

The second way to do this problem is to move the variable with the negative exponent from numerator to denominator or from denominator to numerator depending on its location. Remember a negative exponent indicates a reciprocal. So m^{-5} and m^{-6} trade places and n^{-2} goes to the denominator. Make sure you understand this method before you use it.

$$\left(\dfrac{m^{-5}n^{-2}}{m^{-6}n}\right) = \dfrac{m^6}{m^5 n \cdot n^2} = \dfrac{m}{n^3}$$

Using a separate sheet of paper, divide each problem. Write all answers with positive exponents. Assume no variable in the denominator is 0.

1 $\dfrac{w^5}{w^7}$

2 $\dfrac{10x^4}{10x^7}$

3 $\dfrac{-x^7}{-x^9}$

4 $18a^2 \div 36a^5$

5 $\dfrac{w^{-3}}{w}$

6 $\dfrac{10^{-3}}{y}$

7 $\dfrac{5^{-3}}{5^{-1}}$

8 $\dfrac{1}{x^{-1}}$

9 $\dfrac{x^4 y^3}{x^5 y^3}$

10 $\dfrac{11pr^6}{-11pr^{-7}}$

11 $\dfrac{3^{-3}g}{3^{-1}g^{-6}}$

12 $56abc \div 8a^{-3}bc$

Dividing Polynomials by Monomials

To divide a polynomial by a monomial you need to remember that <u>every</u> term in the numerator is being divided by the denominator. You can "bubble" the terms so as to never forget to divide the last term.

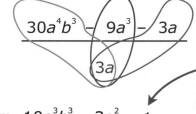

1   Divide $\dfrac{30a^4b^3 - 9a^3 - 3a}{3a}$

Answer: $10a^3b^3 - 3a^2 - 1$

It's a common error to leave out the last term. Remember when dividing if terms cancel you get a 1. A number divided by itself is always one.

2   Divide $\dfrac{-20n^4 + 10n^3 - n}{2n}$

This "2" was in the denominator so it must stay there.

Answer: $-10n^3 + 5n^2 - \dfrac{1}{2}$

Find each quotient. Write all answers with positive exponents. Don't forget to "bubble."

1 $\dfrac{2x^2 + 46}{2}$

5 $\dfrac{75m^4 - 25m^3 - 10m}{5m}$

2 $\dfrac{-9a^3 + 27a^2 - 3a}{3a}$

6 $\dfrac{-35yz^6 + 21yz^5 - 7yz}{7z}$

3 $\dfrac{-h^3 - h}{-h}$

7 $\dfrac{90b^5c^4 + 9b^2}{9bc}$

4 $\dfrac{63v^5 - 3v^3}{-3v}$

8 $\dfrac{6p^6 + 12p^5 - p}{3p^7}$

More Practice

Use a separate piece paper to do the following problems.

1. $(4x^3 + 5x^2 - 3) + (3x^3 + 5xy - 2x^2)$

2. Subtract $(2ab - 3)$ from $(-3ab + 2)$

3. $(18w - 2) - (20w + 4)$

4. From $(9x^2 + 4x + 1)$ subtract $(-9x^2 + 4)$

5. Find the sum: $(5ab + 2)$ and $(5a + b)$

6. $(2x^4)(-3x^5)$

7. $(8ab)(8a^3b)(-2b)$

8. $(6x^3)^3$

9. $(-4a^5)^2$

10. $\left(\frac{1}{3}c^4\right)^3$

11. $-6x(5x^3 - 5x + 1)$

12. $\frac{2}{3}b(18b^4 + 27b^3 - \frac{3}{2}b)$

13. $9ab(9a^5 - 10a^3 + b^4)$

14. $(m + 5)(m - 5)$

15. $(b + 8)(b + 4)$

16. $(x - 6)(x + 9)$

17. $(y - 8)(y - 10)$

18. $(x + y)^2$

19. $(2 - w)^2$

20. $(a - b)(2a + b)$

21. $5(x + 7)(x - 1)$

22. $(4a + b)(4a - b)$

23. $(x + 4)^3$

24. $\dfrac{4a^3}{2a}$

25. $\dfrac{-80b^4}{40b^4}$

26. $\dfrac{5w^6}{w^7}$

27. $18ab^4 \div -36ab^4$

28. $\dfrac{(-2a^3)^5}{-2a^3}$

29. $(8ab + b) \div 4b$

30. $\dfrac{-39v^5 + 13v}{13v}$

31. $\dfrac{-57c^4d^4 + 3cd}{3c^3}$

32. $\dfrac{24a + ab^5 + ac}{-3a}$

Polynomial Thinking Questions

Answer these questions.

1. What are two ways that you can explain why $\dfrac{b^4}{b^4} = 1$ (if $b \neq 0$)?

_____

_____

2. When Lisa simplified this problem $\dfrac{16a - 8}{16}$ she got "$a - 2$." What did Lisa do wrong?

_____

_____

3. If 10^{-2} is the same as $\dfrac{1}{10^2}$, how would you write "40^{-2}"? Explain your thinking.

_____

_____

4. What do we call these binomials? $(x^2 - 25)$; $(m^2 - 49)$; $(y^2 - 1)$? Hint: See p. 153.

_____

_____

5. When Larry simplified this expression $\dfrac{3d^4 - d}{d}$, he got $3d^3$. What did Larry do wrong? What is the correct answer?

_____

_____

6. Show by writing the factors out why $x^4 \div x^6 = \dfrac{1}{x^2}$.

_____

_____

7. Why is $(3^3)(3^2)$ NOT 9^5? Explain your thinking.

_____

_____

Chapter 7

Factoring

In this chapter you will learn **factoring**, a necessary skill needed for solving quadratic equations. Quadratic equations are equations where the highest exponent is a 2. Many equations in science involve solving quadratic equations. From throwing a baseball to determining the curvature of a lens in a satellite, or the movements of the planets, the skills and concepts you learn in this chapter will help you in many future courses and careers.

What is factoring? You have factored many times before when you've been asked, for example, what factors multiply to 36. When you've studied prime numbers you learned that a prime number, like 13, has **only** two factors, 1 and 13.

The Greatest Common Factor

You probably remember how to find the **GCF**, the greatest common factor, of two numbers. We will be finding the greatest common factor of polynomials, too.

1 Find the greatest common factor of 18 and 24.

This is asking what is the biggest factor that 18 and 24 can be divided by.

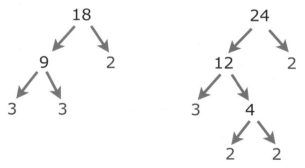

The prime factorization of 18 is $3 \cdot \underline{3} \cdot \underline{2}$ and the prime factorization of 24 is $\underline{3} \cdot \underline{2} \cdot 2 \cdot 2$. Thus, the greatest common factor of 18 and 24 is 6. The number 6 is the largest factor that both numbers can be divided by.

2 Find the GCF of $3a^2b^3$ and $9ab^4$.

The greatest common factor of 3 and 9 is 3. The greatest common factor of "a" and "a^2" is "a," and the greatest common factor of "b^3" and "b^4" is "b^3." So the GCF is $3ab^3$.

> Anytime you are asked to factor, you
> <u>must</u> start by factoring out the GCF of
> the expression (unless the GCF is 1).

3   Factor $4xy^6 + 24xy^3 - 8xy^2$

This is asking you to find the greatest common factor of this trinomial. Use this little story to help:

> A tax collector knocks on the door and wants to tax
> each term with the most each term can contribute as
> long as what is taken out is the same for each term.

The most that can be contributed by each term is $4xy^2$. Each term has at least that many factors. The GCF is $4xy^2$.

Answer: $4xy^2(y^4 + 6y - 2)$

Can you see that factoring is "distributing backwards"? In other words, factoring is rewriting the expression as a multiplication problem.

What is cool about factoring is that you can always check your answer by using the distributive property.

4   Factor $-5w^5z - 10w^4 + 5w^4z$

Here, since the first term has a negative, you can factor out a –5. Each term also has at least w^4.

Answer: $-5w^4(wz + 2 - z)$

Can you see why we could not factor a *z*? Not all the terms had a *z*. Notice the signs have changed so that if you distribute you get your original trinomial. That's why it's important to check your answer.

5   Factor $45mn + 9m - 2y - 5$

This expression cannot be factored, so we call it prime. The GCF is 1, but factoring out the 1 is not necessary since we get the same expression.

GCF Practice

Factor the following polynomials. Do not forget to check each answer. Write the answer underneath each problem.

1) $18c^4 + 9c$

    $9c (\underline{\quad\quad + \quad\quad})$

2) $11a^4 + 121a^3 + 22a^2$

    $11a^2 (\underline{\quad\quad + \quad\quad + \quad\quad})$

3) $-5c - 50$

    $-5 (\underline{\quad\quad\quad\quad})$

4) $12x^2 - 144$

5) $18n^4 - 36n^3 - 18n^2$

6) $25 - 5b^4$

7) $m^4n^2 - 8m^2n$

8) $6v^4 - 42v^3 - 3v$

9) $24y^5 - 36y^3$

10) $63h^4k - 9h^2 - 21h$

11) $14b - 28b^5$

12) $12wy^6 - 36wy^5 - 48y$

13) $-8mn - 96n + 8b - 8$

14) $15a^4 - 225$

15) $80m^2n - 20mn + 40n$

16) $-100n - 200m - 300$

17) $24a^4b^4 + 51a^4b^2 - 39a^4b$

18) $36x^5 - 72x^4 - 108x^3y$

19) $19a^5 - 52$

20) $-21m^4 - 63n^4 - 21mn^3$

Binomial Review

Before we learn more factoring, we need to review multiplying binomials, which is what we learned in the previous chapter.

Using a separate sheet of paper, multiply these binomials.

1   $(w + 5)(w + 6)$

2   $(m + 4)(m + 8)$

3   $(t + 5)(t + 7)$

4   $(y + 1)(y + 4)$

5   $(x - 5)(x - 7)$

6   $(b - 9)(b - 8)$

7   $(m - 7)(m - 7)$

8   $(x - 15)(x - 14)$

9   $(m + 10)(m - 2)$

10   $(n + 18)(n - 4)$

11   $(p + 1)(p - 18)$

12   $(v - 7)(v + 9)$

13   $(x - 11)(x + 12)$

14   $(1 - r)(1 + r)$

15   $(t + 5)(t - 5)$

16   $(v + 9)(v - 9)$

17   $(h - 7)(h + 7)$

18   $(k - 8)(k + 8)$

19   $(11 - m)(11 + m)$

20   $(a + 14)(a - 14)$

21   $(y + 40)(y - 40)$

22   $(b - 8)(b - 8)$

23   $(k + 13)(k + 13)$

24   $(9 + x)(9 + x)$

25   $(a + 14)(a + 14)$

26   $(c - 16)(c - 16)$

Mystery Numbers Game

Answer the following questions.

What two numbers:

1. multiply to 36 and add to 12? _____

2. multiply to 40 and add to 13? _____

3. multiply to 50 and add to 15? _____

4. multiply to 81 and add to 18? _____

What two numbers have:

5. a product of 100 and a sum of 20? _____

6. a product of 15 and a sum of 8? _____

7. a product of –16 and a sum of 0? _____

8. a product of –64 and a sum of 0? _____

9. a product of –24 and a sum of –2? _____

10. a product of 30 and a sum of –11? _____

11. a product of 25 and a sum of –26? _____

12. a product of 56 and a sum of –15? _____

13. a product of 100 and a sum of –29? _____

14. a product of –52 and a sum of –9? _____

15. a product of –52 and a sum of 9? _____

16. a product of –46 and a sum of –21? _____

17. a product of 51 and a sum of –20? _____

18. a product of 72 and a sum of –27? _____

19. a product of –72 and a sum of –6? _____

20. a product of 225 and a sum of –30? _____

Factoring Rules

Factoring Rule I – Factor out the GCF (the greatest common factor), unless it's a 1. Always do this step!

Factoring Rule II – Break the trinomial into the product of two binomials.

1 Factor $x^2 + 8x + 15$

Can you factor out a GCF besides 1? No. Proceed to break the trinomial into the product of two binomials, $(x \quad)(x \quad)$. To figure out the rest, ask yourself, what two numbers multiply to 15 and add to 8. The numbers are 3 and 5, so the two binomials are $(x + 3)(x + 5)$. That is the same answer as $(x + 5)(x + 3)$.

Remember to check your answer by multiplying.

2 Factor $x^2 - 4x - 77$.

Can you factor out a GCF besides 1? Proceed to the next step. What two numbers multiply to -77 and add to -4? The numbers are -11, and 7, because the product of -11 and 7 is -77 and the sum of -11 and 7 is -4. So the answer is $(x - 11)(x + 4)$.

3 Factor $x^2 - 49$.   This is the difference of two perfect squares.

Can you factor a GCF besides 1? Proceed to the next step. Notice there is NO middle term, which means the middle terms cancelled. The numbers that have a product of -49 and a sum of 0 are 7 and -7. The answer is $(x + 7)(x - 7)$.

4 Factor $y^2 + 25$.

Can you factor a GCF besides 1? Proceed to the next step. This is NOT the difference of two perfect squares. Notice the plus sign. There are no two numbers that multiply to a positive 25 and also cancel. The answer is: Prime or not factorable. You cannot factor $y^2 + 25$.

5 Factor $2x^2 + 14x - 36$.

Can you factor a GCF besides 1? Yes, you can factor out a 2.

$2(x^2 + 7x - 18)$. Now, proceed to the next step. What two numbers multiply to -18 and add to 7? 9 and -2.

Answer: $2(x + 9)(x - 2)$

Don't forget the 2.

Remember to check your answer by multiplication.

Using a separate sheet of paper, practice factoring. Remember to follow the rules of factoring and always look for the GCF first.

1 $y^2 + 5y + 4$

2 $x^2 + 6x + 8$

3 $w^2 + 9w + 20$

4 $y^2 + 9y + 14$

5 $p^2 + 11p + 18$

6 $d^2 + 7d + 12$

7 $r^2 + 3r - 10$

8 $k^2 - 3k - 10$

9 $m^2 - 4m - 12$

10 $w^2 + 4w - 12$

11 $g^2 - 13g + 40$

12 $w^2 + 3w - 40$

13 $x^2 - 4x - 21$

14 $y^2 - 9y + 18$

15 $c^2 - 36$

16 $z^2 - 64$

17 $b^2 - 144$

18 $m^2 + 49$

19 $3y^2 + 15y + 18$

20 $5x^2 - 5$

Let's review some other factoring examples that may seem tricky.

6 Factor $x^2 + 2xy + y^2$

Is there a GCF besides 1? No, proceed to factor into the product of two binomials. $(x + y)(x + y)$. What about the signs? Both signs have to be positive. Notice that when you add the middle terms xy and yx you get $2xy$. Always check by multiplying.

← Remember: yx is the same as xy.

7 Factor $8 - 8w^2$

Is there a GCF besides 1? Yes, factor out the 8. You get $8(1 - w^2)$. Can you keep factoring? Yes, you can factor $1 - w^2$ into $(1 + w)(1 - w)$. You must keep it in that order with the 1 first.

Final answer is: $8(1 + w)(1 - w)$.

8 Factor $x^4 - 16$

This is the <u>difference</u> of two perfect squares. Is there a GCF besides 1? No, so proceed to factor into two binomials. $(x^2 - 4)(x^2 + 4)$. Now, notice that one of these binomials is again the <u>difference</u> of two perfect squares. So, …

$(x^2 - 4)(x^2 + 4)$

$(x + 2)(x - 2)(x^2 + 4)$ is your final answer.

Using a separate sheet of paper, practice factoring.

1. $x^2 + 12x + 32$
2. $w^2 - 12w + 32$
3. $m^2 - 4m - 32$
4. $v^2 + 4v - 32$
5. $a^2 + 5a + 6$
6. $b^2 - b - 6$
7. $z^2 + z - 6$
8. $m^2 + 5m - 6$
9. $r^2 - 5r - 6$
10. $w^2 - z^2$
11. $4 - y^2$
12. $1 - 4w^2$
13. $4y^2 - 16$ (Don't forget GCF!)

14. $5m^2 - 5$
15. $2x^2 + 6x - 20$
16. $3y^2 - 363$
17. $4a^2 - 44a + 120$
18. $5c^2 - 500$
19. $169 - h^2$
20. $x^2 + 4xy + 4y^2$
21. $7a^2 + 7a - 42$
22. $5a^2 - 5a - 30$
23. $a^2 + 81$
24. $a^4 - 625$
25. $x(x + 3) + 2(x + 3)$
    Notice each group has $(x + 3)$.

Thinking About Factoring

1   Why is $x^2 + 4$ not factorable? Explain your thinking.

_____

_____

_____

2   When Lisa factored $y^2 - 64$, she got $(y - 32)(y + 2)$. Explain her error.

_____

_____

3   Factor $6 + x - x^2$. Hint: You might want to factor out a "-1" and write your trinomial in standard form.

4   Luis saw a poster on his teacher's bulletin board that read as shown below. Luis wondered if a and b could both equal zero. Give some values for a and b that would give you a product of zero.

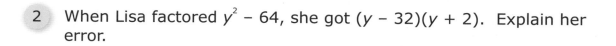

If $a \cdot b = 0$, then $a = 0$, or $b = 0$.

_____

_____

_____

_____

_____

5   How would you factor $y(y + 5) + 2(y + 5)$? Hint: Let $A = (y + 5)$. Factor $y(A) + 2(A)$, then substitute $(y + 5)$ for A.

_____

_____

_____

Factoring Trinomials With a Leading Coefficient

(where there is no GCF other than 1)

Suppose you had to factor $2x^2 + 7x + 6$. You start by trying to factor the GCF, but the GCF is 1, so does this mean this trinomial is not factorable? Actually, this trinomial is factorable. It is the product of $(2x + 3)(x + 2)$. So, let's learn how to factor $2x^2 + 7x + 6$.

1 Factor $2x^2 + 7x + 6$

Steps to Factoring $2x^2 + 7x + 6$

1 Make sure the trinomial is in standard form. Multiply the 2 (leading coefficient) times the 6 (the constant). You get 12.

2 You are going to ask, what two numbers multiply to 12 and add to 7 (the middle term). It helps to write down the factors of 12 until you find the correct pair.

> 12
> $12 \cdot 1$
> $6 \cdot 2$
> $(3 \cdot 4)$

3 Rewrite your trinomials using $3x + 4x$ for $7x$.

The order in which you write the sum does not matter.

$$2x^2 + 7x + 6$$
$$2x^2 + 3x + 4x + 6 \quad (\text{or } 4x + 3x)$$

4 Factor the first two terms and factor the last two terms as shown. This is called **factoring by grouping**.

$$2x^2 + 7x + 6$$
$$\underline{2x^2 + 3x} + \underline{4x + 6}$$

Do not lose this sign.

$$x(2x + 3) + 2(2x + 3)$$

Notice that the binomials in the parentheses are identical and they must be.

5 Factor out the binomial $(2x + 3)$ to arrive at your answer.

$$(2x + 3)(x + 2)$$

See problem 5 on the previous page if you don't see why $(2x + 3)$ is factored out.

Can you show that you arrive at the same answer had you written $7x$ as $4x + 3x$ instead of $3x + 4x$? Try it!

Learning five steps to do these problems may seem overwhelming at first, but it is easier and faster (after you practice a few) than guessing the answer, especially when the problem is harder. Let's try a few more examples.

2   Factor $2x^2 - 13x + 15$.

Is there a GCF? No, so proceed to multiply 2 times 15, which is 30.

Which two numbers multiply to +30 and add to -13? Both numbers would have to be negative.

$2x^2 - 13x + 15$ is rewritten as

30

-1 · -30

-2 · -15

-3 · -10

-5 · -6

$2x^2 - 3x - 10x + 15$. Now factor what is underlined.

$x(2x - 3) - 5(2x - 3)$ Notice how -5 was factored out from the second set. You must end with the <u>same</u> binomial in each set of parentheses.

Answer: $(2x - 3)(x - 5)$

3   Factor $3x^2 - 2x - 1$.

Is there a GCF other than 1? Let's try to factor. Multiply the 3 times the -1. You get -3. What numbers multiply to -3 and add to -2? The two numbers are -3 and 1. So rewrite -2x as -3x and 1x .

$3x^2 - 2x - 1$

$3x^2 + x + -3x - 1$ Now factor what is underlined.

$x(3x + 1) -1(3x + 1)$ Notice how -1 was factored out in order to get the same binomial in both parentheses.

Answer: $(3x + 1)(x - 1)$

Always remember that you can check your answer by multiplying out the binomials.

Practice

Factor the following problems. Check your answer if needed.

(1) $y(y + 4) - 2(y + 4)$

(7) $4y^2 - 5y + 1$

(2) $w(w - 7) + 1(w - 7)$

(8) $5a^2 + 4a - 1$

(3) $3x^2 + 2x + 21x + 14$ Hint: Factor by grouping.

(9) $9x^2 - 6x + 1$

(4) $2w^2 + 13w + 20$

(10) $6y^2 + y - 2$

(5) $6m^2 + 14m + 4$

(11) $6b^2 - 14b - 20$

(6) $2x^2 + x - 15$

(12) $6y^2 + 7y - 5$

Thinking About Factoring

Answer the following questions.

1 If the area of Carmen's bedroom is represented by $x^2 + 4x - 5$ and the length is $(x + 5)$, find an expression to represent the width.

$x + 5$

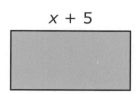

2 The following trinomials are often factored incorrectly. Write the letter of the correct factoring next to each problem.

_____ **1** $x^2 + 5x + 6$ **a** $(x - 2)(x - 3)$

_____ **2** $x^2 + 6x + 5$ **b** $(x + 5)(x - 1)$

_____ **3** $x^2 - 5x + 6$ **c** $(x + 2)(x + 3)$

_____ **4** $x^2 + x - 6$ **d** $(x + 5)(x + 1)$

_____ **5** $x^2 - x - 6$ **e** $(x + 3)(x - 2)$

_____ **6** $x^2 + 4x - 5$ **f** $(x - 3)(x + 2)$

3 Look at the following geometric drawing to answer the questions.

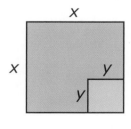 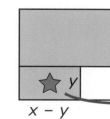 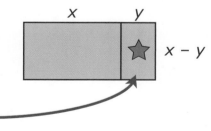

Figure 1   Figure 2   Figure 3

a In Figure 1, write an expression for the area that is leftover if y^2 is removed from x^2. _____

b The piece marked with the star in Figure 2 was rotated and placed in Figure 3.

Find an expression for the area of Figure 3. _____

c   Explain how the drawing on page 175 demonstrates how to factor the difference of two perfect squares.

_____

_____

_____

4   The following trinomials are called "perfect square trinomials." Notice that the last three problems have large leading coefficients. Watch for perfect square patterns to help you factor. (You must still check for a GCF.)

a $x^2 + 6x + 9$ _____ $(x + 3)^2$ _____ ← This is the same as $(x + 3)(x + 3)$.

b $x^2 + 2xy + y^2$ _____

c $y^2 - 14y + 49$ _____

d $a^2 + 10a + 25$ _____

e $x^2 - 6xy + 9y^2$ _____

f $v^2 - 22v + 121$ _____

g $x^2 + 8xy + 16y^2$ _____

h $25x^2 + 40xy + 16y^2$ $(5x + 4y)($ _____ $)$

i $100y^2 + 60y + 9$ _____

j $169x^2 + 156x + 36$ _____

Factoring Challenge

5   Factor completely to become a factoring hero.

$$8bx^3y - 60bx^2y + 28bxy$$

Solving Quadratic Equations

Quadratic equations are commonly used in science. The following are quadratic equations. Look at all three of these quadratic equations. What do they have in common?

$$x^2 + 5x - 24 = 0 \qquad y^2 - 8y = -15 \qquad 2C^2 = -3C + 5$$

You should have noticed that the degree of each polynomial expression within each equation is a 2. We call these "equations of degree 2." Even though we usually think of the prefix "quad" to mean "four," the term "quad" here refers to squaring a variable (x^2), thus the term "quad" for the area of a square.

To solve quadratic equations, we use an arithmetic rule you already know. When two factors multiply to zero (let's assume some numbers are hidden behind the doors below), then you know that at least one or maybe both numbers are 0.

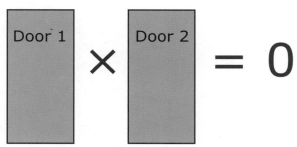

The highest exponent of "2" also tells you that you will get two answers. Sometimes the two answers might be the same and sometimes the answers may be irrational or even imaginary (which you will learn in Algebra II), but you will get two answers or **roots**.

It's also important to know that you may run into quadratic equations that may seem to have no solutions. We will later learn a formula, called the quadratic formula, to help solve those equations.

The standard form of a quadratic equation is written below where the variables a, b and c can be any numbers, as long as $a \neq 0$. Otherwise, if $a = 0$, can you see that it would not be a quadratic equation?

$$ax^2 + bx + c = 0$$

To solve a quadratic equation, follow these steps.

		Steps for Solving Quadratic Equations

1 Solve for y:

$$y^2 = 2y + 63$$

$$y^2 - 2y - 63 = 0$$

$$(y - 9)(y + 7) = 0$$

$$(y - 9) | (y + 7) = 0$$

$$y - 9 = 0 \text{ or } y + 7 = 0$$

Answers: $y = 9$ or $y = -7$

1 Is it a quadratic equation? Yes.

2 Then move every term to one side and set the equation equal to zero. (Keep the second-degree term positive.)

3 Factor. Make sure to factor a GCF if other than 1. Don't drop the equal sign (it's an equation).

4 Set each term equal to zero and solve. Since two factors multiply to zero, then either $(y - 9) = 0$, or $(y + 7) = 0$.

5 Check your answers in the original equation. Does $9^2 = 2(9) + 63$? Does $81 = 18 + 63$? Yes. Does $(-7)^2 = 2(-7) + 63$? Does $49 = -14 + 63$? Yes.

2 Solve for V:

$$3V^2 + 9V = 120$$

$$3V^2 + 9V - 120 = 0$$

$$3(V^2 + 3V - 40) = 0$$

$$3(V - 5) | (V + 8) = 0$$

$$V - 5 = 0 \text{ or } V + 8 = 0$$

3 cannot be 0.

Answers: $V = 5$ or $V = -8$

1 Is it a quadratic equation? Yes.

2 Set equal to 0.

3 Factor completely. Do not drop the equal 0.

4 Solve for the variable.

5 Check your answers.
Does $3(5)^2 + 9(5) = 120$?
$3(25) + 45 = 120$?
$75 + 45 = 120$? Yes.
Does $3(-8)^2 + 9(-8) = 120$?
$3(64) + (-72) = 120$?
$192 + (-72) = 120$? Yes.

3    $-3y = -y^2$

1 Is this a quadratic equation? Yes.

$y^2 - 3y = 0$

2 Set equal to 0. Make sure to make the second-degree term positive.

$y(y - 3) = 0$

3 Factor! Remember: Don't forget the GCF!

$y = 0$ or $y - 3 = 0$

4 Solve for the variable.

Answers: $y = 0$ or $y = 3$

5 Check your answers.
Does $-3(0) = -0^2$? Yes.
Does $-3(3) = -(3)2$?
$-9 = -9$ Yes.

Solve the following quadratic equations. Make sure to check your answers.

1 $x^2 - 4 = 0$

6 $p^2 + 3p = 10$

2 $y^2 + 10y + 9 = 0$

7 $n^2 = -4n + 32$

3 $a^2 - 8a = -15$

8 $-5c = -6 - c^2$

4 $w^2 - 16 = 0$

9 $2x^2 - 10x - 28 = 0$

5 $y^2 - 16y = 0$

10 $y^2 = 25$

Word Problems With Quadratic Equations

The following problems will provide you with more practice solving quadratic equations.

1   In a rectangle the length is three meters longer than the width. If the area of the rectangle is 108 square meters, find the width.

— Notice it says area and not perimeter.

Draw and label a picture (or use a let statement).

$w + 3$

w

Equation: $w(w + 3) = 108$
$$w^2 + 3w = 108$$
$$w^2 + 3w - 108 = 0$$
$$(w + 12)(w - 9) = 0$$
$$w + 12 = 0 \quad w - 9 = 0$$

$w = -12$ or $w = 9$ but wait!

Can the width of a rectangle be –12 meters? No! So discard that answer. The width is 9 meters. Make sure to check your answer. (9m)(12m) = 108 sq m

2   Twice the square of a number plus three times the same number yields –1. Find both numbers.

Let n = the number. Equation: $2n^2 + 3n = -1$
$$2n^2 + 3n + 1 = 0$$
$$(2n + 1)(n + 1) = 0$$
$$2n + 1 = 0 \quad n + 1 = 0 \quad \text{Solving each equation.}$$
$$2n = -1 \quad\quad n = -1$$
$$n = -\frac{1}{2}$$

Check: $2\left(-\frac{1}{2}\right)^2 + 3\left(-\frac{1}{2}\right) = -1?$ $2(-1)^2 + 3(-1) = -1?$

$2\left(\frac{1}{4}\right) + 3\left(-\frac{1}{2}\right) = -1?$ $2(1) + (-3) = -1?$

$\frac{1}{2} + -\frac{3}{2} = -1?$ $2 + (-3) = -1$ Yes!

$-\frac{2}{2} = -1$ Yes!

3   The <u>product</u> of two consecutive even negative integers is 80.
    Use algebra to find both integers.

    Let x = the first consecutive even negative integer
    $x + 2$ = the second consecutive even negative integer

    Equation: $x(x + 2) = 80$
                  $x^2 + 2x = 80$
              $x^2 + 2x - 80 = 0$
            $(x + 10)(x - 8) = 0$
          $x + 10 = 0$ | $x - 8 = 0$
              $x = -10$ | $x = 8$ Discard the 8 as the integers are
                                         supposed to be negative.

    Answers: $x = -10$ and $x + 2 = -8$
    Check: $(-10)(-8) = 80$

Using a separate sheet of paper, solve the following word problems.
Make sure to make a drawing or use a let statement.

1   Paul is eight years younger than his cousin Javier. The product of
    their ages is 33. Find their ages.

2   The product of two consecutive negative odd integers is 99. Use
    algebra to find both integers.

3   A number less the square of the same number equals -20. Find the
    number or numbers that make the statement true.

4   The length of a rectangle is eight more inches than its width. The
    area of the rectangle is 84 square inches. Use algebra to find the
    dimensions of the rectangle.

5   A quadratic equation has these roots {-3, 5}. Write the quadratic
    equation that has those roots.

6   The square of a number minus three times the same number yields
    0. Find the number or numbers that make this true.

7   One positive number is four more than another. The sum of their
    squares is 40. Find the numbers.

8   Find the third consecutive positive integer such that the product of the second integer and the third is 30.

9   When the first of three consecutive integers is multiplied by the third you get one less than six times the second. Find the sets of integers that make this true.

10 Koryndee's parents have a swimming pool with an area of 600 square feet. The length is ten more than the width. What are the dimensions of the pool?

More Thinking About Quadratics

11 When Todd solved the following quadratic, he said the answers were –5 and 3. Is Todd right? Explain your thinking.

$(2n + 5)(n - 3) = 0$ _____

_____

_____

12 Joanna solved the equation below by taking the square root of 49 and she got an answer of 7. Is Joanna right? Explain your thinking.

$x^2 = 49$ _____

_____

_____

13 Solve the following two quadratic equations.

a $4y^2 - 49 = 0$ b $2w^2 = 8w$

Quadratic Equations and the Pythagorean Theorem

You probably recall that the Pythagorean Theorem, $a^2 + b^2 = c^2$, is used to solve for the missing side of a right triangle where a and b stand for the legs of a right triangle and c stands for the hypotenuse of the right triangle. The hypotenuse is the longest side of a right triangle, the side that is always opposite the right angle.

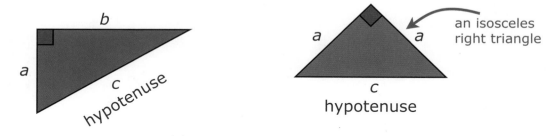

We can use our knowledge of solving quadratic equations to solve problems dealing with the Pythagorean Theorem.

1   In a right triangle the hypotenuse is 10 cm and one leg is 8 cm. Write an equation and solve to find the missing side.

Draw a picture.

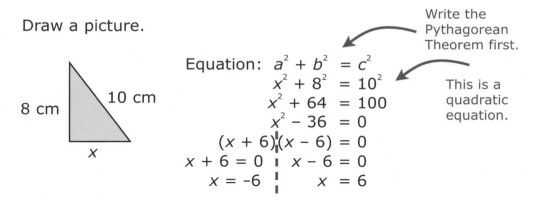

Write the Pythagorean Theorem first.

Equation: $a^2 + b^2 = c^2$
$x^2 + 8^2 = 10^2$
$x^2 + 64 = 100$
$x^2 - 36 = 0$
$(x + 6)(x - 6) = 0$
$x + 6 = 0 \quad | \quad x - 6 = 0$
$x = -6 \quad | \quad x = 6$

This is a quadratic equation.

Notice that because this is a quadratic equation, it has two answers. The side of a triangle cannot be -6, so we eliminate the negative root. Normally, we solve these types of problems by just taking the square root, please remember that when solving an equation of this type, $x^2 = 36$, you do get two answers, $x = \pm\sqrt{36}$ or ± 6.

2 In a right triangle, the hypotenuse is two units more than the smallest leg and one unit more than the medium leg. Find the sides of the right triangle.

Draw a picture.

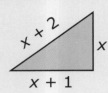

$x + 1$

Equation: $a^2 + b^2 = c^2$

$$x^2 + (x + 1)^2 = (x + 2)^2$$
$$x^2 + x^2 + 2x + 1 = x^2 + 4x + 4$$
$$2x^2 + 2x + 1 = x^2 + 4x + 4$$
$$x^2 - 2x - 3 = 0$$
$$(x + 1)(x - 3) = 0$$
$$x + 1 = 0 \quad \mid \quad x - 3 = 0$$
$$x = \cancel{-1} \quad \mid \quad x = 3$$

Move every term to the left side.

Since the side of a triangle cannot be a negative number, discard the -1.

Answers: The sides of the right triangle are 3, 4, 5 units.

Solve the following problems using a quadratic equation. Make sure to draw a picture (if there isn't one) or use a let statement.

1 A 10' ladder leans against a building touching the bottom of a window as shown below. From the bottom of the window to the ground is 2' more than from the base of the ladder to the base of the building. Find the length from the base of the ladder to the base of the building.

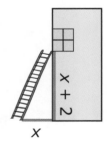

$x + 2$

x

2   In a right triangle, one leg is seven more inches than the smallest leg and the hypotenuse is eight more inches than the smallest leg. Find the dimensions of the right triangle and find its area.

3   In a right triangle, one of the legs is one less than twice the smallest leg. If the hypotenuse is one more than twice the smallest leg, find each side of the right triangle.

4   In an isosceles right triangle, the hypotenuse is 10 meters. Find each leg of the triangle. You can leave your answer in radical form.

Chapter 8

Working With **Radicals**

In algebra you can have equations that give you irrational answers. Remember from Chapter 1, that an **irrational** number is any number whose decimal form is non-terminating <u>and</u> also non-repeating. In this chapter, we will learn how to do operations with square roots. Some square roots will be rational and others will be irrational.

In order to understand square roots, look at the yellow square below.

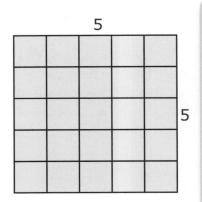

The area of the yellow square is 5^2 or 25 units. $\sqrt{25} = 5$. The symbol $\sqrt{}$ is called the radical. The inverse operation of squaring is taking the square root. Taking a square root never means division. When you see $\sqrt{25}$, it is asking what number times itself is 25. $\sqrt{25}$ is asking for the positive square root or the principal square root. Even though –5 times –5 is also 25, to get the negative square root, you will see $-\sqrt{25} = -5$.

The following numbers are called perfect squares. The quicker you memorize the highlighted perfect squares, the faster you will perform many square root problems (faster than even a calculator).

1, 4, 9, 16, 25, 36, 49, 64, 81, 100, 121, 144, 169, 196, 225, 256, 289, 324, 361, **400**, 441, 484, 529, 576, **625**, ... **10,000**, ...

When you take the square root of a number that is not a perfect square you will get an **irrational** number. You'll be asked to either leave that number inside the radical, in simplest radical form (we will learn this soon), or to round the decimal to a given place value.

To find the square root of a number by using a calculator, look for the square root symbol. In a TI-83 or TI-84 graphing calculator you will find the square root symbol above the x^2 key.

Examples

1   Simplify $\sqrt{49} + \sqrt{81}$ Find each square root first, then add.

$$7 \; + \; 9$$
$$16$$

2   Simplify $-8\sqrt{121}$ No symbol means multiplication.

$$-8 \cdot 11$$
$$-88$$

3   Using your calculator, find the square root of 50 and round to the nearest tenth.

The answer is 7.1. Notice: $\sqrt{49} < \sqrt{50} < \sqrt{64}$. So, $\sqrt{50}$ is definitely closer to 7 than to 8, just slightly larger than 7.

4   Simplify $\left(\sqrt{9}\right)^2$.   Can you see that squaring a square root gives you the number inside the radical?

$$3^2$$
$$9$$

Using a separate sheet of paper, simplify the following problems. Do not use a calculator.

1 $\sqrt{100}$ **6** 18^2 **11** $\sqrt{0}$

2 $\sqrt{144} - \sqrt{81}$ **7** $\sqrt{324}$ **12** $\dfrac{3}{4}\sqrt{16}$

3 $-7\sqrt{196}$ **8** $9\sqrt{36}$ **13** $\left(\sqrt{23}\right)^2$

4 $\left(\sqrt{11}\right)^2$ **9** $-\sqrt{10,000}$ **14**   Round to the nearest hundredth. $\sqrt{143}$

5 $\sqrt{11^2}$ **10** $\sqrt{11 + 25}$ **15**   Round to the nearest tenth. $\sqrt{47}$

Thinking About Radicals

For these problems, you can use a calculator.

1 Is $\sqrt{100-36}$ the same as $\sqrt{100} - \sqrt{36}$? Explain your thinking.

_____

_____

2 Use >, < or =.

a $\left(\sqrt{20}\right)^2$ _____ 20

e $\sqrt{82}$ _____ 9

b 1^{20} _____ $\sqrt{1}$

f $\left(\sqrt{4}\right)\left(\sqrt{25}\right)$ _____ $\sqrt{100}$

c $2^2 \cdot 2^3$ _____ 4^5

g $\left(\sqrt{4}\right) + \left(\sqrt{25}\right)$ _____ $\sqrt{29}$

d $\sqrt{3,600}$ _____ $\sqrt{49} + 53$

h $\sqrt{169}$ _____ $\left(\sqrt{100} + \sqrt{16}\right)$

3 Find the square root of these numbers and write whether the answer is rational (R) or irrational (IR). Round irrational answers to the nearest tenth.

		Square root	R or IR?
a	676	_____	_____
b	28	_____	_____
c	17	_____	_____
d	361	_____	_____
e	50,176	_____	_____

4 Answer the following questions.

a Is the set of perfect squares finite or infinite? Explain your thinking.

_____

_____

b Is it possible to find the square root of a decimal? Explain your thinking. Give an example.

_____

_____

c Is it possible to find a real number answer for $\sqrt{-1}$? Why or why not? Explain your thinking.

_____

_____

d Finish the pattern below. Remember that to multiply monomials with the same base, keep the base the same and add the powers.

$3^2 \cdot 3^2 = 3^4$ $3^{\frac{1}{2}} \cdot 3^{\frac{1}{2}} = $ _____

$9 \cdot 9 = 81$

$3^1 \cdot 3^1 = 3^2$ $\left(3^{\frac{1}{2}}\right)^2 = $ _____

$3 \cdot 3 = 9$

Explain why $3^{\frac{1}{2}}$ is the same as $\sqrt{3}$.

_____

e What do you think are the answers to these problems?

$\sqrt{n^2}$ _____ $\sqrt{n^4}$ _____ $\sqrt{n^6}$ _____ $\sqrt{n^{10}}$ _____ $(n > 0)$

Is there a rule you can write as to how to find the answers when taking the square root of a variable raised to an exponent?

_____

f Show by using an example that $\sqrt{ab} = \sqrt{a} \cdot \sqrt{b}$, but $\sqrt{a} + \sqrt{b} \neq \sqrt{a+b}$. (Let $a > 0$ and $b > 0$.)

_____

_____

Simplifying Square Roots

In this section we will learn how to change square roots into their simplest form. Before the time of calculators, students learned to memorize these popular square roots. $\sqrt{2}$ is about 1.4, $\sqrt{3}$ is about 1.7 and $\sqrt{5}$ is about 2.2. So if you could simplify a square root and end up with any of the above in the problem, then multiplying by hand was easy. However, we still learn how to simplify square roots to make it possible to add, subtract, multiply, and divide problems with square roots. (It doesn't hurt to learn the above facts, too).

When you see the word SIMPLIFY in a square root problem, this is what is being asked.

1   Simplify $\sqrt{12}$.

First, try to break 12 into any factors that are perfect squares. You do not want to use 6 times 2, as neither 6 nor 2 are perfect squares. Break 12 into 4 times 3.

Remember this property.
$$\sqrt{ab} = \sqrt{a} \cdot \sqrt{b}$$

Answer: $2\sqrt{3}$

2   Simplify $\sqrt{48}$.

In this problem, think of the largest perfect square that 48 can be divided by. If you think 4 times 12, you will have more steps since 12 (see above) can be broken down further. So break 48 into 16 times 3.

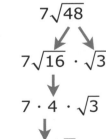

Answer: $28\sqrt{3}$

The numbers in the box below appear frequently in many square root problems, and if you remember these factors you can simplify with fewer steps. But if you don't remember these, just make sure you simplify completely.

$$32 = 16 \cdot 2$$

$$48 = 16 \cdot 3$$

$$72 = 36 \cdot 2$$

Here's the $\sqrt{72}$ done two ways. Can you see which is easier?

$$\sqrt{72}$$
$$\sqrt{9} \cdot \sqrt{8}$$
$$3 \cdot$$
$$3 \cdot \sqrt{4} \cdot \sqrt{2}$$
$$3 \cdot 2 \cdot \sqrt{2}$$
$$6\sqrt{2}$$

$$\sqrt{72}$$
$$\sqrt{36} \cdot \sqrt{2}$$
$$6\sqrt{2}$$

Using a separate sheet of paper, simplify the following square roots.

1 $\sqrt{50}$

2 $-\sqrt{32}$

3 $\sqrt{300}$

4 $\sqrt{98}$

5 $-6\sqrt{400}$

6 $\sqrt{63}$

7 $-2\sqrt{75}$

8 $\sqrt{150}$

9 $\sqrt{500}$

10 $\frac{2}{3}\sqrt{180}$

11 $\sqrt{68}$

12 $\sqrt{441}$

Adding and Subtracting Square Roots

Simplifying square roots will help you perform many square root operations. Adding and subtracting square roots is very much like adding monomials. You must add and subtract only like square roots. Study the examples below.

1 $\sqrt{27} + \sqrt{75}$

You must simplify the square roots first as we did in the last section.

$$\sqrt{27} \quad + \quad \sqrt{75}$$

$$\sqrt{9} \cdot \sqrt{3} \quad + \quad \sqrt{25} \cdot \sqrt{3}$$

$$3\sqrt{3} \quad + \quad 5\sqrt{3} \quad \longleftarrow$$

Now, you're ready to add like square roots. Remember that $3x + 5x$ is $8x$, not $8x^2$.

$$\boxed{8\sqrt{3}}$$

2 $\quad 10\sqrt{98} - 2\sqrt{18} + \sqrt{2}$

$$10 \cdot \sqrt{49} \cdot \sqrt{2} - 2 \cdot \sqrt{9} \cdot \sqrt{2} + \sqrt{2}$$

There's a 1 here.
$$\sqrt{2} = 1\sqrt{2}$$

$$10 \cdot 7 \cdot \sqrt{2} - 2 \cdot 3 \cdot \sqrt{2} + \sqrt{2}$$

$$70\sqrt{2} - 6\sqrt{2} + \sqrt{2} \qquad \text{Now, combine all like square roots.}$$

$$\boxed{65\sqrt{2}}$$

3 $\quad 9 + -7\sqrt{81} + \sqrt{32}$

$$9 + -7 \cdot 9 + \sqrt{16} \cdot \sqrt{2} \qquad \text{Remember the order of operations.}$$

$$9 + (-63) + 4\sqrt{2}$$

$$\boxed{-54 + 4\sqrt{2}}$$

No, you cannot add the −54 to the 2 as they are unlike terms.
Remember that $-54 + 4y$ is NOT $-50y$.

Practice

Simplify the following problems. Show your work.

1 $\sqrt{2} + \sqrt{2} + \sqrt{3}$

7 $2\sqrt{25} + \sqrt{144} - \sqrt{32}$

2 $9\sqrt{5} + \sqrt{20}$

8 $\sqrt{(17)^2} - \sqrt{68}$

3 $2\sqrt{28} - 3\sqrt{63}$

9 $\sqrt{72} + \sqrt{8} - \sqrt{2}$

4 $10 + \sqrt{52}$

10 $\sqrt{3} + \sqrt{300} - \sqrt{27}$

5 $\sqrt{24} + \sqrt{6} + \sqrt{54}$

11 $\sqrt{15} - \sqrt{12} - 2$

6 $-18 + \sqrt{36} - \sqrt{48}$

12 $\sqrt{125} + \sqrt{5} + \sqrt{500}$

Multiplying Square Roots

You can multiply square roots even though the numbers in the radicals might be different. As you saw earlier, $\sqrt{a} \cdot \sqrt{b} = \sqrt{ab}$. Do you see that these are the same rules as for multiplying monomials? And you will use the same procedure for multiplying binomials with square roots. While you cannot add $x + y$, it's okay to multiply x times y (you get xy). You will need to simplify your square roots either before you multiply or after.

1   Find the product and simplify, $\sqrt{3} \cdot \sqrt{6}$.

You get $\sqrt{18}$ Always simplify your answer (unless you're told
                            to round to a given decimal place).

$\sqrt{9} \cdot \sqrt{2}$

$\boxed{3\sqrt{2}}$

2   Simplify $\left(3\sqrt{5}\right)^2$

Write the expression as $3\sqrt{5} \cdot 3\sqrt{5}$ when you're first starting out. Careful, these are NOT binomials! Multiply the outside numbers and multiply the numbers inside the square roots. Just like $3x \cdot 3x = 9x^2$ (here $x = \sqrt{5}$).

You get $9\sqrt{25}$

$9 \cdot 5$

$\boxed{45}$

3   Multiply and simplify $\sqrt{3}(\sqrt{27} + \sqrt{9})$.

This time it's easier to simplify first and then distribute.

$\sqrt{3}(3\sqrt{3} + 3)$

$3\sqrt{9} + 3\sqrt{3}$

$\boxed{9 + 3\sqrt{3}}$

4   Find the product $(\sqrt{3} - 5)(\sqrt{3} + 8)$.

These are binomials. Review how to multiply binomials if you don't remember.

$(\sqrt{3} - 5)(\sqrt{3} + 8)$ First times first, first times second, second times first and second times second.

$\sqrt{9} + 8\sqrt{3} - 5\sqrt{3} - 40$

$3 + 3\sqrt{3} - 40$

$3\sqrt{3} - 37$

From now on, let's remember that $\sqrt{2} \cdot \sqrt{2} = 2$, $\sqrt{3} \cdot \sqrt{3} = 3$, $\sqrt{129} \cdot \sqrt{129} = 129$, etc. In general $\sqrt{x} \cdot \sqrt{x} = x$ $(x \geq 0)$.

Practice multiplying square roots. Make sure to simplify your answer.

1   $\sqrt{5} \cdot \sqrt{10}$

2   $-\sqrt{18} \cdot \sqrt{2}$

3   $(-9\sqrt{5})(9\sqrt{5})$

4   $(3\sqrt{8})(-5\sqrt{3})$

5   $\left(8\sqrt{3}\right)^2$

6   $(4\sqrt{3} + 2\sqrt{5})(7\sqrt{5} + 8)$

More Practice

Use a separate sheet of paper to do the following problems. It's important to master everything we've learned about square roots before moving on.

1 Find $\sqrt{19}$ to the nearest hundredth.

2 What's $\left(\sqrt{7}\right)^2$?

3 Which of these is a perfect square?

   a 9,500   **b** 9,604   **c** 9,506

4 Simplify $-8\sqrt{81}$

5 Simplify $\sqrt{40}$

6 Simplify $\sqrt{625}$

7 Simplify $-8\sqrt{27}$

8 Simplify $-\sqrt{72}$

Add or subtract the following. Make sure to simplify your final answer.

9 $-9 + \sqrt{25}$

10 $\sqrt{3} + \sqrt{3}$

11 $\sqrt{5} + 3\sqrt{5}$

12 $\sqrt{9} + 2\sqrt{3}$

13 $1 - 4\sqrt{24} + \sqrt{6}$

14 $\sqrt{27} + 2\sqrt{3} - \sqrt{3}$

15 $\sqrt{32} + 3\sqrt{2}$

Multiply the following and be sure to simplify your final answer.

16 $\left(-5\sqrt{2}\right)^2$

17 $\left(\sqrt{5}\right)^3$

18 $\sqrt{6} \cdot \sqrt{8}$

19 $3\sqrt{2} \cdot -2\sqrt{3}$

20 $4\sqrt{3} \cdot -2\sqrt{4} \cdot 5\sqrt{5}$

21 $\sqrt{5}(\sqrt{2} - 1)$

22 $-3\sqrt{2}(3\sqrt{5} - 1)$

23 $(2\sqrt{3} + 3\sqrt{5})(2\sqrt{3} + 2\sqrt{7})$

24 $(11 - \sqrt{3})(11 + \sqrt{3})$

Dividing Square Roots

To divide square roots we need to follow the same rules as dividing monomials. We divide the outside numbers with each other and then divide the numbers inside the radicals together. In division, there is an extra step. We must get rid of any radicals that might be left in the denominator. Getting rid of square roots in the denominator is called **rationalizing the denominator** (which means having only a rational number in the denominator).

1   Divide $\dfrac{30\sqrt{10}}{-2\sqrt{5}}$.

Divide the outside numbers. Then divide the numbers inside the radicals. Simplify when possible.

Answer: $-15\sqrt{2}$

2   Find the quotient $\dfrac{6\sqrt{5}}{12\sqrt{5}}$.

Answer: $\dfrac{1}{2}\sqrt{1}$ or $\dfrac{1}{2}$ or .5

3   Divide $\dfrac{\sqrt{3}}{\sqrt{6}}$.

This leaves you with $\sqrt{\dfrac{1}{2}}$ or $\dfrac{1}{\sqrt{2}}$. The answer is not finished.

We need to rationalize the denominator. We can remove $\sqrt{2}$ from the denominator by multiplying both numerator and denominator by $\sqrt{2}$.

$$\frac{1}{\sqrt{2}} \cdot \left(\frac{\sqrt{2}}{\sqrt{2}}\right) = \left(\frac{\sqrt{2}}{2}\right) \quad \text{— This is the answer.}$$

Can you see we're actually multiplying by one and not changing the original problem?

4 Find the quotient $\dfrac{40\sqrt{20}}{-4\sqrt{5}}$.

Always look at a division problem before you start. Here's an example where dividing first is easier than rationalizing the denominator. By dividing first, you arrive at the answer $-10\sqrt{4}$, which equals -20.

5 Divide $\dfrac{7\sqrt{19}}{28\sqrt{3}}$.

You can start by dividing 7 by 28 or reducing it to $\dfrac{1}{4}$.

You now have $\dfrac{\sqrt{19}}{4\sqrt{3}}$. Now, rationalize the $\sqrt{3}$. The 4 is already rational, so don't worry about it for now. Follow along.

$$\dfrac{\sqrt{19}}{4\sqrt{3}} \cdot \dfrac{\sqrt{3}}{\sqrt{3}} = \dfrac{\sqrt{57}}{4 \cdot 3} = \boxed{\dfrac{\sqrt{57}}{12}}$$

6 Divide $\dfrac{12\sqrt{96}}{\sqrt{54}}$.

Simplify first because trying to rationalize $\sqrt{54}$ would take too long.

$$\dfrac{12\sqrt{96}}{\sqrt{54}} = \dfrac{12\sqrt{16 \cdot 6}}{\sqrt{9 \cdot 6}} = \dfrac{12\sqrt{16} \cdot \sqrt{6}}{\sqrt{9} \cdot \sqrt{6}} = \dfrac{12 \cdot 4 \cdot \sqrt{6}}{3 \cdot \sqrt{6}} = \dfrac{48}{3} = \boxed{16}$$

You can cancel here, too.

7 How would you rationalize this denominator $\dfrac{4}{11 + \sqrt{3}}$?

Notice, the denominator is a binomial. Look at problem 24 on page 196 to help you.

Do not look at the next page until you've thought about it.

If you multiply $(11 + \sqrt{3})$ by $(11 - \sqrt{3})$, you will get $121 - 3$, which is 118. $(11 + \sqrt{3})$ and $(11 - \sqrt{3})$ are called **conjugates** of each other.

$$\frac{4}{11 + \sqrt{3}} \cdot \frac{11 - \sqrt{3}}{11 - \sqrt{3}} = \frac{4(11 - \sqrt{3})}{118} = \frac{44 - 4\sqrt{3}}{118} = \frac{22 - 2\sqrt{3}}{59}$$

You could reduce the 4 and the 118 first. This shows how to simplify at the end if you did not reduce first.

Now reduce the fraction by dividing each term by 2.

Practice dividing square roots. Carefully, look at each problem first and make sure to always rationalize your denominator and simplify all answers.

1 $\dfrac{18\sqrt{12}}{-9\sqrt{6}}$

5 $\dfrac{4\sqrt{28}}{-4\sqrt{49}}$

2 $\dfrac{2}{\sqrt{2}}$

6 $\dfrac{8}{4 + \sqrt{2}}$

3 $\dfrac{15\sqrt{90}}{9\sqrt{10}}$

7 $\dfrac{-4}{\sqrt{3} - 2}$

4 $\dfrac{-10\sqrt{40}}{-20\sqrt{5}}$

8 $\dfrac{8}{3 - \sqrt{5}}$

More Practice

Assume all the variables below are greater than zero. Create the best example you can to show that these square root rules really work.

1 $\sqrt{x} \cdot \sqrt{y} = \sqrt{xy}$

4 $x\sqrt{y} + z\sqrt{y} = (x + z)\sqrt{y}$

2 $\sqrt{x^2 y} = x\sqrt{y}$

5 $\left(x\sqrt{y}\right)\left(z\sqrt{c}\right) = xz\sqrt{yc}$

3 $\dfrac{\sqrt{x}}{\sqrt{y}} = \sqrt{\dfrac{x}{y}}$

6 $\dfrac{x}{y\sqrt{z}} = \dfrac{x\sqrt{z}}{y\sqrt{z}\sqrt{z}} = \dfrac{x\sqrt{z}}{yz}$

Thinking With Radicals

1. Anthony thinks that $\sqrt{9}$ is the same as $3\sqrt{3}$ (a typical mistake made by many students). How would you convince him that he's incorrect?

_____

_____

2. Find the length of the diagonal of this square.

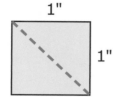

1"

1"

3. Find the length of the diagonal of this rectangle. Simplify your answer.

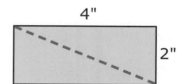

4"

2"

4. The area of this square is 9,800 square meters. Find one side. Simplify your answer.

5. Does the product of two perfect squares always give you a perfect square? Explain your thinking.

_____

_____

6. The area of this circular fountain is represented by $A = \pi r^2$. Use 3.14 for an approximation for π. If the area of the circle is 200.96 square feet, find the radius of the fountain.

7   The square root of 600 is between which two whole numbers? Do not use a calculator.

_____

8   Show how rationalizing the denominator first in these problems helps you combine the following square roots.

a $2\sqrt{3} + \dfrac{6}{\sqrt{3}}$

b $\sqrt{5} + 3\sqrt{5} - \dfrac{5}{2\sqrt{5}}$

9   If $a = 11$ and $b = 25$, evaluate the following expression. Don't forget to simplify.

$$\sqrt{a^2 - \sqrt{b}}$$

10   Is it possible to add a rational number to an irrational number and get a rational number? Is it possible to multiply two irrational numbers and get a rational number? Explain your thinking.

_____

_____

11   If the area of a square is a^2, then $\sqrt{a^2}$ or a represents one side. The volume of a cube with side b is b^3. We can represent one side of this cube by $\sqrt[3]{b}$, or the cube root of b.

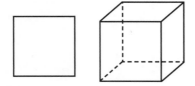

a   If the volume of the cube is 8 cubic inches, find one side. _____

b   If the volume of the cube is 64 cubic inches, find one side. _____

© 2015 The Critical Thinking Co.™ • www.CriticalThinking.com • 800-458-4849

The Quadratic Formula

There are many times when we cannot solve a quadratic equation by factoring. For those times, we can use a formula called the **quadratic formula**. Using the formula will help us review how to work with square roots.

The Quadratic Formula

$$x = \frac{-b \pm \sqrt{b^2 - 4ac}}{2a}$$

You might remember that the general form of a quadratic equation is $ax^2 + bx + c = 0$, where a, b are the coefficients of the first two terms and c is a constant. It's important to remember that $a \neq 0$ or the equation would no longer be a quadratic. Let's look at the examples below.

1   Solve $x^2 + 3x + 1 = 2$.

Remember to let the equation equal 0 and make sure it's in standard form. So subtract 2 from each side.

$$x^2 + 3x - 1 = 0 \longleftarrow$$ Don't forget to try to factor it. If you can't, then proceed to use the quadratic formula.

So $a = 1$ (the coefficient of x^2)
   $b = 3$ (the coefficient of x)
   $c = -1$ (the constant)

$$x = \frac{-b \pm \sqrt{b^2 - 4ac}}{2a} \quad \text{or} \quad \frac{-3 \pm \sqrt{3^2 - (4 \cdot 1 \cdot -1)}}{2 \cdot 1}$$

It really helps to put parentheses around $4ac$.

$$x = \frac{-3 \pm \sqrt{9 - (-4)}}{2} = \frac{-3 + \sqrt{13}}{2} \quad \text{or} \quad \frac{-3 - \sqrt{13}}{2}$$

The $\pm$ gives you two answers.

A check for the first answer is shown below. Using a separate sheet of paper, check the second answer.

Is $\left(\dfrac{-3+\sqrt{13}}{2}\right)^2 + 3\left(\dfrac{-3+\sqrt{13}}{2}\right) + 1 = 2?$ or $\left(\dfrac{-3}{2}+\dfrac{\sqrt{13}}{2}\right)^2 + 3\left(\dfrac{-3}{2}+\dfrac{\sqrt{13}}{2}\right) + 1 = 2?$

$\left(\dfrac{-3}{2}+\dfrac{\sqrt{13}}{2}\right)\left(\dfrac{-3}{2}+\dfrac{\sqrt{13}}{2}\right) + 3\left(\dfrac{-3}{2}+\dfrac{\sqrt{13}}{2}\right) + 1 = 2?$ Now, multiply the binomial.

$\dfrac{9}{4} - \dfrac{3\sqrt{13}}{4} - \dfrac{3\sqrt{13}}{4} + \dfrac{13}{4} - \dfrac{9}{2} + \dfrac{3\sqrt{13}}{2} + 1 = 2?$ Multiply every term on both sides of the equation by 4.

$9 - 3\sqrt{13} - 3\sqrt{13} + 13 - 18 + 6\sqrt{13} + 4 = 8?$

$4 \quad + \quad 4 \quad = 8$ Yes!

---

2 Solve the following quadratic equation by using the quadratic formula.

$3y^2 - 10y + 5 = 0$

$a = 3,\ b = -10$ and $c = 5$

$y = \dfrac{-(-10) \pm \sqrt{(-10)^2 - (4 \cdot 3 \cdot 5)}}{2 \cdot 3} = \dfrac{10 \pm \sqrt{100 - (60)}}{6} =$

$\dfrac{10 \pm \sqrt{40}}{6} = \dfrac{10 \pm 2\sqrt{10}}{6} = \dfrac{5 \pm \sqrt{10}}{3}$ so the two answers are:

Divide each term by 2. $\dfrac{5 + \sqrt{10}}{3}$ or $\dfrac{5 - \sqrt{10}}{3}$

The more you practice using the quadratic formula the more you'll remember it. Just be sure you use it when it's absolutely necessary. It's more important to be great at factoring when you can factor!

Practice

Using a separate sheet of paper, solve the following quadratic equations. Remember to write your equation in standard form first. Simplify your answer.

$$x = \frac{-b \pm \sqrt{b^2 - 4ac}}{2a}$$

1. Solve $y^2 + 3y - 10 = 0$ by factoring AND by using the quadratic formula.

2. Solve $x^2 + 11x = -18$ by factoring and by using the quadratic formula.

3. In $y^2 - 4 = 0$, $a =$ _____, $b =$ _____ and $c =$ _____.

4. Solve $y^2 - 4 = 0$ by factoring and by using the quadratic formula.

5. In $4x^2 - 2x = 0$, $a =$ _____, $b =$ _____, and $c =$ _____.

6. Solve $4x^2 - 2x = 0$ by factoring or by using the quadratic formula.

7. Solve $x^2 + 3x + 1 = 0$.

8. Solve $y^2 - 7y = 2$.

9. Solve $2x^2 - 5x + 1 = 0$.

10. Solve $4n^2 + 8n + 1 = 0$.

11. Larry tried to solve this quadratic equation, $20x^2 + 160x + 300 = 0$, by using the quadratic formula using $a = 20$, $b = 160$, and $c = 300$. Was this the most efficient way to solve this equation? Explain your thinking.

_____

_____

12. Some quadratic equations such as this one, $4x^2 - 2x + 2 = 0$, will give you answers that are not rational and also not irrational. These answers or roots are called "imaginary." Can you see why? Explain your thinking.

_____

_____

Chapter 9

Linear Functions

What Is a Function?

In algebra, when you pair or map numbers, you form what is called a **relation**. A relation is actually a set of ordered pairs (x, y), for example, (5, -3), (5 , 5), (-3, 4), (0, 5), (0, 1), etc. The x's in the ordered pairs are called the input or **domain** and the y's are called the output or **range**. A **function** is a special type of relation where given an input you will get the <u>same</u> output for that given input every time.

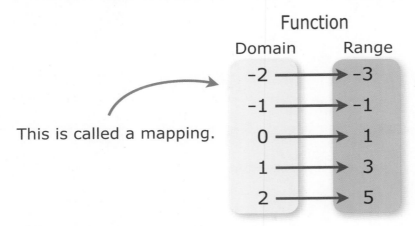

This is called a mapping.

The ordered pairs above are (-2, -3), (-1, -1), (0, 1), (1, 3), and (2, 5). Because it is a function, the next time you input 2, you will get 5 and only 5.

Not a Function

Domain   Range

-2 ——→ -3
-1 ——→ -1
0 ——→ 1
1 ——→ 3
2 ——→ 5

Notice that in the relation above the input -1 has two outputs. The ordered pairs (-1, -1) and (-1, 5) make this fail to be a function. A good example of a function in real life is a classroom of ninth graders matched to their birthdays. Every time you mention someone's name that person has a unique birthday. The person cannot have two birthdays. However, it's possible for other people in the class to have the same birthday. See the example of a function where that happens on the next page.

As you see by this example, both Pat and Luis share the same birthday. So this still fits the definition of a function, for every input (*x*) there is only ONE output (*y*) that corresponds to that input.

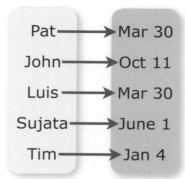

Functions are very important in mathematics. Often a very easy way to check if a set of ordered pairs is or is not a function is to perform what is called a "vertical line test." In the graph below, *y* = 2*x*, notice that if we pick a point on the graph (the green point) there is no other point above or below that point or for any other point of that graph. That makes it a function. However, notice on the graph on the right there that there is a point on the graph below the green point, so it's not a function.

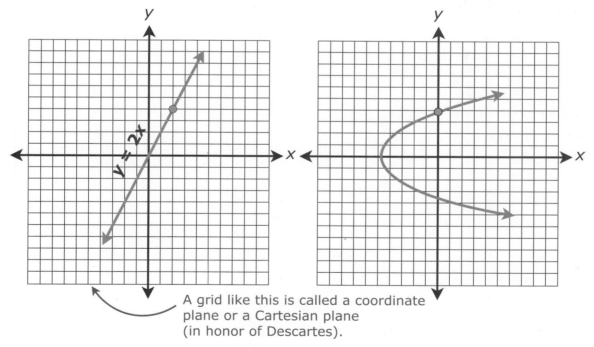

A grid like this is called a coordinate plane or a Cartesian plane (in honor of Descartes).

Because *y* = 2*x* is a function, we can write it with the notation *f*(*x*) = 2*x*. This is read as "*f* of *x*" and not "*f* times *x*." Just remember that *f*(*x*) is another way of saying *y*. The notation should remind you that you're working with a function. You might see also see *g*(*x*) or any other variable that is a function or *x*.

Thinking About Functions

Answer the questions below.

1   Given these ordered pairs: (–3, 4), (–4, 8), (–5, 10), (–3, 8)

    a   The domain is _____ and the range is _____ .

    b   Is the set of ordered pairs a function?   Explain your thinking.

    _____

2   The drawing below represents a relation.   Is this relation a function?
   Explain your thinking.

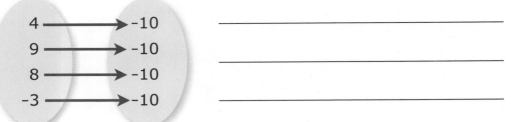

    _____

    _____

    _____

3   Perform a vertical line test to determine if the graphs below represent
   a function or just any relation.   Explain your thinking.

    _____

    _____

    a   b

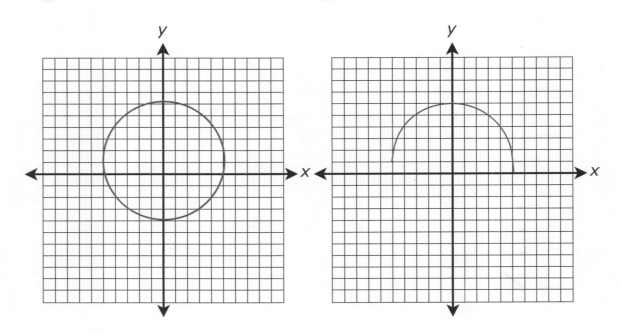

4　Given the domain choices below, which value for *x* would make this relation, (3, 5), (4, 6), (*x*, 5), (10, 8), a function? Explain your thinking.

> Domain Choices
>
> **10**
> 　　**4**
> 　**8**

_____

_____

_____

5　Look at this table of values.

x	y
-2	-7
-1	-4
0	-1
1	2
2	5

a　Can you determine the equation?

_____

b　Do these ordered pairs represent a function?

_____

c　If a function, write it in function notation.

_____

6　A one-to-one function is a function that has one input mapping to one and only one output, but also has each output mapping back to only one and only one input. Does the table of values above represent a one-to-one function? Explain your thinking.

_____

_____

7　Is $y = x^2$ a function? Fill out the rest of this table and explain your thinking.

x	-2	-1	0	1	2
y	4				

_____

_____

_____

Linear Functions

A **linear function** is a function with an equation of the form $y = mx + b$, or $f(x) = mx + b$, where m are b are constants. When the equation is written as $y = mx + b$, the coefficient m is the **slope** or the steepness of the line and the constant b is the **y-intercept** or where the line crosses the y-axis. Not all lines are functions as we will see shortly.

Given an equation of this form, $y = mx + b$, let's learn how to graph it.

1 Graph $y = 3x + 1$

Make a table of values. So if $x = -3$, you plug in or substitute -3 for x into the equation, $y = 3(-3) + 1 = -8$. Substituting the other x values in the domain, we finish the table. Label the equation on the line.

Domain Range

x	$f(x) = y$
-3	-8
-2	-5
-1	-2
0	1
1	4
2	7
3	10

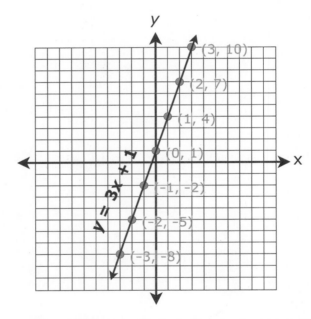

We could have written our equation as $f(x) = 3x + 1$ since it's a function. If you see $f(4)$, it's the same as plugging in or substituting 4 into our equation. In this case, $f(4) = 3(4) + 1$ or 13. It's another way of saying "evaluate the equation for $x = 4$."

Notice on the table that as the x values go up by one unit, the y values go up by 3 units each time. Our function is **linear** if as the x values go up by one unit the y values consistently go up by the same amount.

Let's take a closer look at the last equation and its graph. The equation $y = 3x + 1$ is written in the form, $y = mx + b$. This is called the **slope-intercept** form of an equation. We know, even without graphing it, that it will cross or intercept the y-axis at 1 or at (0,1). We also know that the line will rise to the right because the **slope** (the number in front of the x) is a positive 3. The slope controls the steepness of the line and which way the line rises. Notice that from one point to the next, the line goes over to the right 1 and up 3. We will do more with slope later, but keep these ideas in mind as you practice graphing the next few equations.

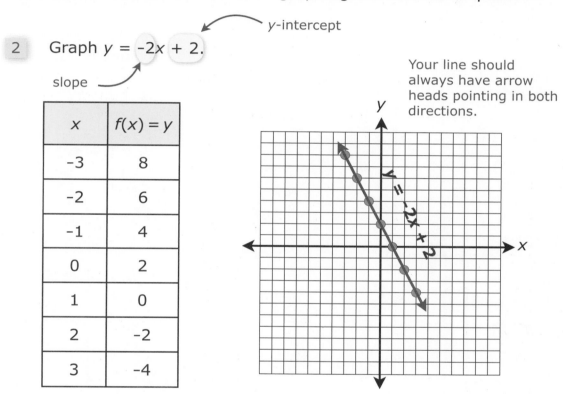

2   Graph $y = -2x + 2$.

x	$f(x) = y$
-3	8
-2	6
-1	4
0	2
1	0
2	-2
3	-4

Your line should always have arrow heads pointing in both directions.

Can you see that the line crosses the y-axis at 2 or (0, 2)? Can you see that the top arrow on the line is pointing toward the left? This is because it has a negative slope.

If you look at the table, can you see that as the x values (the domain) go up by one unit, the y values (the range) decrease by 2 units each time? That constant change in the range is what makes this another example of a linear function.

The slope-intercept form of an equation ($y = mx + b$) makes it easy to make a table of values and can help you graph even without a table as we will see shortly. You can always change an equation to slope-intercept form by solving for y.

3 Change this equation to slope-intercept form. Make a table of values and answer the questions below.

$9 - y = 3x$

You need to solve for y. Subtract 9 from both sides.

$-y = 3x - 9$

Now, multiply (or divide) every term by –1.

$y = -3x + 9$ Now it's in slope-intercept form.

x	f(x) = y
-3	18
-2	15
-1	12
0	9
1	6
2	3
3	0

a What is the slope? The slope is –3.

b Where will the line cross the y-axis? At 9, or point (0,9).

c As the domain changes by one unit, what does the range do? It decreases consistently by 3 (or –3 each time).

d How will the line look? Choose one.

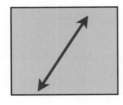 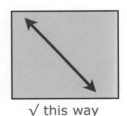

√ this way

e Write the equation using function notation. $f(x) = -3x + 9$

f Can you find $f(5)$? $f(5) = -3(5) + 9 = -6$

g Is it possible for $f(2)$ to equal 3 and also equal another value? No, it's a function, so for every x value there is only ONE value associated with that x value.

Practice

Do the following problems.

1   Change the following equations to slope-intercept form ($y = mx + b$).
    Identify the slope (m) and the y-intercept (b).

   a $2y = 4x + 10$ d $8x + 2y = 6$ g $2x - y + 5 = 0$

   $m = $ _____, $b = $ _____ $m = $ _____, $b = $ _____ $m = $ _____, $b = $ _____

   b $-y = -3x - 2$ e $-2x + y = 10$ h $4y - 3x = 8$

   $m = $ _____, $b = $ _____ $m = $ _____, $b = $ _____ $m = $ _____, $b = $ _____

   c $2x + y = 7$ f $\frac{3}{4}y = 12x + 6$ i $3x + \frac{1}{2}y = 1$

   $m = $ _____, $b = $ _____ $m = $ _____, $b = $ _____ $m = $ _____, $b = $ _____

2   Make a table of values and graph the following equations. Make sure
    to label the equation on the line.

   a $y = -2x + 1$

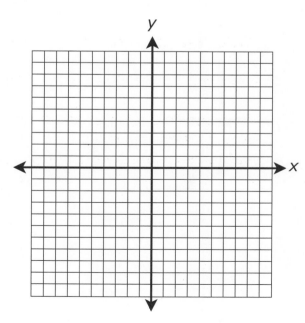

x	$f(x) = y$
–3	
–2	
–1	
0	
1	
2	
3	

b) $-y + x + 5 = 0$

x	f(x) = y
-3	
-2	
-1	
0	
1	
2	
3	

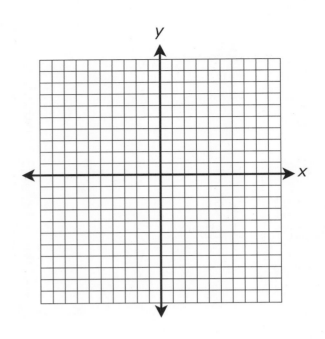

c) $2y = -4x$

x	f(x) = y
-3	
-2	
-1	
0	
1	
2	
3	

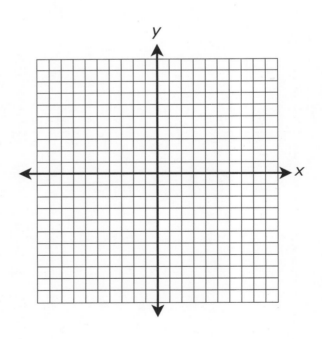

In this equation, what is the *y*-intercept? _____

d) $y = 3$

x	f(x) = y
-3	
-2	
-1	
0	
1	
2	
3	

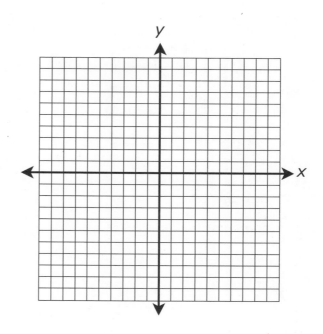

In this equation, what is the slope? _____

e) $x = 3$

y can be any value you want since x is always 3.

x	f(x) = y
3	
3	
3	
3	
3	
3	
3	

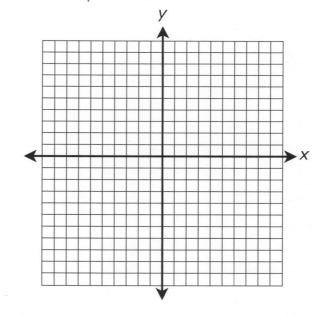

Is this a function? Explain your thinking.

_____

_____

What Is Slope?

Slope is defined as the rate of change (the number of units up or down divided by the number of units going right or left).

$$m = \frac{\text{rise}}{\text{run}} = \frac{\Delta y}{\Delta x}$$

Δy divided by Δx means vertical change (y) divided by the horizontal change (x).

When the equation is written in slope-intercept form, then the slope is the number in front of the x. For example, in this equation, $y = \frac{3}{2}x - 2$, the slope is $\frac{3}{2}$. You know the y-intercept is –2, so if you use that as your starting point, you can graph the next point by going up 3 units and over to the right 2 units. When you have at least three or four points, then draw your line and label the equation.

While you can draw a line with only two points, the more points, the more accurate the line.

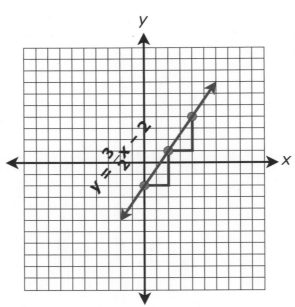

Because $\frac{3}{2} = \frac{-3}{-2}$, from –2 (the y-intercept), you can also go down on the y-axis 3 units and to the left 2 units.

When your equation is in slope-intercept form you can now graph it without a table of values.

Let's look at one example where the slope is negative.

1   Graph $y = -\frac{2}{5}x - 4$.

The slope is $\frac{-2}{5}$ *or* $\frac{2}{-5}$. You can give the negative to either the numerator or the denominator, but NOT both as that would make it a positive. So start at -4, the y-intercept. Go down 2 units and to the right 5 units. You can also go up 2 units and to the left 5 units.

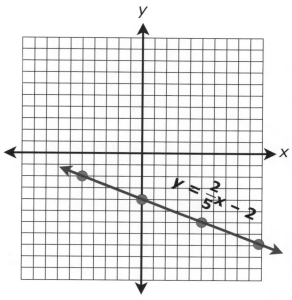

2   Graph $3y = 6x$.
Be sure to solve for y. So dividing both sides by 3, $y = 2x$.

The y-intercept is 0 and the slope is 2. Change 2 to $\frac{2}{1}$ or $\frac{-2}{-1}$.

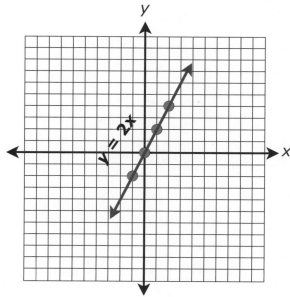

Zero Slope and Undefined Slope

Suppose you have an equation such as $y = 0x + 5$ or $y = 5$. This means that the slope is 0, or $\dfrac{0}{n}$ where $n \neq 0$. You would start at the y-intercept, which is 5, and not move up any units while you move sideways either left or right. Thus the graph of the equation is a horizontal line.

If you have a slope where the denominator is 0, then the fraction is empty set or undefined. You can move up as many units as you want, but because the zero is in the denominator you never move right or left, thus the graph is a vertical line. Vertical lines start with "$x =$" and have no y variable. For example, if $x = 4$, then the vertical line intersects the x axis at 4 or (4, 0). Vertical lines, as you know, are not functions.

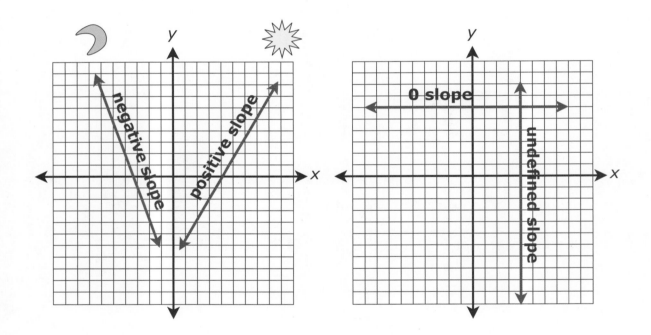

Horizontal lines have 0 slope.

Vertical lines have Ø or undefined slope.

Graphing Practice

Using graph paper, graph the following equations by using the slope-intercept method. State the slope (*m*) and the *y*-intercept (*b*).

1 $y = 7$ $m =$ _____, $b =$ _____

2 $y = \frac{1}{4}x$ $m =$ _____, $b =$ _____

3 $x = -3$ $m =$ _____, $b =$ _____

4 $y = x$ $m =$ _____, $b =$ _____

5 $y = -x$ $m =$ _____, $b =$ _____

6 $y = -x + 5$ $m =$ _____, $b =$ _____

7 $y = -\frac{1}{2}x + 3$ $m =$ _____, $b =$ _____

8 $y = 5$ $m =$ _____, $b =$ _____

9 $x = -4$ $m =$ _____, $b =$ _____

10 $\frac{3}{4}y = -6x + 12$ $m =$ _____, $b =$ _____

Answer the following questions.

11   Graph $y = 3x + 5$ and $y = 3x - 2$ on the same coordinate plane. What types of lines are these? Does it have anything to do with their slopes? Explain your thinking.

_____

_____

12 Graph $y = \frac{3}{4}x + 2$ and $y = -\frac{4}{3}x + 5$ on the same coordinate plane.

What do you notice about these two lines? Does it have anything to do with their slopes? Explain your thinking.

_____

_____

Parallel lines have the <u>same</u> slope.

Perpendicular lines have <u>negative reciprocal</u> slopes
(Find the reciprocal of the slope and change the sign.)

Perpendicular lines make 90° angles.

13 Which of the following equations is parallel to $y = 5x + 6$?

  a $y = 6x + 5$ b $y = -5x + 6$ c $y = 5x$ d $y = 4x + 6$

14 Which of the following equations is parallel to $3x + y = 2$?

  a $y = -3x + 5$ b $y = 3x + 2$ c $y = 3$ d $y = \frac{1}{3}x + 4$

15 Which of the following equations is perpendicular to $y = 4x$?

  a $y = -4x$ b $y = 4$ c $y = -\frac{1}{4}x + 9$ d $y = \frac{1}{4}$

16 Are these two lines perpendicular? $y = 5$ and $x = 5$. Explain your thinking.

_____

_____

17 Write an equation that is parallel to $2x - y = 3$. Explain how you know it's parallel without graphing it. Use function notation.

_____

_____

Writing Equations for Linear Functions

To write a linear equation you need to know the slope and y-intercept. You can arrive at the equation if: 1) You are given only two points, or 2) You are given one point and the slope.

If you are given two points you can find the slope. You can graph the two points and determine the slope by counting the change in y and dividing it by the change in x, but if the points are fractions or decimals or very big numbers, using the slope formula is the way to go.

> To find the slope given two points,
> (x_1, y_1) and (x_2, y_2), use the slope formula:
>
> $$\frac{(y_2) - (y_1)}{(x_2) - (x_1)}$$

First, let's practice how to find the slope given two points.

1   Find the slope of the line that passes through (-2, 3) and (4, 5).

It doesn't matter which y value you pick first, as long as the first x value you pick first corresponds to that y value.

$$\frac{(5) - (3)}{(4) - (-2)} = \frac{2}{6} = \frac{1}{3}$$

It helps to keep the parentheses.

2   Find the slope of the line that passes through (-3, -5) and (-2, -1).

$$\frac{(-5) - (-1)}{(-3) - (-2)} = \frac{-4}{-1} = 4$$

Find the Slope

Find the slope of the line that connects the following points.

1 (0, 4) and (5, 6)

8 (9, –2) and (7, –3)

2 (–2, –4) and (8, 2)

9 (10, 2) and (12, 4)

3 (–3, 8) and (0, 5)

10 (–1, 5) and (–3, –8)

4 (8, 3) and (2, 3)

11 (–7, –2) and (–9, –4)

5 (–2, 0) and (–2, 5)

12 (0, 0) and (–5, –6)

6 (8, –4) and (9, –5)

13 (14, –20) and (16, –24)

7 (–3, 6) and (0, 9)

14 (3, 0) and (0, –12)

Now that we know how to find the slope of a line given two points, finding the equation of the line that goes through those two points requires one more step.

1 Write the equation of a line that goes through (-3, 2) and (-4, -1).

First, find the slope: $\dfrac{(2) - (-1)}{(-3) - (-4)} = \dfrac{3}{1} = 3$

Now, that we know the slope is 3, pick one of the ordered pairs (either one) and plug that point into the variables x and y and substitute 3 for m (slope).

$y = mx + b$ Let's pick (-3, 2) for x and y.

$2 = 3(-3) + b$ Now, solve for b.

$2 = -9 + b$

$11 = b$

The equation is: $y = 3x + 11$.

2 Write the equation of a line that goes through (0, 5) and (-2, 6).

First, find the slope: $\dfrac{(6) - (5)}{(-2) - 0} = \dfrac{1}{-2} = -\dfrac{1}{2}$

Notice that (0, 5) is actually the y-intercept!

The equation is: $y = -\dfrac{1}{2}x + 5$.

In case you did not notice that the y-intercept is one of the given points, find it by solving for b. Plugging in (-2, 6) and using $-\dfrac{1}{2}$ as the slope, this is what you get:

$y = mx + b$

$6 = -\dfrac{1}{2}(-2) + b$

$6 = 1 + b$

$5 = b$

Find the Equation

Find the equation of the line that passes by these points. These are all functions, so you can replace $f(x)$ for y at the end if you want.

1   (4, 5) and (3, 3)

6   (4, 4) and (5, -2)

2   (-2, 6) and (-4, 8)

7   (-5, 3) and (-8, 6)

3   (1, 4) and (-3, 8)

8   (5, 1) and (4, 1)

4   (0, 3) and (4, 0)

9   (3, -8) and (6, -2)

5   (-6, -2) and (-4, 1)

10   (9, 0) and (0, 3)

Point-Slope Formula

It is also possible to write a linear equation if you have the slope and only one point. Obviously, if you graph the one point and use the slope, you can find the next point on the graph, but again, without a graph it's still possible to find the equation. Remember the slope formula.

$$\frac{(y_2) - (y_1)}{(x_2) - (x_1)} = m$$

Multiplying both sides by $[(x_2) - (x_1)]$, we get:

$$y_2 - y_1 = m\,[(x_2) - (x_1)].$$

Let (x_1, y_1) represent the point we are given and replace (x_2, y_2) with (x, y), since (x, y) represents every other point on the line.

That gives us:

Point-Slope Formula

$$y - (y_1) = m \cdot [x - (x_1)]$$

1 Use the point-slope formula to write the equation of a line that passes through (–3, 4) and has a slope of 2.

$$y - 4 = 2(x - (-3))$$

$$y - 4 = 2x + 6 \qquad \text{Solving for } y.$$

Equation: $y = 2x + 10$

2 Use the point-slope formula to write the equation of a line that passes through (2, –10) and has a slope of $\frac{3}{4}$.

$$y - (-10) = \frac{3}{4}(x - 2)$$

$$y + 10 = \frac{3}{4}x - \frac{3}{2} \qquad \text{Solving for } y.$$

Equation: $y = \frac{3}{4}x - 11\frac{1}{2}$

Point-Slope Practice

Use the point-slope formula to find the equation of the line that passes through these points with the given slope.

1 (-3, 4); $m = 2$

5 (1, 10); $m = -4$

2 (-1, -1); $m = 5$

6 (-4, 5); $m = -\frac{1}{2}$

3 (4, -3); $m = \frac{1}{2}$

7 (0, 8); $m = 3$

4 (2, 4); $m = 0$

8 (-2, -2); $m = \frac{3}{4}$

More Practice

Using a separate sheet of paper, practice working with linear functions.

1. Write an equation of a line with slope of -3 and a y-intercept of 8.

2. Find the slope of a line that passes through (0, 6) and (20, -4).

3. Find the slope of a line that passes through (-5, 5) and (-5, 8).

4. Vertical lines have _____ (zero or undefined) slope.

5. Horizontal lines have _____ (zero or undefined) slope.

6. Solve for y: $3x - y = 8$.

7. Write an equation of a line that passes through (1, 1) and (6, 6).

8. Write an equation for a line that passes through (-2, 5) and (-3, 9).

9. Use the point-slope form to write an equation that passes through (3, 4) and has a slope of -5.

10. Use the point-slope form to write an equation that passes through (4, 0) and has a slope of $\frac{3}{4}$.

11. Write an equation of a line that is parallel to $y = 2x + 6$, but passes through the point (-3, 4).

12. Write an equation of a line that is perpendicular to $y = 2x + 6$ and passes through the point (-3, 4).

13. If $f(x) = 3x + 9$, find $f(-2)$.

14. This linear function, $f(x) = 5x$ has a y-intercept of _____.

For problems 15-24, give an explanation along with your answer.

15. A line that is parallel to $y = 3x + 10$ would have a slope of _____. Explain your thinking.

16. A line that is perpendicular to $y = 3x + 10$ would have a slope of _____. Explain your thinking.

17. Is the point (-3, 4) on the line $y = 2x + 2$? Explain your thinking.

18. Does the line $y = 3x + 8$ pass by the origin? Explain your thinking.

19. Are these lines parallel: $y = -2x + 8$ and $2y = 4x + 8$? Explain.

20. Are these lines perpendicular? $y = 3x + 8$ and $2x + 6y = 10$. Explain your thinking.

21. Give an example of a linear equation that is not a function.

22. Is it possible to tell from looking at an equation if it is a linear function or not? Explain your thinking.

23   Slope is usually called the rate of change. Explain what this means.

24   True or False? All linear equations of the form "$y = mx$" go through the origin. Explain your thinking.

Linear Function Applications

The following examples represent some real life applications to linear functions.

1   A flower shop sells roses for $6 with a $15 delivery fee. Write a function where r represents the cost of one rose and c the total cost. Determine how many roses were bought if Paulo spent $231 on roses for his grandmother.

$$c = f(r) = 15 + 6r$$

$231 = 15 + 6r$ Solving for r.
$216 = 6r$
$36 = r$

He bought 36 roses.

2   Membership to the local gym costs $150 for the initial fee plus $40 every month. Let g = total cost per month and T = the total cost of the membership. Write a function to represent the total cost. Determine how many years Julia belonged to the gym if so far she's paid $2,070.

$$T = F(g) = 150 + 40g$$

$2,070 = 150 + 40g$ Solving for g.
$1,920 = 40g$
$48 = g$

48 months = 4 years. Julia has belonged to the gym 4 years.

A graphing calculator can help you solve many of these problems or at least help you check them. The graphing calculator is a tool to help you think. It's not a tool to do work you do not understand, so keep that in mind. If you have a TI-83 or TI-84, the following section will help you see how linear functions have applications in the real world.

Graphing Linear Functions on a Calculator

If you have a TI-83 or TI-84 calculator (TI-89 calculators are often not allowed in many classrooms and not on state exams), let's review some basic functions we need to know before we start working with linear functions. You can refer to your instruction booklet and even better, there are many great Internet sites with instructions and problems to practice using a graphing calculator.

How to Clear the Memory

Go to (2ND) (+).
Go to 7 (scroll or press (7)) (ENTER).
RESET RAM Go to 2.
Done.

Warning: This process will erase any programs or data you have stored on the calculator.

How to Return to the Home Screen

Go to (2ND) (MODE) (puts you in QUIT).

The Difference Between Delete and Clear

Delete (DEL) gets rid of the last entry you typed whereas (CLEAR) gets rid of everything you've typed.

The Negative Sign IS NOT the Subtraction Sign

The negative sign is the key under the 3, and the subtraction sign is above the plus sign. Do not get these confused.

The Window Setting

The (WINDOW) key (top row, next to (Y=)) is set at Xmin= -10, Xmax= 10, Xscl=1 (units by 1), Ymin= -10, Ymax = 10, Yscl= 1 (units by 1), Xres= 1 (how dark). So the screen is set 10 units on either side of the x- and y-axis. If your equation is not visible under these settings, you can try the (ZOOM) key. (ZOOM) (0), called Zoom Fit, resets the window settings for you or you can change the window settings yourself. After you press (ZOOM) (0), go to (WINDOW) and you will see that the settings were changed. Be aware of that before you try graphing another equation.

How to Graph a Linear Function

The very top left key is (Y=). The calculator will not graph anything that is not a function. To graph a linear function, make sure you've solved for *y*.

1   Graph $f(x) = y = 3x - 6$ on your graphing calculator.

Make sure your windows are set to the default setting. Clear the memory of your calculator if needed.

Go to (Y=) and type $3x - 6$. The (x) is the key under (MODE). Make sure you used the subtraction sign and not the negative sign.

Now, go to (TRACE). (TRACE) and (GRAPH) both give you the graph but notice that (TRACE) gives you the points on the line. As you press the right scroll key, you will see other points on your line.

Now, press (2ND) (GRAPH) (TABLE). You are now seeing the table of values for your function. Can you find the *y*-intercept on the table?

Using the table can you find $f(-22)$? The answer is -72.

How to Change the Units on the Table of Values

If you want to change your table settings so that the table of values goes up or down by .5 units, go to (2ND) (WINDOW) (puts you in Table Set) and change ΔTbl =1 to ΔTbl =.5.

Later on, you'll be able to graph two equations and determine where they intersect. But remember, learning everything by using a pencil and paper first will make you appreciate the graphing calculator more.

Try graphing the following equations on your calculator.

1    $y = 4x + 9$
2    $2y = -7x - 10$ ◄—— (To type a fraction in the calculator, use the division key, but to be safe, surround the fraction with parentheses).
3    $25x - y = 200$
4    $y = x$
5    $y = -x$
6   Do Example 2 (page 228) on the graphing calculator. Use *x* instead of *g*. Find what Julia spent in 6 years (72 months) using the calculator.

Scatterplots

There are many applications of linear functions in science and other fields. Often we need to know if our data is behaving in a linear manner or not. A scatterplot is a graph of points that can help us determine if our two variables have a correlation (are they affecting each other or not?)

1   Mr. Reilley asked ten of his students how long they studied for their Biology midterm and then compared that to their results. Here's his data.

Hours Studying	Midterm Grades
2	93
0.5	72
3	97
1	89
3	99
5	100
0	58
2	91
2.5	95
0.25	78

While Mr. Reilley knows that the hours of studying does not always directly result in great scores, he was interested in that correlation (how the two are related). He was also interested if the relationship between both variables is linear or not.

To Make a Scatterplot of This Data

Clear the memory.
2ND 0 (CATALOG) and go down the list to Diagnostic ON and press ENTER.
Press STAT.
ENTER.
Under L1 type the hours studying: 2 ENTER, .5 ENTER, etc.
Scroll to the right with the right arrow key.
Under L2 type the midterm scores.
2ND Y= (STAT PLOT) and press ENTER.
Scroll to the left and select ON.
Go to ZOOM 9 (top middle key) ENTER.
You will now see the scatterplot.

```
Plot1 Plot2 Plot3
On  Off
Type:▩ ⋰ ⊞ ⊞ ⊞ ⋰
Xlist:L1
Ylist:L2
Mark: ▫ + ·
Color:  BLUE
```

How to Determine the Line of Best Fit

Next, to determine if the points are close to a linear function, do the
following.

Go to STAT and scroll right to CALC.
Go down to 4 (LinReg (ax + b)) ENTER and
ENTER again.

```
LinReg
y=ax+b
a=7.411798896
b=72.93228713
r²=.7034060157
r=.8386930402
```

The equation or line of best fit is $y = 7.41 + 72.93$.
a is the slope and b is the y-intercept.

The r is called the correlation coefficient. The correlation coefficient will
be between −1 to 1 or $-1 \leq r \leq 1$. The closest that value is to 1 the more
positive the correlation. From our data the correlation coefficient is .8.
It's a strong correlation.

Mr. Reilley concluded from his results that studying more resulted in
better grades.

Don't forget that to see the correlation coefficient, you need to go first to
the CATALOG and press Diagnostic ON.

A word of caution. If you need to graph a function after you've done
a scatterplot, when you press Y= you will need to unhighlight PLOT.
Otherwise, you won't be able to graph.

Types of Correlations

NO CORRELATION

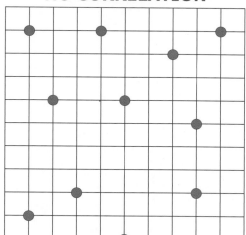

HIGH POSITIVE CORRELATION

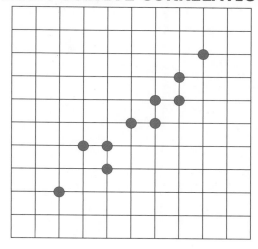

HIGH NEGATIVE CORRELATION

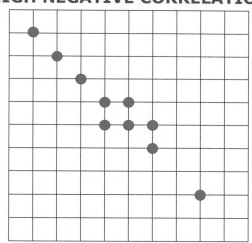

LOW POSITIVE CORRELATION

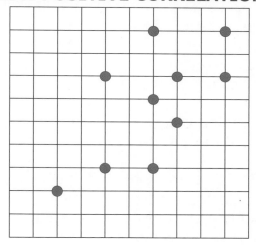

LOW NEGATIVE CORRELATION

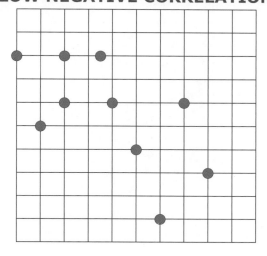

Calculator Practice

If you don't have a graphing calculator, you may try some of the problems by hand, changing the units on your grid, or skip this section. Use a separate sheet of paper.

1 In your graphing calculator, graph $y = 4x - 2$.

     a Use the table of values (2ND GRAPH) to find the y-intercept.

     b Is the ordered pair (−15, −62) a point on the graph?

     c What is the x-intercept (where the line touches the x-axis)?

2 Go to Y= and under Y1 type $y = 3x + 10$. Scroll down and under Y2 type $y = 3x - 7$. Now graph them (Press TRACE). What do you notice? (Go to ZOOM 5 (ZSquare) to make sure the units are the same for both the x- and the y-axis.)

3 Graph $y = 10x + 200$ on your graphing calculator. Remember to use Zoom Fit to see the graph or change the window settings. On the table of values, find $f(25)$.

4 Venissa wants to join a yoga class. The membership is $50 for the initial fee and $12 a class. Write an equation to represent this linear function. If she only has $250 for yoga classes, how many classes can she attend? Use the graphing calculator to answer the question.

5 An ice cream shop kept track of how many ice creams were sold and the high temperature of each day. Here are their results for 10 days. Make a scatterplot. Determine the line of best fit and the correlation coefficient. Is there a correlation?

Temperature (Fahrenheit)	95	80	89	103	105	79	80	80	69	65
No. of Ice Creams Sold	195	100	120	220	205	110	105	106	72	50

Suggested Projects

6 Is there a correlation between the length of a person's hand (from wrist to index finger) and the length of the person's feet? Make a table of values and find the correlation.

7 Is there a correlation between the circumference of someone's head and their height? Make a table of values and find if there is a correlation.

Chapter 10

Systems of Equations and Inequalities

What is the solution to $x + y = 10$? Can you see that there are infinite answers to one equation with two unknowns. How about if you are asked to find an x and a y that satisfies both of these equations?

This brace is optional but it's sometimes used to remind you that you are working with a system.

$$\begin{cases} x + y = 10 \\ x - y = 2 \end{cases}$$

The solution to both equations is now $x = 6$ and $y = 4$ and that is the only solution that works for both equations. While you can use trial and error to figure out what solution works for more than one equation, there are three methods that can be used to solve what we call a "system of equations" (think "solar system"—more than just one planet). A system of equations is often referred to as "simultaneous equations" (two or more equations being solved at the same time). The three methods are 1) **Graphing**, 2) **Elimination**, and 3) **Substitution**.

Method 1 — Graphing

Graphing each equation on the same coordinate plane will locate the solution set.

1 Graph $x + y = 10$
$\qquad\qquad y = -x + 10$
$\qquad\qquad\qquad\qquad$ (Solving for y.)

Graph $x - y = 2$
$\qquad\qquad -y = -x + 2$
$\qquad\qquad\quad y = x - 2$

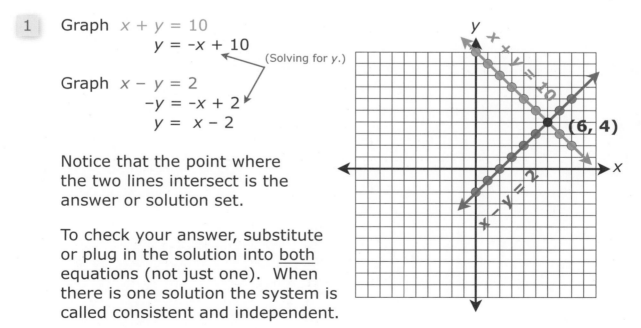

Notice that the point where the two lines intersect is the answer or solution set.

To check your answer, substitute or plug in the solution into both equations (not just one). When there is one solution the system is called consistent and independent.

Are you thinking of what happens if the lines are parallel? Or if the equations look different, but they are actually the same line?

2 Solve the following system of equations by graphing.

$$\begin{cases} -3x - y = 3 \\ 6x + 2y = 8 \end{cases}$$

Graph $-3x - y = 3$
$-y = 3x + 3$
$y = -3x - 3$

Graph $6x + 2y = 8$
$2y = -6x + 8$
$y = -3x + 4$

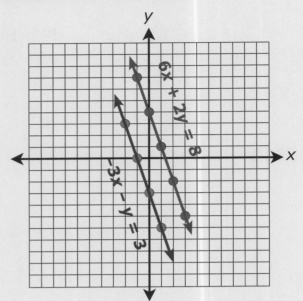

Notice that the lines are parallel (they have the same slope), so there is no intersection. This system of equations has no solution. The system is called inconsistent.

3 Solve the following system of equations by graphing.

$$\begin{cases} 8x + 4y = 12 \\ 2x + y = 3 \end{cases}$$

When you solve each equation for y you will get $y = -2x + 3$ for both equations.

Both equations are the same line, so there are infinite solutions. This system is called consistent and dependent.

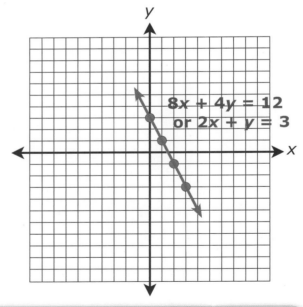

Consistent Systems
→ Independent – one solution (intersecting lines)
→ Dependent – infinite solutions (one line)

Inconsistent System → NO solution – (lines are parallel)

Graphing Practice

Solve the following systems of equations by graphing. Make sure to label each equation on the line and label the point of intersection if there is any. Write whether the system is consistent (what type?) or inconsistent on the line provided below.

1   $3x - y = 3$
    $x + y = 5$

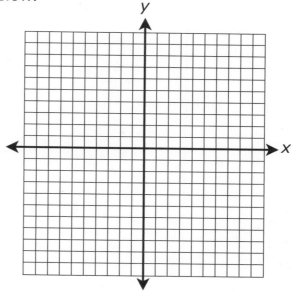

_____

2   $y = 4$
    $x + y = -1$

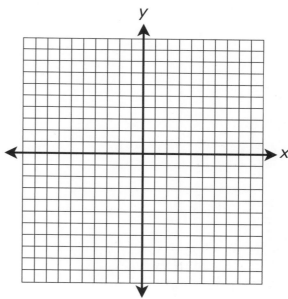

_____

3   Show a check here for problem 1. Always write the original equation before you do a check.

4 $y = -x + 5$
  $y - x = -3$

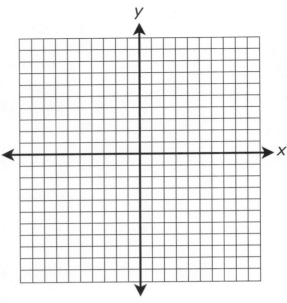

_____

5 $3x + 2y = -6$
    $x + y = -2$

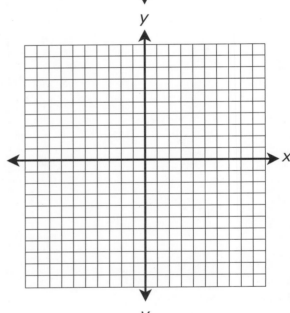

_____

6 $x + 2y = -10$
    $2y = -x + 6$

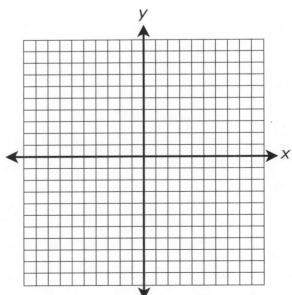

_____

⑦ $y = 3x + 2$
       $2y - 6x = 4$

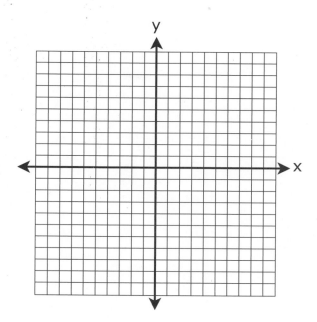

_____

Method 2 – Elimination

We can also solve a system of equations by using algebra. This is helpful when our numbers are too large to fit in a coordinate plane, or you are working with decimals or fractions.

1   Solve this system of equations algebraically.

        $x - y = 4$
       $5x + y = 2$

First, make sure your two equations are lined up so the same variables are above each other and the constants are also above each other. The goal is to try to add the equations to eliminate one of the variables. Notice what happens when both equations are added.

$$x - y = 4$$
$$\underline{5x + y = 2}$$
$$6x = 6$$
$$x = 1$$

Now that we know $x = 1$, we take <u>either</u> equation and substitute 1 for x.

$x - y = 4$
$1 - y = 4$ (solve for y)
   $-y = 3$
    $y = -3$
The solution is (1, -3).

To check the solution, you MUST check it into both equations and not just one of them.

Check: $x - y = 4$ $5x + y = 2$

        $1 - (-3) = 4$ Yes! $5(1) + (-3) = 2$? Yes!

What happens if adding down does not cancel one of the variables? In algebra, you can "legally" change an equation to make one of the variables cancel by multiplying one or both equations by a term of your choosing (that is multiplying each term by the same number).

2 Solve this system of equations algebraically.

$3x + 2y = 6$
$5x - 3y = -28$

You can see that adding down does not eliminate a variable, so we can either try to get the x's to cancel or try to get the y's to cancel. We could eliminate x by multiplying the top equation by 5 and the bottom equation by -3 so that we end up with $15x$ on the top equation and $-15x$ on the bottom equation. We can instead eliminate y by multiplying the top equation by 3 and the bottom equation by 2 to get $6y$ on the top equation and $-6y$ on the bottom equation. We will use the last option. Either way will work.

$3(3x + 2y = 6)$ ⟶ $9x + 6y = 18$
$2(5x - 3y = -28)$ ⟶ $\underline{10x - 6y = -56}$
                             $19x \quad\quad = -38$
                                 $x = -2$

Substitute $x = -2$ into either equation. If the top equation is chosen, $3x + 2y = 6$, then $3(-2) + 2y = 6$, then $-6 + 2y = 6$, $2y = 12$ and $y = 6$. The solution is $(-2, 6)$.

Check: $3x + 2y = 6$ $5x - 3y = -28$

      $3(-2) + 2(6) = 6$? $5(-2) - 3(6) = -28$?

         $-6 + 12 = 6$? Yes! $-10 - 18 = -28$? Yes!

3   Solve this system of equations algebraically.

$3x = 4y + 26$
$2y = -x + 2$

We need to organize our equations so that the same variables and the constants are on top of each other.

$3x - 4y = 26$
$x + 2y = 2$

Now we can either multiply the bottom equation by -3, or we can multiply the bottom equation by 2. We will use the first option this time.

$$
\begin{array}{rcl}
3x - 4y = 26 & \longrightarrow & 3x - 4y = 26 \\
-3(x + 2y = 2) & \longrightarrow & \underline{-3x - 6y = -6} \\
& & -10y = 20 \\
& & y = -2
\end{array}
$$

Substituting $y = -2$ into the second equation,

$$
\begin{array}{rcl}
x + 2y & = & 2 \\
x + 2(-2) & = & 2 \\
x - 4 & = & 2 \\
x & = & 6.
\end{array}
$$ The solution is (6, -2).

Can you check this solution on your own? Rewrite each equation first.

When you are using x's and y's, you can write your answer as an ordered pair. Often you will use other variables, especially when you are working with real-life applications.

Elimination Practice

Using a separate sheet of paper, solve these equations algebraically by using the elimination method. Check your answers to the odd problems.

1. $x + y = 15$
     $x - y = 1$

11. $5x + y = 0$
      $x + 5y = 0$

2. $x + y = 9$
     $-x + 3y = 11$

12. $4x + 3y = 10$
      $5x + 2y = 9$

3. $3x + y = 15$
     $-x - y = 5$

13. $4w - z = 3$
      $-4w + 5z = 9$

4. $a + 2b = -5$
     $3a + 2b = -3$

14. $y = -3x - 8$
      $9 - 3x = y$

5. $a + b = 3$
     $5a + 2b = 0$

15. $4a + b = 7$
      $8a - 8b = -36$

6. $3x + 4y = -4$
     $2x - y = -10$

16. $8r + 3s = 0$
      $12r + 4s = 1$

7. $x + 10y = 3$
     $4y - x = 4$

17. $8x + y = -24$
      $9x + 11y = -27$

8. $-2p + 3q = 15$
     $-2p + 3q = 3$

18. $4x + 2y = 3$
      $x - y = 0$

9. $2x + 4y = 80$
     $x + y = 10$

19. $18a + 27b = 9$
      $9b + 6a = 3$

10. $4x + 2y = 19$
     $3x + 4y = 13$

20. $-x + y = 20$
      $3x + 5y = -300$

Method 3 – Substitution

Another way to solve a system of equations algebraically is to use substitution. A good time to use substitution is when one equation has a variable alone on one side, but you can always solve for one variable to use this method.

1 Solve the following system of equations by using substitution.
$y = 2x$
$y + 3x = 25$
Since $y = 2x$, take $2x$ and substitute it into the y of the second equation.

$y = \boxed{2x}$

$ y + 3x = 25$
$\boxed{2x} + 3x = 25$
$\ 5x = 25$
$\ x = 5$

Now take $x = 5$, and it's easier to substitute it into the first equation. If $y = 2x$ and $x = 5$, then $y = 10$. The solution is (5, 10).

2 Solve the following system of equations by using substitution.
$a = -b$
$4b - a = -25$

Since $a = -b$, you can substitute $-b$ for the a in the second equation.

$a = \boxed{-b}$
$4b - a = -25$ Be careful with the sign!

$4b - (-b) = -25$
$5b = -25$
$b = -5$

So if $b = -5$ then $a = -(-5)$ or 5. The solution is $a = 5$, and $b = -5$.

See if it also checks in the second equation.
$4b - a = -25$
$4(-5) - 5 = -25?$
$-20 - 5 = -25?$ Yes!

3 Solve the following system of equations by using substitution.

$y + 3x = 13$
$6y + x = -7$

While elimination is easier here, you can still use substitution. Solve for one of the variables. Let's say you choose the first equation to solve for y.

$y + 3x = 13$ so $y = -3x + 13$

$6y + x = -7$
So $6(-3x + 13) + x = -7$ Notice the need for parentheses.
$-18x + 78 + x = -7$ All of y is $-3x + 13$.
$-17x + 78 = -7$
$-17x = -85$
$x = 5$

If $y + 3x = 13$ and $x = 5$, then $y + 3(5) = 13$, and $y = -2$.

Again, it helps to check both equations.

Using a separate sheet of paper, practice solving by using substitution. Check the odd problems.

1 $y = 3x$
$x + 2y = 14$

6 $3x + 4y = -7$
$x = y + 7$

2 $x = -y + 1$
$x + 3y = 9$

7 $y = -4x$
$18 + y + x = 3$

3 $5a - 2b = 3$
$2a = b$

8 $a + b = 4$
$2a + b = -2.5$

4 $y = 3x + 6$
$y + x = 6$

9 $2y + x = -22$
$x - y = 11$

5 $w = -z$
$5w + 4z = 2$

10 $w + y = 19.4$
$2w + y = 36.4$

Using Systems to Solve Real-Life Problems

Many of the word problems we solved previously can now be solved with two variables. The following is an example best solved by a system of equations.

1   At the local supermarket Susan was getting ready to make breakfast for her summer camp. She bought 5 gallons of milk and 10 loaves of bread, and paid $42.50. Later that afternoon she went back and bought 3 more gallons of the same milk and 5 more loaves of the same bread, and paid $23.00. What was the price of milk, and what was the price of bread?

Don't forget a let statement.

Let m = cost of one gallon of milk
  b = cost of one loaf of bread

$5m + 10b = \$42.50 \longrightarrow 5m + 10b = 42.50$
$3m + 5b = \$23.00 \longrightarrow -2(3m + 5b = 23.00)$

$$
\begin{aligned}
5m + 10b &= 42.50 \\
-6m - 10b &= -46.00 \\
\hline
-m &= -3.50 \\
m &= 3.50
\end{aligned}
$$
  The price of one gallon of milk is $3.50.

Substitute into either equation. Let's use the second one.
$$3m + 5b = 23.00$$
$$3(3.5) + 5b = 23.00$$
$$10.5 + 5b = 23.00$$
$$5b = 12.5$$
$$b = 2.5$$
  The price of one loaf of bread is $2.50.

Just as before, it's a good idea to check your answers in <u>both</u> equations.

Check:
$5m + 10b = 42.50$ $3m + 5b = 23$
$5(3.5) + 10(2.5) = 42.50?$ $3(3.5) + 5(2.5) = 23?$
$17.5 + 25 = 42.50?$ Yes! $10.5 + 12.5 = 23?$ Yes!

2   Mrs. Sanchez needed 5 pounds of trail mix for a class picnic. Dried fruit costs $6 a pound, and organic oats cost $4 per pound. The total she paid was $24. How many pounds of each did she buy?

Let x = the ounces of dried fruit
    y = the ounces of organic oats

$$x + y = 5$$
$$\$6x + \$4y = \$24$$

You can use elimination or substitution. We'll use substitution.

Since $x + y = 5$, then $y = 5 - x$ (or $x = 5 - y$)

$$6x + 4(5 - x) = 24$$
$$6x + 20 - 4x = 24$$
$$2x + 20 = 24$$
$$2x = 4$$
$$x = 2$$

So she used 2 pounds of dried fruit and 3 pounds of organic oats. Remember she used 5 pounds altogether.

Check: $x + y = 5$ $\$6x + \$4y = \$24$
         $2 + 3 = 5$? Yes! $6(2) + 4(3) = 24$?
                                  $\$12 + \$12 = \$24$? Yes!

3   The sum of two numbers is 54. The larger is twice the smaller. Find the numbers.

Here's an example where you can use one variable or two.

With one variable: With two variables:
Let x = one number   Let x = one number
    $2x$ = larger number y = larger number
Equation: $x + 2x = 54$ Equations:
            $3x = 54$ $x + y = 54$
            $x = 18$ $y = 2x$
larger number = 36   You can use substitution and arrive at the equation on the left.

Word Problems

Using a separate sheet of paper, solve the following word problems. Use a system of equations and solve using graphing, elimination, or substitution. Don't forget to check your answers.

1   The sum of two numbers is 35, and their difference is 15. Find the numbers.

2   The sum of the ages of two sisters is 34 years. The older sister is 6 years older than the younger sister. Find their ages.

3   There are a group of chickens and elephants standing together. Someone counted 30 heads and 70 feet. If each chicken had 2 legs and each elephant had 4 legs (just to let you know the elephants had not stomped on the chickens yet ...), how many of each were there?

4   A juice machine at school contains 200 coins, in nickels and dimes only. If there is a total of $18.10 in the machine, how many nickels were in the machine?

5   Mr. Powers ordered three electric pencil sharpeners and four packs of pens for the teachers in the Social Studies Department for a total of $69. The next day his secretary ordered from the same company two electric pencil sharpeners and 2 packs of pens, and this order was $42. If the prices had not changed, how much was each electric pencil sharpener and each pack of pens?

6   On the first evening of a musical production, The Hangar Theatre sold 200 adult tickets and 300 child tickets, and made $1,450. The next night they sold 400 adult tickets and 100 child tickets for a total $2,150. How much were the adult tickets? How much were the child tickets?

7   Ms. Boruchowitz ordered 10 packs of gel pens and 10 packs of highlighters for her 4th grade class for a total of $280. The next day she realized she needed more and ordered 3 packs of gel pens and 4 highlighters for a total of $92. How much did she pay for the pack of gel pens?

8   Mr. Santí ordered 9 pounds of coffee. He paid $15 a pound for the Gimme Decaf brand and $12 a pound for the Ethiopian brand. In total he paid $120. How many pounds of each did he buy?

9   Veni bought 6 ounces total of chia seeds and flax seeds. The chia seeds were $7.50 an ounce and the flax seeds were $8.80 an ounce. The total she paid was $47.60. How many ounces of each did she buy?

10 The sum of two numbers is 47. The larger number is 19 less than twice the smaller number. Find both numbers.

11 At the Ithaca Library Sale, children's paperback books are 60¢ and all children's hardback books are $2.50. Juanita bought 27 children's books altogether, and she spent $39. How many of each type did she buy?

12 For this year's junior prom, Luke and Tamar spent $95 in roses and carnations. Luke remembered that the number of roses was 10 less than three times the number of carnations. Tamar could only remember that the carnations cost 50¢ each and the roses $1.00 each. How can they figure out how many of each they bought?

13 On September 5th, just before school started, a local store sold 20 regular graphing calculators and 5 color graphing calculators for a total of $2,850. The very next day they sold 30 regular graphing calculators and 2 color graphing calculators for a total of $3,450. If the prices were the same for both days, what was the price for each type of graphing calculator?

14 Write a word problem to match this system of equations and solve it.

$$x + y = 18$$
$$\$2x + \$4y = \$50$$

15 Use your knowledge of "substitution" as a strategy to solve these two systems of three equations with three unknowns.

a $x + y + z = 14$
    $z = x + y$
    $y = x + 1$

b $a + b = -8$
    $a - b + c = 0$
    $b + c = -1$

Graphing Inequalities

To graph inequalities on the coordinate plane, you might want to review how to graph equations. In this section, you can use a graphing calculator once you learn to graph inequalities by hand.

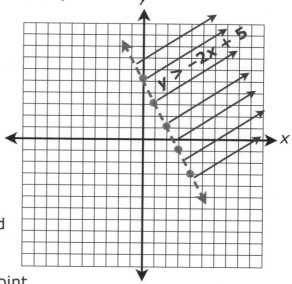

1 Graph $2x + y > 5$.

Solve for y:
$$y > -2x + 5$$

The y-intercept is 5 and the slope is $\frac{-2}{1}$. When you draw the line, you must use a dashed line since the inequality has a greater than sign. Now, you need to shade a region of the plane. To determine which side of the dashed line to shade, we test a point.

Test (0, 0) which is an easy point to test (your testing point must not be on the dashed line).

In $y > -2x + 5$, is $0 > -2(0) + 5$? No, so shade the side away from (0, 0). Write the inequality on the shaded region.

> For < or > use a dashed line.
>
> For ≤ or ≥ use a solid line.

The different kinds of lines are used to indicate whether or not the points on the line are part of the solution set. For < or >, the points on the line are not part of the solution set, whereas for ≤ or ≥, the points on the line are part of the solution set.

Any point on the shaded region makes the inequality true. Test the points below to see if this is true.

A point on the shaded region. Try (5, 8)

A point right on the dashed line. Try (1, 3)

A point not on the shaded region. Try (-3, -3)

2   Graph $\frac{2}{3}x - y \geq 1$.

Solve for y: $-y \geq -\frac{2}{3}x + 1$

Remember to switch
the inequality symbol $y \leq \frac{2}{3}x - 1$
when multiplying or
dividing by a negative.

Every point on the line will work
this time. Test a point not on
the line to determine which way
to shade. You can test (0, 0)
again since (0, 0) is not on the line.

In $\frac{2}{3}x - y \geq 1$, is $\frac{2}{3}(0) - 0 \geq 1$? No, so shade the side away from
this point.

3   Paulo and Seth want to raise at least $400 to have spending money
for their trip to Disney World. They want to sell chocolate bars
for $2 and bracelets for $4. Graph an inequality to represent the
different quantities of chocolate bars and bracelets that will help
Paulo and Seth raise $400 or more.

Let x = number of chocolate bars sold
   y = number of bracelets sold

$2x + 4y \geq 400$

Solve for y:

$y \geq -\frac{1}{2}x + 100$

Let's think about the results of this graph (done in a graphing
calculator). To graph an inequality in a graphing calculator, scroll
with the left arrow key to the left of the Y1= and keep pressing
"Enter" until you see the symbol ◣ – greater than. The graphing
calculator does not differentiate between > or ≥. By the way, the
symbol ◤ is the less than symbol. You can also graph by hand.

Thinking About Paulo and Seth's Problem

1 Why is the graph done in quadrant I?

_____

_____

_____

2 Is every point on the line shown an answer to this problem? Why or why not? Explain your thinking.

_____

_____

_____

3 Show how the point (100, 50), one of the points shown, satisfies the inequality.

4 Name one point that satisfies the inequality and one that does not. Show work for each one.

5 Circle which of the following statements is true.

   a The more chocolate bars sold, the less bracelets that need to be sold.

   b The more bracelets sold, the less chocolate bars that need to be sold.

   c If no bracelets were sold, then at least 200 chocolate bars need to be sold.

   d all of the above.

Graphing Practice

Graph the following inequalities. Remember to check one point in order to determine which way to shade. Label the inequality on the shaded region.

1 $y > 3x - 5$

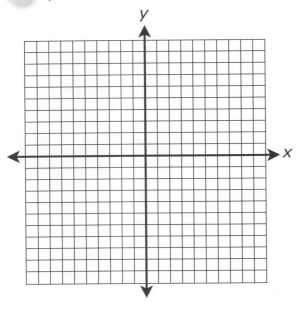

2 $y < 6$

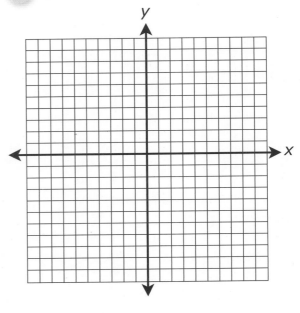

3 $2x - 4y \leq 8$

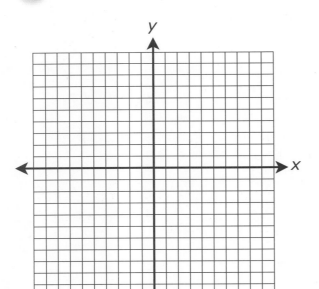

4 $-y > x$

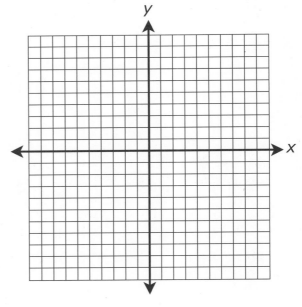

5   $3y - x < 6$

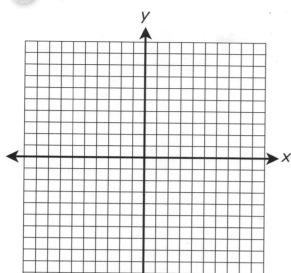

6   $x > -4$

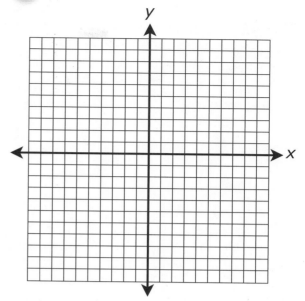

Solve the following problems by graphing an inequality, and answer the questions.

7   Luis wanted to start a greeting card business because he's very artistic. Every month, he would spend no more than $150 total on both paper and markers. His father said he would supply the envelopes. He would like to sell his cards at $3 each and postcards at $2 each.

    a   Write an inequality to represent what he must sell to make a profit.

    b   Use graph paper or a graphing calculator to graph the inequality.

    c   List three ordered pairs that will yield a profit (remember, your answers must be whole numbers since he cannot sell half a postcard or a quarter of a greeting card).

8   Min-ji has 10 skeins of yarn, each one 220 yards long. She wants to make scarves and hats for presents. Each scarf takes 190 yards of yarn, and a hat takes 150 yards.

a   Write an inequality to represent the possible scarves and hats she could knit.

b   Using graph paper or a graphing calculator, graph the inequality. You will need to change the window settings. Hint: Use Xmin = 0, Xmax = 20, Ymin = 0, Ymax = 15.

In a graphing calculator, type your equation using fractions. To change a decimal to a fraction in a graphing calculator: When the decimal is on the screen, go to (MATH), (FRAC), then (ENTER).

c   If Min-ji decided to make only scarves, what is the greatest number of scarves that she could knit?

d   If Min-ji decided to make only hats, what is the greatest number of hats that she could knit?

e   If Min-ji sold her scarves for $8 and her hats for $5, with the yardage she has, would she make more money selling only scarves, only hats, or both? Explain your thinking.

_____

_____

_____

_____

Systems of Inequalities

A system of inequalities is two or more inequalities solved on the same coordinate plane. The solution will be the shaded area both inequalities have in common. Let's look at a couple of examples and one application.

1 Graph this system of inequalities. State one point in the solution set.

$y > x$
$y \geq -4x - 3$

Graph $y = x$ and test the point (2, 5) which satisfies $y > x$ since 5 > 2. Why could we not use (0, 0) as a test point? Notice the line is a dashed line.

Then graph $y = -4x - 3$. Test the same point (2, 5), which satisfies the second inequality, $5 \geq -4(2) - 3$. Notice the line must be solid.

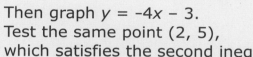

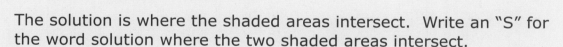

The solution is where the shaded areas intersect. Write an "S" for the word solution where the two shaded areas intersect.

The point (1, 8) is a point in the solution set.

$y > x$	$y \geq -4x - 3$
8 > 1? Yes!	$8 \geq -4(1) - 3$? Yes!

Answer the following questions based on this example.

1 Explain why (–1, 1), a point on the line $y = -4x -3$, satisfies both inequalities?

_____

_____

2 Does the point (0, 0) satisfy both inequalities? Why or why not?

_____

2 Graph this system of inequalities. State one point in the solution set.

$-2y > 2x - 10$
$2x \geq y + 4$

Solve for y in the first inequality, and write it in slope-intercept form.

$y < -x + 5$ Notice how dividing by a negative reverses the inequality symbol.

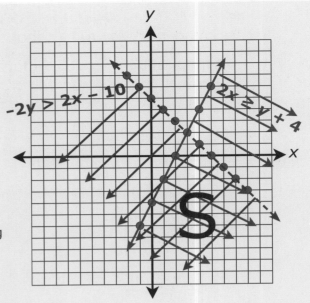

Test the point (0, 0) in the first inequality. $-2(0) > 2(0) - 10$?
It does satisfy the inequality, so shade in the direction of (0, 0).

Solve for y in the second inequality.

$-y + 2x \geq 4$
$-y \geq -2x + 4$ Again, notice how dividing by a negative reverses the inequality symbol.
$y \leq 2x - 4$

Test the point (0, 0) in the second inequality. $2(0) \geq 0 + 4$?
It does not satisfy the inequality, so shade the side away from (0, 0).

The point (4, -5) is a point in the solution set.

$-2y > 2x - 10$ $2x \geq y + 4$
$-2(-5) > 2(4) - 10$? $2(4) \geq -5 + 4$
$10 > 8 - 10$? Yes! $8 \geq -1$? Yes!

Answer the following questions.

1 Is the point (-1, 10) in the solution set of the problem above?

_____

2 Is it possible for a system of inequalities to NOT have a solution? Explain your thinking.

_____

_____

3 Larisa wants to make at least $80 a month babysitting and doing gardening work for a neighbor. She gets paid $10 an hour for gardening and $8 for babysitting. However, her mom does not want her to work more than 40 hours a month because Larisa has to also concentrate on her school work.

Write a system of inequalities to represent this real life situation.

Let b = hours babysitting
g = hours gardening

$8b + 10g \geq 80$
$b + g \ < 40$

Solving for g on the first inequality:

$10g \geq -8b + 80$

$g \geq -\dfrac{4}{5}b + 8$

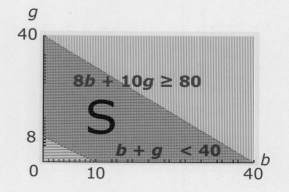

Solving for g on the second inequality:

$g < -b + 40$

To make $80 or more and do both jobs, Larisa needs to babysit at least 10 hours, or garden at least 8 hours, or work some combination of the two that is on or above the line connecting (0, 8) and (10, 0). Remember she must not exceed 40 hours in total.

Answer the following questions.

1 How much will Larisa make if she babysits exactly 10 hours and gardens 8 hours? Show work.

2 How much money can Larisa make if she babysits 20 hours and gardens 20 hours?

3 If she wants to make the most money possible, but work 40 hours or less to please her mom, what should she do?

_____

_____

Systems of Inequalities Practice

Graph each system of inequalities.

1 $y \geq 4$
   $-y + 1 < -x$

2 $y > 2x - 4$
   $y < 1$

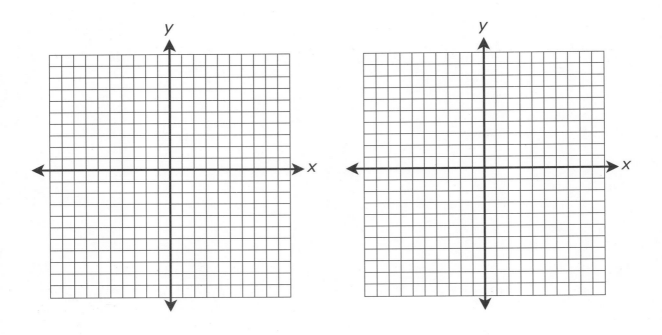

3 $y \leq x + 3$
   $-y < x + 5$

4 $y > 3x + 4$
   $y < 3x - 5$

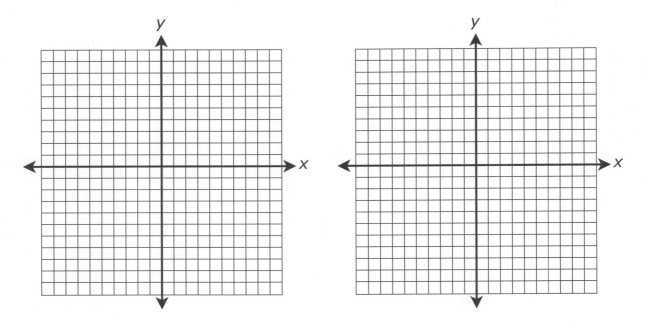

5 $y > -x$
   $-y < x + 2$

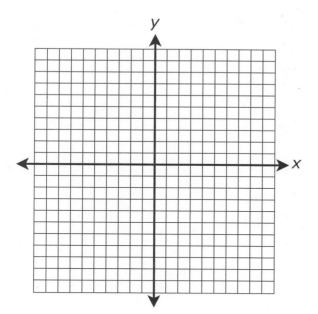

6 $x > -2$
   $y \leq 2$

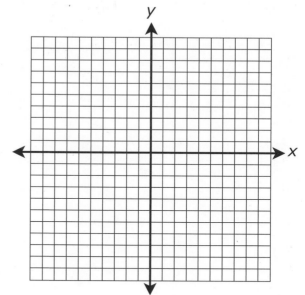

7 $6x + 4y > -4$
   $x + 2y \leq 2$

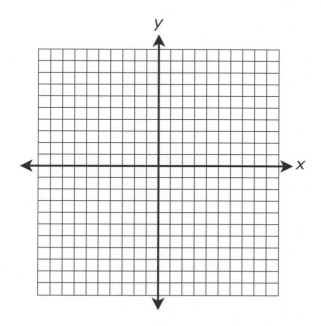

8 Name two points in the solution set of problem 7, and show these points satisfy both inequalities.

9   $x + y > 10$
    $-y < 5$

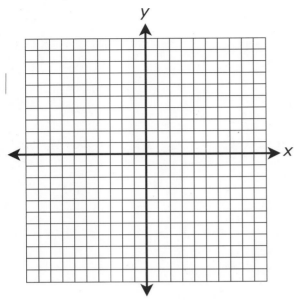

Using graph paper or a graphing calculator, answer the following questions.

10   Trumansburg Middle School's auditorium only seats 400 people. For the upcoming musical, tickets are $4 for adults and $2 for students. If the school wants to raise at least $800, show the possible solutions that meets these requirements.

   a   Show the system of inequalities.

   b   If the auditorium was only filled with students, would the school make enough money? Explain your thinking.

   _____

   _____

   c   What is the most money the musical could make on tickets given these requirements? Explain your thinking.

   _____

   _____

11 Joanna got a $60 gift card to an online store that sells movies and songs. She wants to buy at least 20 items with this card. Songs are $1 and movies are $3.

a Write a system of inequalities to represent what Joanna can buy.

b Graph the system of inequalities. Use graph paper or a graphing calculator.

c Show one possible solution to this problem.

d Assume that Joanna wants to buy twice as many songs as movies, show one possible solution to spend as much of the $60 as possible.

e Joanna decided to buy 15 movies and 17 songs. Can she do it? Explain your thinking.

_____

_____

_____

12   Several ninth grade classes are having an end of the year party for students and parents. Ms. Burton is in charge of buying pizza. She cannot spend more than $240 on two kinds of pizza: cheese pizza and pepperoni pizza. She's been told to buy at least 10 pepperoni pizza pies. If cheese-only pizza pies cost $8.00 each and pepperoni pizza pies cost $10.50, answer the questions below.

a   Write a system of inequalities representing what Ms. Burton must buy. Let y = the number of pepperoni pizzas, and x = the number of cheese only pizzas.

b   Label the inequalities on the graph below. Label the axes and identify the indicated points.

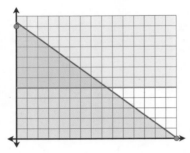

c   Using the graph above and your inequalities, complete the table of Ms. Burton's possible purchases.

Cheese pizzas	Pepperoni	Total Amount
_____	10	$185
_____	22	$239
12	_____	$232.50

d   Assume you want to get the most pizzas using as much of the $240 and meet the conditions above, how many of each type would you buy and why? Explain your thinking.

_____

_____

System of Inequalities Challenge

Solve this system of inequalities. Use different colors for shading.

$$-y \le -2x + 5$$
$$y + x < 6$$
$$x > 0$$
$$y < 5$$

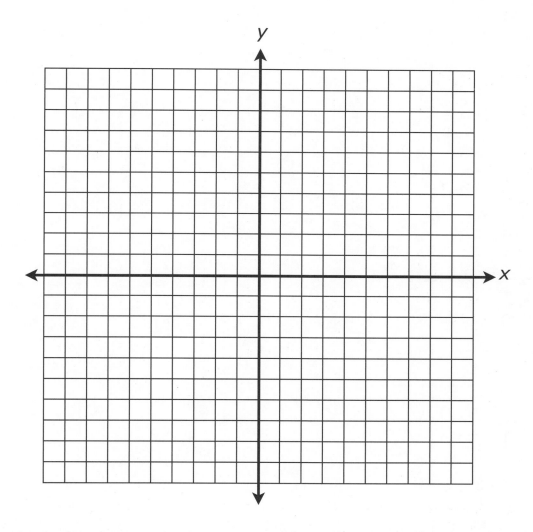

Name one point in the solution set and show how it satisfies all the inequalities.

Chapter 11

Other Types of **Functions**

In this chapter we will investigate other functions. Remember when you have a function you can use the notation $f(x) = y$.

Absolute Value Functions

In Chapter 1, page 5, we learned the definition of absolute value. Remember that the absolute value of any number is always positive. Let's look how to graph the following absolute value equation.

1    $f(x) = |x|$

Let's make a table of values.

x	$f(x) = y$
-3	3
-2	2
-1	1
0	0
1	1
2	2
3	3

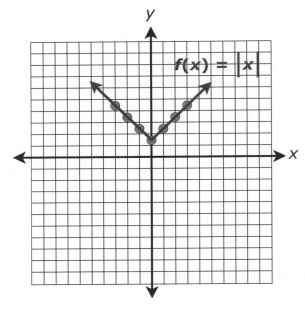

The domain of this function is: all real numbers, because you can use any x value you want. The range is: $y \geq 0$ because the y values will always be greater than or equal to zero.

Notice the shape of this graph is a V not a U. Why is this a function? If you recall for every input there is a unique output associated with that input. If you do the "vertical line test" you will see that there is no point above or below any point on the graph. Now, look at the equation below.

$$y = |x - 4|$$

Before you see the graph on the next page, do you think the graph will be moved to the left or to the right, up or down from (0, 0)?

2   Graph $y = |x - 4|$

Let's make a table of values for $y = |x - 4|$.

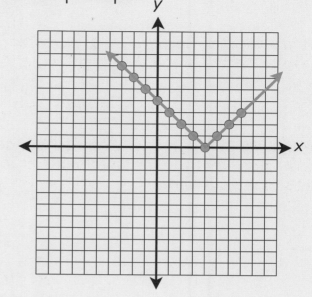

x	f(x) = y
-3	7
-2	6
-1	5
0	4
1	3
2	2
3	1
4	0
5	1
6	2
7	3

Can you see why the graph moved to the right 4 spaces from its original position? At $x = 4$, $y = 0$.

This point (4, 0) is called the **vertex** or **turning point** of this function.

Graph the following absolute value functions. Before you graph, use your thinking skills to predict what the graph will look like.

1   $f(x) = |x| - 3$

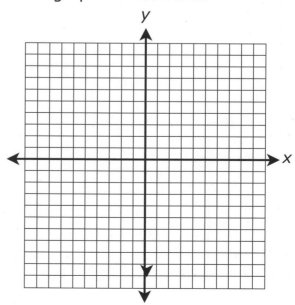

2 $f(x) = |x + 2|$

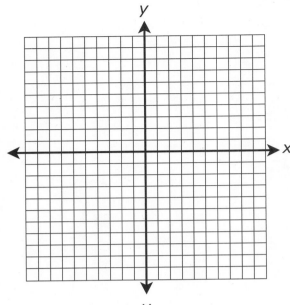

3 $f(x) = -|x|$

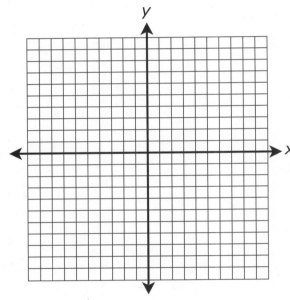

4 $f(x) = |x + 2| - 3$

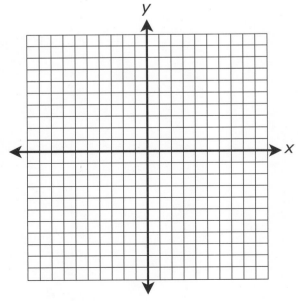

Graphing Absolute Value Functions on a Calculator

You can use the graphing calculator to graph absolute value functions. Remember, the more you do with paper and pencil, the more you will understand these concepts. However, if you have a graphing calculator, let's learn these steps so that you can use it as a tool to check your work and engage in more thinking.

To graph $y = |x + 2| - 3$ in the graphing calculator, follow these steps. Make sure you have cleared and/or deleted any old equations you had left from the last time you used it and have the right window settings.

Go to (Y=)
Then go to (MATH)   This stands for absolute value.
Scroll to NUM — notice in the menu 1: abs (
Press (ENTER)
Type "$x + 2$)" and scroll to the right to move beyond the absolute value symbol, then
Type "$- 3$"
(TRACE) or (GRAPH)

As before, to see the table of values, press (2ND) (GRAPH).

Notice how the function moved to the left two units and down 3 units when compared to the parent (most basic) function of $y = |x|$.

Using graph paper, graph these absolute value functions.

1. $f(x) = \frac{1}{2}|x|$

2. $f(x) = -2|x|$ Pay attention to how the sign and the number in front of the absolute value symbol affects the graph.

3. $f(x) = -|x - 3|$

4. $f(x) = |x| + 4$

5. $f(x) = \frac{1}{4}|x| - 2$

Graphing Match

Write the letter of the graph that matches the function.

_____ ① $f(x) = |x + 5|$ _____ ② $f(x) = |x - 5|$ _____ ③ $f(x) = -|x + 5|$

_____ ④ $f(x) = \frac{1}{5}|x|$ _____ ⑤ $f(x) = 5|x|$ _____ ⑥ $f(x) = |x - 2| + 3$

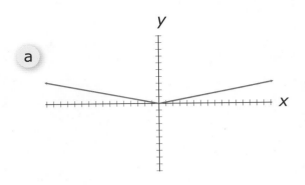

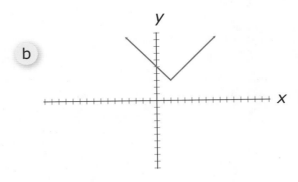

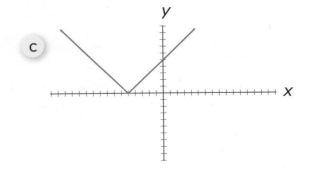

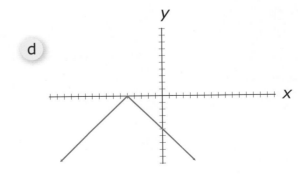

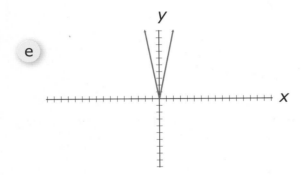

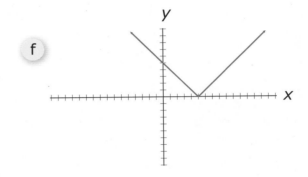

Thinking About Absolute Value

Answer the following questions about absolute value.

1. Is $|a + b| = |a| + |b|$? Explain your thinking.

   _____

   _____

2. Is $|a \cdot b| = |a| \cdot |b|$? Explain your thinking.

   _____

   _____

3. If $f(x) = a|x|$, how does the coefficient a affect the graph of the absolute value function?

   _____

   _____

   _____

4. Is the equation $x = |y|$ a function? Why or why not? Make a table of values and graph if you need to.

   _____

   _____

5. Explain the difference between these two functions. $y = |x| + 4$ and $y = |x| - 4$. How do both compare to $y = |x|$?

   _____

   _____

   _____

6. Write an equation where the parent function $y = |x|$ has been moved to the left 6 units and down 3 units.

   _____

Quadratic Functions

A quadratic function is an equation of the form $y = ax^2 + bx + c$, where a, the coefficient of x^2, does not equal zero. Can you see that if a equals zero the function would be linear and not quadratic? The graph of a quadratic equation is called a **parabola**. Not all parabolas are functions, only those that start with $f(x)$ or $y =$. Parabolas are everywhere, as you will see in many of the applications we will work through later.

Let's first look at the parent (most basic) function of a parabola.

1 Graph $f(x) = x^2$.

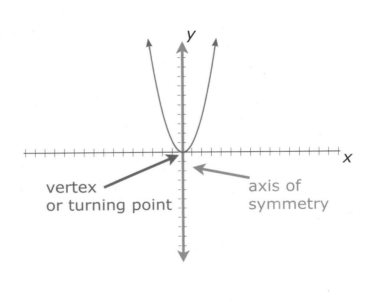

x	$f(x) = y$
-3	9
-2	4
-1	1
0	0
1	1
2	4
3	9

vertex or turning point

axis of symmetry

Notice that our parabola has symmetry. In this example, the y-axis ($x = 0$) is the axis of symmetry. The parabola has a **vertex** or **turning point** which is where the graph makes its turn. In this example the vertex of our parent function is (0, 0), and this point is a "minimum" point as it is the lowest point of the graph. If the parabola opens up, its vertex is called a **minimum** point, and if the parabola opens down, its vertex is called a **maximum** point.

When a parabola is written as $y = ax^2 + bx + c$, it is written in standard form. This form gives us lots of information about the parabola as you will see in the next example.

2 Graph $f(x) = x^2 - 6x + 5$. Find the vertex and axis of symmetry.

When a parabola is in standard form, the axis of symmetry is $x = -\dfrac{b}{2a}$. Since $a = 1$ and $b = -6$, then the axis of symmetry is $x = -\dfrac{-6}{2\cdot1} = 3$. The axis of symmetry is $x = 3$ (it's an equation).

Now, we know the vertex IS on the axis of symmetry so substitute or plug in 3 for x in your equation to find the y that corresponds to 3.

$y = (3)^2 - 6(3) + 5 = -4$. So the vertex is (3, –4).

Either by making a table of values or using your graphing calculator you will get your graph which should look like this. Put arrow heads on your parabolas. The graphing calculator doesn't do that, but you should!

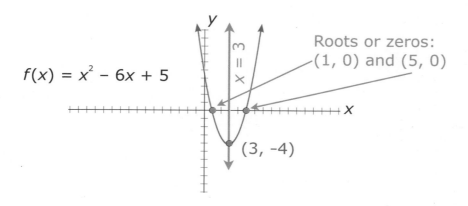

$f(x) = x^2 - 6x + 5$

Roots or zeros:
(1, 0) and (5, 0)

(3, –4)

There's one more important fact you can gather when the equation is written in standard form. You can find where the parabola crosses the x axis. In the figure above you can see that it crosses the x-axis in two points. The x value of those x-intercepts are called the **roots** or **zeros** of a parabola.

If the parabola, like the parent function, only touches one point of the x-axis, then it has one root. A parabola which sits above the x-axis, having no common points with the x-axis, would have no real roots.

To find the roots or zeros of $y = x^2 - 6x + 5$, let $y = 0$ (remember $y = 0$ is the x-axis) and solve for x.

$0 = x^2 - 6x + 5$
$0 = (x - 1)(x - 5)$
$x = 1$ or $x = 5$

The zeros and roots are $x = 1$ and $x = 5$. The points $(1, 0)$ and $(5, 0)$ are the x-intercepts of the graph. Look at the graph again.

With the vertex, axis of symmetry, and the roots, you can sketch the parabola without a table of values or even a graphing calculator.

Standard form of a quadratic equation is $y = ax^2 + bx + c$.

Axis of symmetry is $x = -\dfrac{b}{2a}$. This is the x value of the vertex point so substitute to find the y of vertex.

Set the equation equal to zero to find the roots or zeros.

Sketch the following parabolas by finding the axis of symmetry, vertex, and zeros. Don't forget $f(x) = y$.

1 $f(x) = x^2 - 8x + 12$

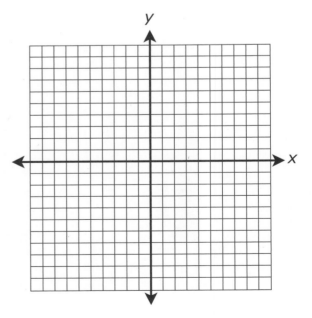

© 2015 The Critical Thinking Co.™ • www.CriticalThinking.com • 800-458-4849

2 $f(x) = x^2 - 8x + 7$

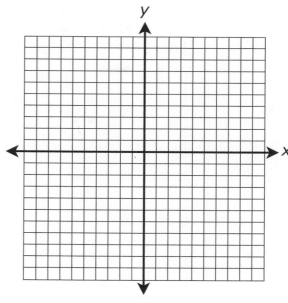

3 $f(x) = x^2 - 9$

Hint: $b = 0$

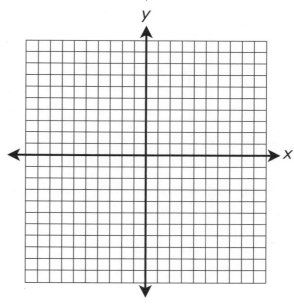

4 $f(x) = x^2 + 2x + 1$

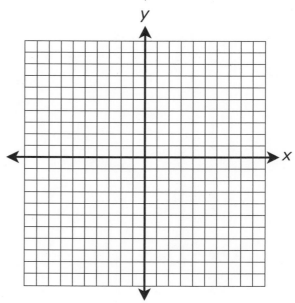

5 $f(x) = -x^2 + 1$

This parabola has a maximum point.

6 $f(x) = x^2 + 3x - 4$

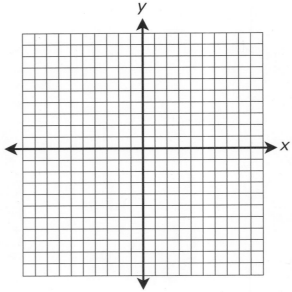

7 $f(x) = x^2 - 3x - 10$

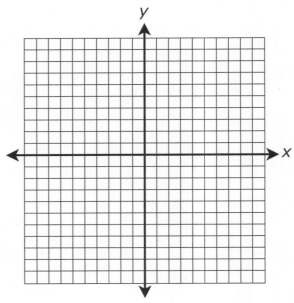

Thinking About Parabolas

Answer the following questions.

1 How do you know (before graphing) if the graph of an equation is a line? Explain your thinking.

_____

_____

2 How do you know (before graphing) if the graph of an equation is a parabola? Explain your thinking.

_____

_____

3 Graph $f(x) = x^2 - 3x$ using the table of values provided.

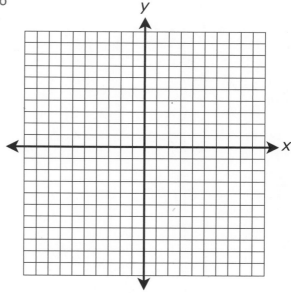

You don't need to graph this point.

x	$f(x) = y$
-3	
-2	
-1	
0	
1	
2	
3	

4 What is the axis of symmetry? _____. Show that you get the same results as $x = -\dfrac{b}{2a}$.

5 Find the vertex. _____

6 What are the roots or zeros of this parabola? _____
Show you get the same results by setting equal to 0 and solving.

Vertex Form of a Quadratic Equation

Sometimes a quadratic equation is written in vertex form instead of standard form. It's important to recognize this form as it will help you determine, very easily, the vertex and the axis of symmetry by just looking at the equation.

The vertex form of a quadratic equation is $y = (x - h)^2 + k$, where the vertex is (h, k) and the axis of symmetry is $x = h$. Notice sign.

1. Determine the vertex and axis of symmetry of this parabola without graphing it.

$$f(x) = (x - 3)^2 + 8$$

Change sign. Keep sign.

The vertex is $(3, 8)$ and the axis of symmetry is $x = 3$.

2. Determine the vertex and the axis of symmetry of this parabola without graphing it.

$$f(x) = (x + 4)^2 - 5 \qquad \text{In vertex form: } f(x) = (x - {-4})^2 - 5.$$

The vertex is $(-4, -5)$ and the axis of symmetry is $x = -4$.

To go from vertex form to standard form, you would simplify the equation and write it as $f(x) = ax^2 + bx + c$, so you can then find the roots or zeros of the parabola.

3. Determine the vertex, axis of symmetry, and the zeros of this parabola without graphing it.

$$f(x) = (x + 2)^2 - 1$$

The vertex is $(-2, -1)$ and the axis of symmetry is $x = -2$.

Simplify $(x + 2)^2 - 1$ and you get $x^2 + 4x + 4 - 1$ so the standard form is $f(x) = x^2 + 4x + 3$. Setting this equal to 0 and solving:

$$0 = (x + 1)(x + 3)$$
$$x = -1 \text{ or } x = -3 \text{ so these are the roots or zeros.}$$

Vertex Practice

Find the vertex and the axis of symmetry of these functions.

1    $f(x) = (x + 6)^2 - 3$ Vertex: _____   Axis of symmetry: _____

2    $f(x) = 3(x - 5)^2 + 1$ Vertex: _____   Axis of symmetry: _____

3    $f(x) = \frac{1}{2}(x + 2)^2 - 7$ Vertex: _____   Axis of symmetry: _____

4    $f(x) = \left(x + \frac{3}{4}\right)^2 + 9$ Vertex: _____   Axis of symmetry: _____

5    $f(x) = (x - 3)^2$ Vertex: _____   Axis of symmetry: _____

6   Explain why the coefficients in problems 2 and 3 do not affect the vertex or the axis of symmetry.

_____

_____

Each of the parabolas below are translations of the parent function $f(x) = x^2$. Write an equation in vertex form given the vertices below.

7   Vertex (-4, 9)   Equation in vertex form: ___$y = (x + 4)^2 + 9$___
                                       or $f(x)$ ⟶

8   Vertex (-1, 1)   Equation in vertex form: _____

9   Vertex (4, -8)   Equation in vertex form: _____

10   Vertex (0, -2)   Equation in vertex form: _____

11   Vertex (-2, 0)   Equation in vertex form: _____

12   Graph the following functions with each set on the same coordinate plane, and explain how they differ. You can do it by hand with graph paper or use the graphing calculator.

    a $y = x^2$ $y = -x^2$

_____

b $y = x^2$ $y = x^2 + 4$ $y = x^2 - 4$

_____

_____

c $y = x^2$ $y = (x + 4)^2$ $y = (x - 4)^2$

_____

_____

d $y = x^2$ $y = 4x^2$ $y = \frac{1}{4}x^2$

_____

_____

13   Write an equation in vertex form for each of these parabolas. Each one is a translation of the parent function $y = x^2$. State the domain and range of each function.

a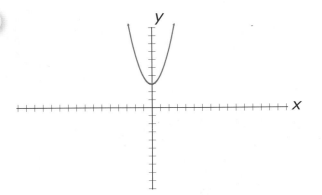

Equation: $y = x^2 + 3$

Domain: $x \in$ all real numbers

Range: $y \geq 3$

b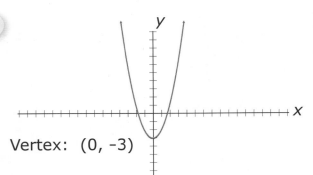

Vertex: (0, –3)

Equation:

Domain:

Range:

c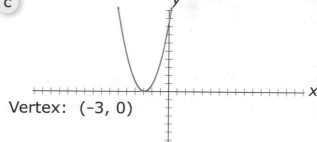

Equation:

Domain:

Range:

Vertex: (–3, 0)

d

Equation:

Domain:

Vertex: (–3, 2)

Range:

e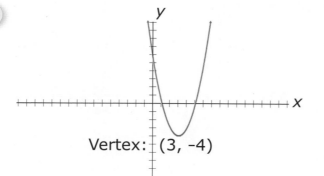

Equation:

Domain:

Range:

Vertex: (3, –4)

14 Take the vertex form of the last equation shown (13e) and change it to standard form and find the zeros.

Applications of Parabolas

Parabolas have many applications in everyday life. From the curvature of bridges, the path of a baseball, to the curvature of lenses for eye glasses and telescopes, parabolas are found in many different fields of study. Press the water button at a water fountain and you will see a parabola.

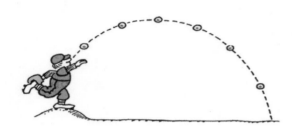 

1. Carmen shoots a small rocket she made in technology class into the air. The equation for the path of her rocket is $h = 8t - t^2$, where h is the height in feet and t is the time in seconds. Answer the following questions.

   a. What is the height of Carmen's rocket after 1 second?

   Substitute 1 for t.
   $h = 8(1) - 1^2$. So the height is 7 feet.

   b. At what time or times is her rocket 15 feet from the ground?

   Substitute 15 for h.
   $15 = 8t - t^2$ Now solve this quadratic. Set it equal to 0.
   $t^2 - 8t + 15 = 0$
   $(t - 5)(t - 3) = 0$
   $t = 5$ or $t = 3$.
   So at 3 seconds and at 5 seconds her rocket is 15 feet from the ground.

   c. At what time does it reach its maximum height? What is the maximum height?

   First, find the vertex by finding the axis of symmetry.
   $x = -\dfrac{b}{2a}$. Here x is t. $a = -1$ and $b = 8$, so $-\dfrac{b}{2a}$ is 4.

   So at 4 seconds it reaches its maximum height. Now plug in 4 for t and find the height.

   $h = 8(4) - 4^2$
   $h = 32 - 16$, so the maximum height is 16 feet.

d   At what time does Carmen's rocket hit the ground?

Let $h = 0$ as the height on the ground is 0 feet.
$0 = 8t - t^2$
$0 = t(8 - t)$ Remember the GCF.

$t = 0$ seconds (when it originated from the ground)
$t = 8$ seconds (when it returns to the ground)

By the way, this is the sketch of the path of Carmen's rocket.

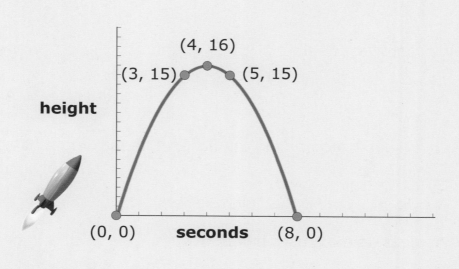

Answer the following questions based on this example.

1   What is the height of the rocket at 2 seconds? Explain how you got your answer.

_____

_____

2   What is the <u>equation</u> for the axis of symmetry? _____

3   Is the vertex of this parabolic path a maximum or a minimum? Explain your thinking.

_____

_____

Parabola Word Problems

Read the following problems carefully and answer the questions.

1. During a fireworks display, a flare was shot from the ground and traveled the path given by the equation $h = -4t^2 + 16t$, where h stands for height in meters and t stands for time in seconds. Show your work.

   a. How high was the flare at half a second?

   b. How high was the flare at three seconds?

   c. At how many seconds did the flare hit its maximum height?

   d. What was its maximum height?

   e. At how many seconds did the flare hit the ground?

   f. Graph the function on graph paper or with a graphing calculator.

2 A missile is shot from the ground at an initial velocity of 96 ft/sec. Its path is expressed by the equation $h = -16t^2 + 96t$, where h is the height in feet and t is the time in seconds.

a How high is the missile at one second?

b How high is the missile at $1\frac{1}{2}$ seconds?

c At how many seconds does it reach its maximum height?

d At how many seconds does it return to the ground?

3 Kurt threw a ball from a window 4 meters above the ground. The path of the ball he threw can be determined by the equation $h = -t^2 + 4$, where h is the height in meters and t is the time in seconds.

a Sketch a picture to help you understand the problem. Don't forget to label the axes.

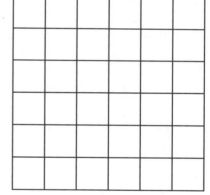

b At 1 second, what is the height of the ball?

c How much time elapsed before the ball hit the ground? Explain your thinking.

_____

_____

Exponential Functions

In the previous section you learned that the parent function of a quadratic equation is $y = x^2$. In an exponential function the base will be a number greater than 0 (but not 1, as 1 to any power is just 1) and the variable will now be the exponent. $y = 2^x$ is an example of an exponential function. Exponential functions model many situations in real life such as compound interest, bacteria growth, radioactive decay, population growth, etc.

Let's look at the graph of $y = 2^x$

x	$f(x) = y$
-3	$2^{-3} = \frac{1}{8}$
-2	$2^{-2} = \frac{1}{4}$
-1	$2^{-1} = \frac{1}{2}$
0	$2^0 = 1$
1	$2^1 = 2$
2	$2^2 = 4$
3	$2^3 = 8$

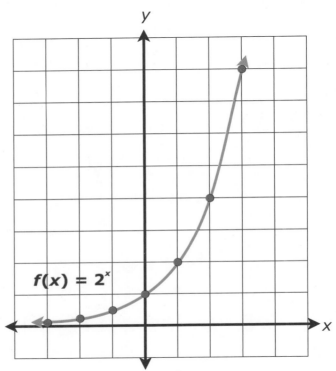

Notice that this graph is a smooth curve that rises very quickly and never crosses the x-axis.

Answer these questions based on this graph.

1. What is the domain (x-values) and the range (y-values) of this function?

_____

2. Find $f(-4) =$ _____

3. Find $f(4) =$ _____

Exponential Growth and Decay

As you've seen with the previous exponential function, the y values increased very quickly. The y values can also decrease very quickly which is why we often hear the expression "growing exponentially" or "decreasing exponentially." While the growth or rate of change of a linear function is constant, in exponential functions the increase or decrease happens very quickly.

The general form of an exponential growth or decay function is $y = a(1 \pm r)^x$ where a is the initial amount you start with and r is rate. If the function represents exponential growth, you will add the rate to 1; and if the function represents exponential decay or decrease, you will subtract the rate from 1. The x power represents the time. You must make sure that the time you use for the variable x matches the time indicated by the rate. You may use a graphing calculator for these problems.

1   Emelina invests $500 in a bank that pays 1.5% interest a year. This interest is compounded annually. If she does not add to her savings or withdraw any of that amount, how much would she have after three years?

   The formula is $y = a(1 + r)^x$ where a is $500 (her initial amount), $r = .015$ (percent changed to a decimal) and $x = 3$ years. We use $1 + r$ because her savings will be increasing.

   Substituting these values into our formula and using a calculator results in:

   $y = 500(1 + .015)^3$ and $y = \$522.84$ (rounded to the nearest cent)

2   Carlos bought a new car for $19,000. The rate of depreciation is 2% per <u>month</u> (this means the car loses 2% of its value per month). How much is Carlos's car worth after $2\frac{1}{2}$ <u>years</u>?

   The formula is $y = a(1 - r)^x$ where a is $19,000, the rate is .02 (percent changed to decimal) and $x = 30$ months (2.5 years must be changed to months. The units must match.)

   $y = 19,000(1 - .02)^{30}$ and $y = \$10,364.20$ (rounded to the nearest cent)

It's important to be aware that in some textbooks the general equation form of exponential growth or decay is given by $y = ab^x$ where you are given a (the initial amount) and b as the "exponential factor." The variable x is the time. You will then be given these parameters for b: If $b > 1$, then it's exponential growth (remember how we added the 1 to our previous formula. And if b is between 0 and 1 (remember how we subtracted our rate from 1), then it's exponential decay. It's useful to know this as you can tell, given an initial amount of $5,000 and a rate of 3% per year and a time of 4 years, that: $y = 5,000(1.03)^4$ represents exponential growth and that $y = 5,000(.97)^4$ represents exponential decay. You know this just by looking at your b or exponential factor in the formula.

3   A spelling competition starts out with 4,000 students and with each round half the students are eliminated. How many students remain after 5 rounds?

The students are decreasing so use the exponential decay formula $y = a(1 - r)^x$.

$y = 4,000(1 - .5)^5$ The answer is 125 students.

Notice what is happening:
    Round 1   Round 2   Round 3   Round 4   Round 5
4,000 ⟶ 2,000 ⟶ 1,000 ⟶ 500 ⟶ 250 ⟶ 125

Let's look at what the graph looks like.

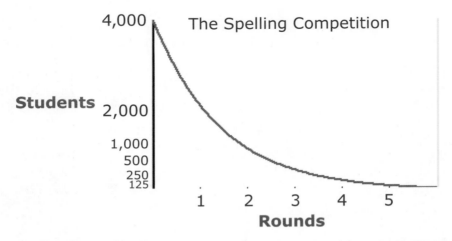

Can you see why the graph can never go below the x-axis? Why?

_____

Exponential Word Problems

Using graph paper, do the following problems. For most of these problems you do need a calculator with an exponent key $\wedge$. Round your answers to the nearest hundredths.

1 Graph $y = 3^x$

2 Bacteria can multiply very fast. Suppose you start with 10 bacteria cells and each one doubles every hour, how many bacteria would be there after one day? Since they double, your rate is 100% or 1. Notice one day changed to 24 hours. Here's the formula.

$y = 10(1 + 1.0)^{24}$

You're adding 100% of what you had before. 100 becomes 200, 200 becomes 400, etc.

3 Joaquín kept his grandmother's 1956 Oldsmobile as an investment since it was in perfect condition. The initial price his grandmother paid was $1,000. The car has increased in value by an average of 7.5% per year. How much will this car worth after 60 years?

4 A pesticide no longer in use has a half-life of 15 years. A substance's half life is the amount of time it would take for half the amount of the substance to decay. This is why some chemicals no longer in use can still be hazardous to our health. Assume that 200 grams of this chemical were spread on a farm, how many grams still remain after 5 years since it was spread? Here's the formula.

$y = a(1 - .5)^{t/h}$ where y = final amount, a = initial amount, t = interval of time, and h = half life (15 yrs)

5 Hakim invested $5,500 in a special account that earns 3% interest per year. If he does not deposit or withdraw any money, how much will he have after 5 years?

6 In a town, the population is growing at a rate of 2% per year. If currently the town has 1,500,600 people, how many people can be expected to live in this town in 9 months? (Hint: 9 months is .75 of a year).

7 Does this equation represent an exponential growth or decay? $y = (.96)^5$? Explain your thinking.

Functions Review

Answer the following multiple choice questions about the functions we've learned about in this chapter. Remember $y = f(x)$.

1 Which equation represents the graph of $y = |x|$ after it has translated down 5 units?

   a $y = |x| + 5$ b $y = |x + 5|$ c $y = |x| - 5$ d $y = |x - 5|$

2 Which equation represents the graph of $y = x^2$ after it has been translated 4 units to the left?

   a $y = (x + 4)^2$ b $y = x^2 - 4$ c $y = (x - 4)^2$ d $y = x^2 + 4$

3 Which of the following is an exponential function?

   a $y = x^2$ b $y = 5x + 2^3$ c $y = 3^x$ d $y = (x + 2)^2$

4 Which of the following is a quadratic function?

   a $y = 3x - 5$ b $y = 4x^2$ c $x = y^2$ d $y = x$

5 Which of the following shows an exponential decay equation?

   a $y = 4(.97)^3$ b $y = 4(1.07)^3$ c $y = 4(2.03)^3$ d $y = 4(1+.04)^3$

Answer the following question.

6 In Cascadilla Park the squirrel population is increasing rapidly. It is believed that in 2010 the population was 1,000 squirrels. The population is increasing at 12% a year. What is the expected population for each of these years?

2010	2011	2012	2013	2014	2015	2016
1,000	1,120					

   a Write an exponential equation for the problem. _____

   b Why would a linear equation not work for a problem like this? Explain your thinking.

   _____

Thinking About Patterns – A Helpful Guide

Fill out the following tables using the given functions below. Then read the tips on how to tell these functions apart.

1
$$f(x) = 3x$$

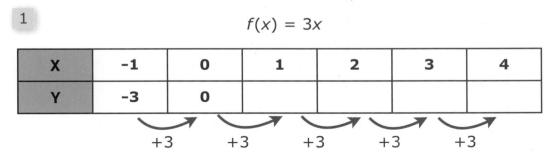

X	-1	0	1	2	3	4
Y	-3	0				

+3   +3   +3   +3   +3

TIP: This is a linear equation. The difference between successive outputs is always constant. That rate of change is the slope. This equation is also called a direct variation. A direct variation is a linear equation of the form $y = mx + 0$. Direct variation equations always go through the origin. Notice the y-intercept is where $x = 0$.

2
$$f(x) = -4x + 5$$

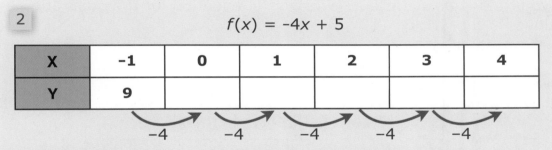

X	-1	0	1	2	3	4
Y	9					

−4   −4   −4   −4   −4

TIP: This is a also a linear equation. The difference between successive outputs is always constant. Notice that the rate of change is the slope of the equation. The y-intercept is where $x = 0$.

3
$$f(x) = x^2$$

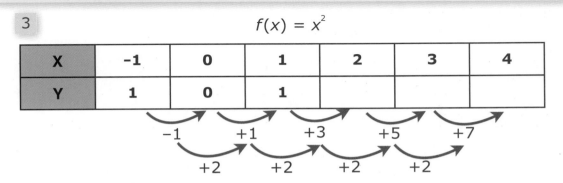

X	-1	0	1	2	3	4
Y	1	0	1			

−1   +1   +3   +5   +7

+2   +2   +2   +2

TIP: This is a quadratic equation. The second difference between outputs is a constant. This means: First find the difference between the outputs as shown, and then find the difference of those differences as shown.

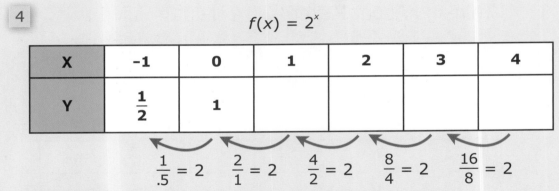

4 $f(x) = 2^x$

X	-1	0	1	2	3	4
Y	$\frac{1}{2}$	1				

$\frac{1}{.5} = 2 \qquad \frac{2}{1} = 2 \qquad \frac{4}{2} = 2 \qquad \frac{8}{4} = 2 \qquad \frac{16}{8} = 2$

TIP: This is an exponential function. The ratio between successive outputs is a constant.

Use the tips above to determine what type of functions are represented by these tables of values (linear, quadratic, or exponential). For the linear functions, write the equation. Also try writing an equation for the exponential functions. In an exponential function where $x = 0$ will give you the initial coefficient. Writing the equation for the quadratic functions is more tricky.

1

X	-1	0	1	2	3	4
Y	5	10	15	20	25	30

_____

_____

2

X	-1	0	1	2	3	4
Y	$\frac{1}{3}$	1	3	9	27	81

_____

_____

③

X	−1	0	1	2	3	4
Y	−8	0	8	16	24	32

_____

_____

④

X	−1	0	1	2	3	4
Y	5	4	5	8	13	20

_____

_____

⑤

X	−1	0	1	2	3	4
Y	5	3	1	−1	−3	−5

_____

_____

⑥

X	−1	0	1	2	3	4
Y	$\frac{2}{3}$	2	6	18	54	162

_____

_____

7

X	-1	0	1	2	3	4
Y	4	9	16	25	36	49

_____

_____

8

X	-1	0	1	2	3	4
Y	$\frac{7}{2}$	3	$\frac{5}{2}$	2	$\frac{3}{2}$	1

_____

_____

9

X	-1	0	1	2	3	4
Y	$\frac{1}{4}$	1	4	16	64	256

_____

_____

10

X	-1	0	1	2	3	4
Y	25	30	35	40	45	50

_____

_____

Graphing a System of Functions

Linear and Quadratic Functions

Now that you are familiar with how to graph quadratic and linear functions, you can solve a system of equations such as this one.

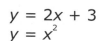   Graph this system of equations.

$y = 2x + 3$
$y = x^2$

The solution is (-1, 1)
and (3, 9)

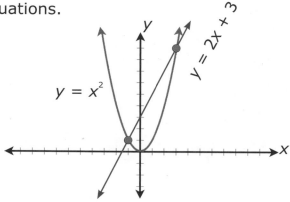

Check:

(-1, 1)	(3, 9)
$y = 2x + 3$	$y = 2x + 3$
$1 = 2(-1) + 3$ Yes!	$9 = 2(3) + 3$ Yes!
$y = x^2$	$y = x^2$
$1 = (-1)^2$ Yes!	$9 = 3^2$ Yes!

You can solve this equation algebraically by substitution. If $y = 2x + 3$ and $y = x^2$ then substituting x^2 for y gives you the following:

$x^2 = 2x + 3$.
$x^2 - 2x - 3 = 0$
$(x - 3)(x + 1) = 0$
$x = 3$ or $x = -1$

Solve the quadratic equation by setting it equal to zero.

Now substituting these values for x in order to get the corresponding y values, you get (3, 9) and (-1, 1).

Whenever solving by graphing is difficult, you can use an algebraic method to find the solution.

Think about this:
Does a line and a parabola on the same coordinate plane always intersect? If yes, do they always intersect in two points?

Graphing Practice

Answer the following questions.

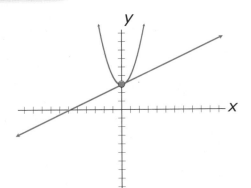

1 Boris graphed this system of equations in his graphing calculator. What is the solution?

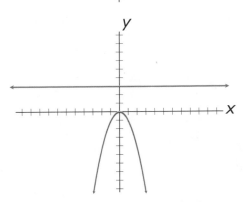

2 Heidi graphed this system of equations in her graphing calculator. What is the solution?

Solve the following systems by graphing or by using algebra. Use your own graph paper.

3 $y = x^2 + 5$
$y = 6$

4 $y = 2x^2 - 1$
$y = x - 1$

5 $y = -x + 1$
$y = x^2 + x - 2$

6 $y = -1$
$y = x^2 - 4x + 3$

7 $y = -4$
$y = -x^2$

8 $y = -2x + 4$
$y = (x - 2)^2$

9 $y = x^2 - 5x + 7$
$y = 2x + 1$

10 $y = -2x + 4$
$y = -x^2$

Chapter 12

Working With **Algebraic Fractions**

An **algebraic fraction** is a fraction that has an algebraic expression in the numerator or the denominator. As you saw in the chapter on polynomials, the rules that apply to arithmetic will hold true when you work with variables. When you started learning about fractions back in elementary school, you learned how to reduce or simplify them, and that is where we start, but it's a lot more fun!

When you reduce $\frac{8}{24}$ and get $\frac{1}{3}$, this is what is really taking place.

$$\frac{8}{24} = \frac{\overset{1}{\cancel{2}} \cdot \overset{1}{\cancel{2}} \cdot \overset{1}{\cancel{2}}}{\underset{1}{\cancel{2}} \cdot \underset{1}{\cancel{2}} \cdot \underset{1}{\cancel{2}} \cdot 3} = \frac{1}{3}$$

You are breaking up the 8 and the 24 into <u>factors</u>. Remember $2 \div 2$ is 1, so you must write a 1 in the numerator in the example above.

You must also remember that you may never divide a fraction by zero. If you do the answer is undefined or ∅.

[1]   Reduce $\dfrac{x^2 + 7x + 12}{x + 3}$. $x \neq -3$ or the denominator would be zero.

You MUST turn the numerator into factors because ONLY <u>factors</u> can be canceled. Remember to check for a GCF when you factor.

Factor the numerator: $\dfrac{\overset{1}{\cancel{(x + 3)}} \cdot (x + 4)}{\underset{1}{\cancel{(x + 3)}}}$ $(x + 3)$ is a factor group that cancels with the factor group $(x + 3)$ in the denominator.

Answer: $(x + 4)$ or $x + 4$

The use of parentheses is optional here.

In order to cancel, the factor groups must be identical. If you had $\dfrac{(y + 10)}{(y + 2)}$, that would be the final answer. The answer is NOT $y + 5$.

2 State for which value of x this expression is undefined. Then reduce.

$$\frac{y + 10}{2x + 5}$$

When you're asked what value makes an expression undefined, just set the denominator equal to 0 and solve for the variable. This will tell you the value you do not want the variable to be. In this case, set $2x + 5 = 0$.

Solving for x gives you $x = -\frac{5}{2}$, so the answer is $x \neq -\frac{5}{2}$.

Next notice that we cannot factor the numerator or the denominator, so the fraction cannot be reduced. NO, you cannot divide the 10 by 5. The operation next to those numbers is not a multiplication symbol.

3 Reduce $\dfrac{2x^2 - 50}{4x - 20}$. Restrict the variable. ⟵

This is another way of asking what value makes the fraction undefined. You are asked to state that the variable cannot be that value.

Let $4x - 20 = 0$ and solve for x, so $x \neq 5$.

Now to reduce you must factor. Remember to always look for the GCF.

$$\frac{2x^2 - 50}{4x - 20} = \frac{2(x^2 - 25)}{4(x - 5)} = \frac{\overset{1}{2} \cdot (x + 5) \cdot \overset{1}{(x - 5)}}{\underset{2}{4} \cdot \underset{1}{(x - 5)}} = \frac{(x + 5)}{2}$$

Notice three factor groups in the numerator and two factor groups in the denominator.

You can also write your answer as $\frac{1}{2}(x + 5)$ or take one half of x and one half of 5 and write your answer as $\frac{x}{2} + \frac{5}{2}$ or even $\frac{1}{2}x + 2\frac{1}{2}$. Remember $\dfrac{(x + 5)}{2}$ means both x and 5 are being divided by 2.

Restricting the Variable

For which value or values of the variable is the fraction undefined?

1 $\dfrac{4}{w}$

2 $\dfrac{-7}{8 - y}$

3 $\dfrac{x + 8}{x + 4}$

4 $\dfrac{4x}{2c + 4}$

5 $\dfrac{-8}{d^2 + 1}$

6 $\dfrac{21}{p^2 - 9}$

7 $\dfrac{w}{w - 4}$

8 $\dfrac{x}{4}$

9 $\dfrac{g + 10}{4 - h}$

10 $\dfrac{5}{3x + 2}$

11 $\dfrac{-5}{8 + 2x}$

12 $\dfrac{3}{14 - 2x}$

Simplify the following algebraic fractions. Restrict the variable when needed.

13 $\dfrac{8w}{-4}$

14 $\dfrac{3x + 15}{x + 5}$

15 $\dfrac{x - 9}{9 - x}$

16 $\dfrac{y^2 - 16}{y + 4}$

17 $\dfrac{x^2 + 10x + 21}{x^2 + 8x + 15}$

18 $\dfrac{x^2 - 3x + 2}{2x - 4}$

19 $\dfrac{8c + 48}{4c + 24}$

20 $\dfrac{-4a - 32}{-8a + 64}$

Thinking About Simplifying

A common mistake made by students when first learning how to simplify (or reduce) is to cancel terms of the expression that are not factors. Let's take a look at this problem.

$$\frac{y + 12}{6}$$

Why is the answer NOT $y + 2$? Let $y = 6$ for example. Then the numerator turns into 18 which divided by 6 is 3. Then it cannot equal $y + 2$, as $6 + 2$ is 8. You can try other numbers to convince yourself that except for the number 0, the value of the expression is not $y + 2$.

Canceling illegally is often called "term chopping." Only cancel factor groups. Again the 12 above is "tied" to the variable y by an operation other than multiplication. Therefore, it cannot be canceled.

Try these:

1. Savannah took the expression $\frac{2a + 8}{2}$ and got $a + 8$ by canceling the 2. Let $a = 3$ and test if her answer is correct. Then show how to simplify correctly. Notice $2a$ is attached to the 8 by a plus sign.

   _____

   _____

   _____

2. In the problem $\frac{x - 9}{9 - x}$, a student wrote an answer of 1. Let $x = 10$ to show what the correct answer should be. Explain your thinking.

   _____

   _____

3. Try another value for x besides 9 in the problem above. Will $\frac{a - b}{b - a}$ always result in the same answer? Explain your thinking.

   _____

   _____

4   Timothy suggested that every time he sees either $\dfrac{a-b}{b-a}$ or $\dfrac{a+b}{b+a}$, he will write "-1." Is he correct? Explain your thinking.

_____

_____

_____

5   Explain why $\dfrac{4a-8b}{4}$, which results in $a - 2b$, is NOT term chopping?

_____

_____

6   A student let $x = 0$ and tried to prove that $\dfrac{x+4}{x+3}$ equals $\dfrac{4}{3}$. How many values should one try to be certain what the correct answer is?

_____

_____

_____

7   Simplify this monster algebraic fraction. Remember the GCF.

$$\frac{3a^2b^3x^2 - 18a^2b^3x + 15a^2b^3}{9a^2bx^2 - 27a^2bx - 90a^2b}$$

8   In the problem above, restrict all the variables that may make the fraction undefined.

_____

Multiplying and Dividing Algebraic Fractions

Let's review what we know already from multiplying and dividing fractions.

1   Simplify $\dfrac{\cancel{7}^{\,1}}{\cancel{8}_{\,1}} \cdot \dfrac{\cancel{4}^{\,1}}{\cancel{100}_{\,25}} \cdot \dfrac{\cancel{-8}^{\,-1}}{\cancel{14}_{\,2}} = \dfrac{-1}{50}$

Remember you can cancel any factors in the numerator with any factors in the denominator.

You can multiply straight across, but it's a lot easier to cancel first.

2   Simplify $\dfrac{2x^2}{4y} \div \dfrac{16x^3}{-7y^3}$, $x \neq 0$ and $y \neq 0$

When you divide fractions, you turn the problem into a multiplication problem by changing the fraction that follows the division symbol into its <u>reciprocal</u>.

$$\dfrac{\cancel{2x^2}^{\,1}}{\cancel{4y}_{\,2}} \cdot \dfrac{-7\cancel{y^3}^{\,y^2}}{16\cancel{x^3}_{\,x}} = \dfrac{-7y^2}{32x} = -\dfrac{7y^2}{32x}$$

Write the negative in the front. A negative divided by a positive makes the fraction negative.

Now, let's look at some problems with more algebraic fractions.

3   Simplify $\dfrac{y^2 - 36}{y + 9} \cdot \dfrac{y^3 + 14y + 45}{y - 6} \cdot \dfrac{1}{y^2 + 11y + 30}$

$$\dfrac{\cancel{(y + 6)}\cancel{(y - 6)}}{\cancel{(y + 9)}} \cdot \dfrac{\cancel{(y + 5)}\cancel{(y + 9)}}{\cancel{(y - 6)}} \cdot \dfrac{1}{\cancel{(y + 6)}\cancel{(y + 5)}} = 1$$

When all the terms cancel, the answer is 1. Remember when you cancel, you are dividing.

It's really important that before you start factoring to rewrite the problem. It's easy to lose track of your factors if you're not neat, or if you cannot read your own handwriting. Also, using parentheses may help you remember that you are canceling factor groups.

4   Simplify $\dfrac{x + 1}{x^2 - 121} \cdot \dfrac{-4ab}{2x + 2} \div \boxed{\dfrac{-8ab^3}{x + 11}}$ You need the reciprocal of this fraction since it follows division.

$$\dfrac{(\cancel{x + 1})}{(\cancel{x + 11})(x - 11)} \cdot \dfrac{\overset{}{\cancel{-4ab}}}{2(\cancel{x + 1})} \cdot \dfrac{(\cancel{x + 11})}{\underset{2 \quad b^2}{\cancel{-8ab^3}}} = \dfrac{1}{4b^2(x - 11)}$$

Notice that when everything cancels in the numerator you still have a factor of 1. For your final answer you may distribute the denominator but it's optional to do that.

Practice multiplying and dividing algebraic fractions. Do not worry about restricting the variables.

1    $\dfrac{5ab}{-8} \cdot \dfrac{72}{b^3}$

5    $\dfrac{18a}{a + 7} \div \dfrac{36a}{7 + a}$

2    $\dfrac{x + 1}{x^2 - 1} \cdot \dfrac{2x}{10x}$

6    $\dfrac{-9}{x^2 - 144} \div \dfrac{3}{12 - x}$

Remember:
$(12 - x) = -(x - 12)$

3    $\dfrac{a^2 + b^2}{a^2 - b^2} \cdot \dfrac{a + b}{a - b}$

7    $\dfrac{1 - x^2}{x - 1} \div \dfrac{x + 1}{x}$

4    $\dfrac{c + 4}{c^2 - 16} \cdot \dfrac{6c^2 - 24c}{2c + 8}$

More Practice

Using a separate sheet of paper, simplify the following algebraic fraction problems. Do not worry about restricting the variables.

1) $\dfrac{x^2 - 49}{x + 1} \cdot \dfrac{7}{x + 7} \div \dfrac{x - 7}{x + 1}$

2) $\dfrac{w - 1}{1 - w} \div \dfrac{w + 10}{w^2 - 100} \cdot \dfrac{1}{w - 10}$

Only use the reciprocal of the fraction that follows division.

3) $\dfrac{-3x^4}{x + 1} \div 6$

Don't forget to put a "1" under the 6 first!

4) $\dfrac{x^2 + 5x - 24}{x^2 - 13x + 30} \cdot \dfrac{x^2 - 12x + 20}{x^2 - 169} \div \dfrac{x^2 + 6x - 16}{x + 13}$

5) $\dfrac{2x + 12}{-4x - 28} \cdot \dfrac{7x + 56}{x^2 + 14x + 48} \div \dfrac{x + 5}{x + 7}$

6) $\dfrac{2x^2 + x - 6}{2x^2 + 3x - 9} \div \dfrac{1}{x^2 - 9}$

7) $\dfrac{81 - x^2}{x^2 - 6x - 27} \cdot \dfrac{x + 3}{x + 9} \div \dfrac{1}{4}$

8) $\dfrac{4wz}{w^3 z} \cdot \dfrac{10}{2w^2 z} \cdot \dfrac{8w^5}{w} \div \dfrac{4z}{-1}$

9) $\dfrac{x^3 - x}{8x^2} \cdot \dfrac{4}{x - 1} \div \dfrac{x + 1}{3}$

10) $\dfrac{a^2 - 9b^2}{a^2 + ab - 6b^2} \cdot \dfrac{a - 2b}{a^2 - 6ab + 9b^2}$

Adding and Subtracting Algebraic Fractions

Adding and subtracting algebraic fractions follows the same principles you've learned before. Remember that to add and subtract fractions, the denominators must be the same. The denominator you choose must be the **least common denominator (LCD)**. To find the LCD when you have variables is not hard as long as you remember that the LCD must contain the other denominators as factors.

1 Simplify $\dfrac{3}{5x} + \dfrac{9}{10x}$

It's always a good idea to check if any of your fractions can be reduced before you start. In this example, you can't reduce either fraction.

The least common denominator is $10x$. Notice that $10x$ has the factors 5 and x. While you could multiply both denominators and get $50x^2$, it's always better to use the LCD. Now, let's see how to proceed.

$$\dfrac{3}{5x} + \dfrac{9}{10x}$$

2   1

$$\dfrac{6 + 9}{10x} = \dfrac{15}{10x} = \dfrac{3}{2x}$$

ASK: What does $5x$ need to multiply by to become $10x$? It needs 2, so multiply 3 by 2. $10x$ just needs to multiply by 1 to become $10x$ so the numerator stays a 9.
Make sure to reduce your answer.

2 Simplify $\dfrac{-4}{x} - \dfrac{2}{y}$

Since x and y are different values and you don't know if y or x are multiples of each other, you must use xy as your LCD. For example, if $x = 3$ and $y = 7$, you would use 21 as the LCD. Now, watch the subtraction sign between the fractions.

$$\dfrac{-4}{x} - \dfrac{2}{y}$$

y   x

$$\dfrac{-4y - 2x}{xy}$$

ASK: What does x need to multiply by to become xy? It needs y. And on the second fraction, what does y need to become xy? It needs the factor "x."

So that is our answer since it cannot be simplified further. Yes, you could factor out a -2 from the numerator, but in this example it's not necessary.

3 Simplify $\dfrac{5}{x-6} - \dfrac{x-1}{x-6}$.

Both denominators are the same. Notice the subtraction sign. You must distribute the subtraction sign to the numerator that follows it, so please use parentheses.

$$\frac{5-(x-1)}{x-6} = \frac{5-x+1}{x-6} = \frac{6-x}{x-6} = \frac{-1(x-6)}{(x-6)} = -1$$

4 Simplify $\dfrac{1}{5x^2} + \dfrac{4}{15x} - \dfrac{1+x}{60}$.

The LCD is $60x^2$ since it has all the other denominators as factors.

$$\frac{12(1)+4x(4)-x^2(1+x)}{60x^2} = \frac{12+16x-x^2-x^3}{60x^2} \quad \text{final answer}$$

5 Simplify $\dfrac{3}{w+5} - \dfrac{3}{w+10}$.

The LCD is NOT "$w+10$." The LCD is $(w+5)(w+10)$ since we don't know what w is. If $w=1$, then $w+5$ is 6 and $w+10$ would be 11. The LCD of 6 and 11 would be 66.

$$\frac{3(w+10)-3(w+5)}{(w+5)(w+10)} = \frac{3w+30-3w-15}{(w+5)(w+10)} = \frac{15}{(w+5)(w+10)}$$

You don't need to distribute the denominator unless you want to.

When in doubt about the LCD, use a value to substitute before you decide. Watch out for problems that have a subtraction sign as the numerator that follows the subtraction sign will change signs. If it helps you, put a -1 to help you remember to distribute the negative as you did in the polynomial chapter. Always try to simplify your final answer.

Practice

Simplify the following algebraic fractions. Don't worry about restricting the variable.

1 $\dfrac{3}{10a} + \dfrac{4}{20a}$

6 $\dfrac{6}{x} - \dfrac{2}{x^2} + \dfrac{3}{x^3}$

2 $\dfrac{1}{3w^2} - \dfrac{4}{6w^3}$

7 $\dfrac{a - b}{2a} - \dfrac{2}{4a^2}$

3 $\dfrac{5}{x} - \dfrac{10}{2y}$

Remember $x^2 - 4$ is $(x + 2)(x - 2)$

8 $\dfrac{2}{x^2 - 4} + \dfrac{1}{x + 2}$

4 $\dfrac{7}{a} + \dfrac{2}{b} + \dfrac{3}{c}$

9 $\dfrac{5}{x^2 - 25} - \dfrac{1}{x - 5}$

5 $\dfrac{3}{15c} - \dfrac{4}{20c}$

10 $\dfrac{4}{y + 7} - \dfrac{3}{y + 8}$

Proof Why 1 = 2

Let $x = y$.

Let's multiply both sides by x,

so then $x^2 = xy$.

Now subtract y^2 from each side,

and you get $x^2 - y^2 = xy - y^2$.

So factoring $(x - y)(x + y) = y(x - y)$.

Divide both sides by $(x - y)$ and you get

$x + y = y$

Now, since $x = y$, then $2x = x$.

Dividing by x gives you $2 = 1$!

Are all these steps legal? How could we come up with 2 = 1? Explain your thinking.

_____

_____

_____

_____

Hint: In the past few problem sections you were not asked to restrict the variable to save you time, but always keep in mind: Restricting the variable is very important.

Solving Equations With Algebraic Fractions

In Chapter 2 you learned how to get rid of fractions and decimals when working with equations. This chapter follows the same rules as before but with denominators that may contain variables. We must make sure that in all these problems, zero is never on any of the denominators.

1   Solve for y ($y \neq 0$).

$$\frac{1}{y} + \frac{1}{4} = \frac{2}{y}$$

These are the steps you need to follow.

1   Find the LCD of ALL the denominators. In this equation it's $4y$.

2   Multiply each term on BOTH sides by the LCD. This will get rid of all the denominators because you have an equation. NOTE: In the previous sections when you have expressions you never do away with the denominators (unless you are able to reduce at the end).

3   Be careful with the subtraction sign if there is any as you will need to distribute the negative (see the example 2).

4   Solve the equation.

$$\frac{(4y)1}{y} + \frac{(4y)1}{4} = \frac{(4y)2}{y}$$

Use your canceling skills.

Solve the equation.

$$4 + y = 8$$
$$y = 4$$

You can check your answer by substituting into the original equation.

$$\frac{1}{y} + \frac{1}{4} = \frac{2}{y}$$

Is $\dfrac{1}{4} + \dfrac{1}{4} = \dfrac{2}{4}$? Yes!

2 Solve for w ($w \neq 2$).

$$\frac{2w}{w-2} - \frac{3}{4} = 1$$

The LCD is $4(w-2)$.

$$\frac{4(w-2)\,2w}{w-2} - \frac{4(w-2)\,3}{4} = \frac{4(w-2)\,1}{}$$

Don't forget to multiply the right side of the equation.

Notice the sign.

$$8w - 3(w-2) \;=\; 4w - 8$$
$$8w - 3w + 6 \;=\; 4w - 8$$
$$5w + 6 \;=\; 4w - 8$$
$$w \;=\; -14$$

It will help you to take that subtraction sign and in the example above, place it in front of the 3 to make sure you distribute the negative.

3   Solve for x ($x \neq 2$).

$$\frac{x-1}{7} = \frac{6}{x-2}$$

A proportion is two ratios that are equal. $\dfrac{a}{b} = \dfrac{c}{d}$

The product of the means (bc) equals the product of the extremes (ad). $ad = bc$

The problem above is a <u>proportion</u> problem. When a fraction equals another fraction you have a proportion problem which you've solved in pre-algebra math classes. You can multiply both sides by the LCD, which is $7(x - 2)$, or you can cross multiply. But, be careful, you can cross multiply ONLY when you have one fraction equal to another fraction.

$$(x - 1)(x - 2) = 42$$
$$x^2 - 3x + 2 = 42$$
$$x^2 - 3x - 40 = 0$$
$$(x + 5)(x - 8) = 0$$
$$x = -5 \text{ or } x = 8$$

Solve the quadratic equation.

Always check your answers as sometimes one of them may not work.

Equation Practice

Solve these equations. Restrict the variable.

1. $\dfrac{1}{x} + \dfrac{15}{2} = 8$

2. $\dfrac{10}{4y} - \dfrac{1}{2} = 1$

3. $\dfrac{y}{3} - \dfrac{3y + 1}{6} = -\dfrac{1}{2}$

4. $\dfrac{x + 5}{8} = \dfrac{3}{x}$

5. $\dfrac{12}{x + 4} - \dfrac{20}{x + 4} = -4$

6. $\dfrac{2}{w} + \dfrac{w + 4}{5w} = \dfrac{9}{10}$

7. $\dfrac{3}{x + 4} = \dfrac{x + 9}{2}$

8. Check #7.

9. $\dfrac{9}{4} - \dfrac{1}{a + 3} = 2$

10. $\dfrac{81}{x^2} = 9$

Thinking About Fractions

Solve the following problems.

1 $2y - \dfrac{24}{y + 2} = \dfrac{12y}{y + 2}$

Do both solutions work? Why or why not? Explain your thinking.

_____

_____

2   The Egyptians solved many equations with fractions. Some of the problems had applications to the price of barley and other products, but remember they were great at surveying the land and building pyramids, so their knowledge of mathematics was extensive. Here's another problem from the Rhind Papyrus, the most famous collection of Egyptian mathematics, written about 1650 BCE. This one has variables in the denominator.

$\dfrac{2}{3} = \dfrac{1}{2n} + \dfrac{1}{6n}$

3   Dividing by zero as an impossibility was first noted by a philosopher named George Berkeley in 1734 in an article called *The Analyst*. Brahmagupta (598-668) tried much earlier to give zero a proper value but failed to explain why division by 0 is undefined. The Mayan civilization was one of the first civilizations to have a symbol for 0. Use the Internet to embark on a search for the history of zero.

Revisiting Work Problems

On Chapter 4, p. 110, we had a work problem that we are now able to do with algebra instead of trial and error. Math problems with people working at different rates create equations with fractions.

1   Tina works half as fast as Jane. Working together they can finish a job in 8 hours. What is the rate of each girl?

Let Jane's rate per hour be $\dfrac{1}{x}$; then Tina's rate is $\dfrac{1}{2x}$. In 8 hours they complete the entire job (100% or 1). Unlike the equation we used before, this one might be easier to understand.

Together $\dfrac{1}{x} + \dfrac{1}{2x} = \dfrac{1}{8}$ One-eighth of the job would be completed in one hour.

The LCD is $8x$. Multiplying every term of the equation by $8x$, we get

$$8 + 4 = x \quad \text{and} \quad x = 12.$$

Jane's rate is $\dfrac{1}{12}$ and Tina's rate is $\dfrac{1}{24}$. It would take Jane alone 12 hours and Tina 24 hours what together they can do in 8 hours. Team work!

2   Paula can paint a room in 2 hours and Tom can paint it in 3 hours. How long would it take them to paint the room together?

Paula's rate is $\dfrac{1}{2}$ of the room in one hour. Tom's rate is $\dfrac{1}{3}$ of the room in one hour, so together $\dfrac{1}{x}$ of the room would be done.

$$\frac{1}{2} + \frac{1}{3} = \frac{1}{x}$$

Solve the equation. Multiplying each term by the LCD ($6x$), you arrive at $x = \dfrac{6}{5}$, which is 1 hour and 12 minutes.

More Practice

Using a separate sheet of paper, solve the following problems. Do not restrict the variable unless asked.

1    $\dfrac{8}{x} \cdot \dfrac{x^2 - 144}{x - 12} \div \dfrac{x + 12}{x^3}$

2    $\dfrac{-4a^3}{a + b} \cdot \dfrac{b + a}{b - a} \cdot \dfrac{1}{4a}$

3    $\dfrac{8 - x}{x + 3} \cdot \dfrac{-10}{x - 8} \cdot \dfrac{1}{-20}$

4    $\dfrac{a}{a + 3} = \dfrac{3}{4}$ Restrict the variable.

5    $3 + \dfrac{7}{y} = \dfrac{y + 3}{2} - 1$ Restrict the variable.

Solve the following work problems. Show a let statement or make a table to organize your information.

6   A construction worker can put siding on a house in 12 hours, and his partner can do the same work alone in 10 hours. How long would it take them working together?

7   Joan can prepare a meal for 12 people in 3 hours, and Lucinda can prepare the same meal for the same amount of people in 4 hours. If they could work together, how long would it take them to do this job?

8   It took Joe and Jim working together 6 hours to mow Mr. Sanchez's lawn. Joe is more experienced, and he is twice as fast as Jim. Find each of their rates.

9   Carmen can paint a barn in 10 hours. Sara wants to help, and so does her twin sister Camila. Camila is three times as fast as Sara. Together all three work together and finish the job in 6 hours. What is the rate of the twins?

10   Show a check for problem 9.

Thinking About Algebra

A Message From the Author

As we approach the end of this algebra workbook, it is my hope that the algebra tools you have learned will give you the confidence to help you succeed in future math courses and in other fields of study. You may hear people tell you that they had trouble with algebra in school, or that they did not need algebra after high school or after college. As a teacher, I've heard comments like this many times from friends who later would ask me to help them figure out their new salary because they did not know how to solve a proportion problem, or needed help finding the missing side of a right triangle when there were variables involved. As you think about algebra you need to remember that algebra is all about thinking. The calculators and computers you have access to will help you perform operations more quickly, but they won't replace your thinking. Here's an example of a task that is still best done by hand WITH ALGEBRA.

How to Change a Repeating Decimal to a Fraction

Change .17171717... or $.\overline{17}$ to a fraction

Notice that this repeating decimal has <u>two</u> numbers that repeat.

Let $x =$ .17171717...

Then multiply both sides of the equation by 100 (we use 100 because we need to move the decimal place two places since two numbers repeat). Write $100x = 17.171717...$ on top of our $x = .171717...$ LOOK:

$$100x = 17.171717...$$
$$x = .171717...$$

Decimal tails fall out!

$$99x = 17$$

$$x = \frac{17}{99}$$

You can try dividing this fraction in the calculator to verify your answer. For fun, change the following repeating decimals to fractions.

1 .1111...   2 .123123...   3 .030303...   4 .99999... (hmm!)

Algebra
by T. Husted

If you cannot speak at all,
If your language is not theirs.
If you cannot be heard,
Or even understood,
You can always count
Beyond the numbers one and two.
It's the beating of your heart,
That gives meaning to the unknown
In this uncertain life,
Full of variables and questions,
Do not lose your identity,
Or commute when you're not ready.
Be patient!
For you will soon graph
The sunset with your lines.
And reach those higher slopes
Where your vision will be vast.
You will see the beauty of the universe
With goodness, love,
With algebra.

Terri Husted did not speak English when she came to this country.
Math was the only language she understood. She has tried to
make algebra her students' favorite subject for over 30 years.

Glossary

Abscissa	Seldom used term for the x values of ordered pairs
Absolute Value	The distance a number is away from zero. The absolute value of a number is always positive.
Associative Property	A rule that states that $(a + b) + c = a + (b + c)$ and that $(ab)c = a(bc)$. So that grouping in addition and multiplication does not affect the answer. The property does not work for subtraction or division.
Axis of Symmetry	In a parabolic function, the vertical line that divides the parabola in half so that each side is a mirror image of the other
Base	The number or variable that sits under an exponent. In 5^3 the base is the 5.
Binomial	A polynomial with two terms
Braces	Inclusion symbols { } most often used with set notation
Closure Property	A set has closure property or is said to be "closed" for a given operation if, when performing the operation, the result is in the original set
Coefficient	A number that multiplies a variable. In an expression such as $3x^2$, the 3 is called the coefficient.
Commutative Property	A property that states that $a + b = b + a$ and that $ab = ba$. The commutative property does not work for subtraction or division.
Complement	For a given subset of a set, the set of all elements in the set that are outside the subset. For the set of even whole numbers, the complement of {0, 2, 4, 6, 8} would be all the even numbers larger than 8.
Conjugate	In a binomial involving radicals, the conjugate of $(a + \sqrt{b})$ is $(a - \sqrt{b})$. For the purposes of this book, $b > 0$.

Constant	A number by itself with no variable next to it
Disjoint	Two sets that have no elements in common
Distributive Property	A property that states that $a(b + c) = ab + ac$. Also, $a(b - c) = ab - ac$.
Domain	The x values in a set of ordered pairs
Empty Set or Null Set	A set with no elements or members
Equal	Having the same quantity
Equation	Two expressions that are connected with an equal sign
Equivalent	Two sets are equivalent if they have the same number of elements
Evaluate	To substitute or "plug in" a value for a variable in an algebraic expression and then find the value of the expression
Exponent	The small, raised number next to a base that determines how many times the base is to be multiplied by itself
Expression	Numbers and/or variables with the operations $+$, $-$, $\times$ or $\div$ that are not connected with an equal sign or an inequality
Fallacy	An argument that may sound right, but it's based on illogical steps
Function	A set of (x, y) values where each x is paired to a unique y. While one value of y may be paired other x values, in a function, a given x always results in the same y.
Identity	Any number or symbol after an operation that does not change the number before the operation; 0 is the identity for addition and 1 is the identity for multiplication
Improper Set	The set that is an exact copy of a given set. The improper set of $\{-3, 2, 8\}$ is $\{-3, 2, 8\}$.

Inequality	A sentence with any of these symbols: $>$, $<$, $\geq$, $\leq$, or $\neq$
Intersection	For two or more sets, the set of only those elements common to both or all sets
Let Statement	A way of identifying what a variable stands for.
Line of best fit	The line that most closely aligns with a set of points on a graph
Linear	Refers to any graph that creates a line or any equation where the highest exponent is 1
Monomial	A polynomial with one term
Ordinate	Seldom used term for the y values of ordered pairs
Parabola	A two-dimensional symmetrical "U" (or upside down U) shape created by graphing a quadratic equation
Polynomial	An expression having one or more terms consisting of numbers and variables with whole number exponents, with terms separated by addition or subtraction
Property	A rule that always works
Proportion	Two fractions that equal each other
Quadratic	A second-degree equation
Radical	An expression that uses a root, such as a square root, cube root, etc., designated by the symbol $\sqrt{}$
Range	The y values in a set of ordered pairs
Reciprocal	The reciprocal of $\frac{a}{b}$ is $\frac{b}{a}$, as long as neither number is 0. Two reciprocals always multiply to 1.
Relation	Any set of ordered pairs or mapping of two sets
Roster	A list of the elements of a set
Root(s)	Another word for the answer or answers to a quadratic equation

Satisfies	To make an equation or inequality a true statement
Scatterplot	In statistics, a graph of the points taken from a table with two variables. The points are not connected.
Set	A collection or group of objects or numbers
Simplify	To find the answer in simplest form
Slope	The steepness of a line; the vertical change divided by the horizontal chage
Solution Set	Another term for the answer to a problem
Solve	To find the answer to an equation involving variables, or to find the answer to a word problem
Standard Form	In polynomials, organizing the terms from largest degree to smallest degree
Subset	A set whose elements all belong to another set. A subset can also be the empty set or the improper set.
System of Equations or Inequalities	Two or more equations or inequalities solved together
Trinomial	A three-term polynomial
Union	For two or more sets, the set of all elements of every set listed
Variable	A symbol or letter that stands for a number
Vertex	In a parabola or absolute value function, the point where the graph makes a turning point
Vertical Line Test	A test to determine if a graph represents a function. If you pick any point on a graph and there is no point above or below that point, then it is the graph of a function.
x-intercept	Any point $(x, 0)$ where a line or curve touches the x-axis
y-intercept	Any point $(0, y)$ where a line or curve touches the y-axis

Reference

Laws of Exponents

$x^a \cdot x^b = x^{a+b}$

$(x^a)^b = x^{ab}$

$(xy)^a = x^a y^a$

$x^{-a} = \dfrac{1}{x^a}, x \neq 0$

$\dfrac{x^a}{x^b} = x^{a-b}, x \neq 0$

$x^0 = 1, x \neq 0$

Special Products

$(a + b)^2 = (a + b)(a + b) = a^2 + 2ab + b^2$

$(a - b)^2 = (a - b)(a - b) = a^2 - 2ab + b^2$

$(a + b)(a - b) = a^2 - b^2$

$(a + b)^3 = (a + b)(a + b)(a + b) = a^3 + 3a^2b + 3ab^2 + b^3$

$(a - b)^3 = (a - b)(a - b)(a - b) = a^3 - 3a^2b + 3ab^2 - b^3$

Properties of Equality

Operations

Addition: If $x = y$, then $x + a = y + a$

Subtraction: If $x = y$, then $x - a = y - a$

Multiplication: If $x = y$, then $xa = ya$

Division: If $x = y$ and $a \neq 0$, then $\dfrac{x}{a} = \dfrac{y}{a}$

Reflexive property: $a = a$

Symmetric property: If $a = b$, then $b = a$

Transitive property: If $a = b$ and $b = c$, then $a = c$

Basic Number Properties

Commutative: $a + b = b + a$
$a \cdot b = b \cdot a$

Associative: $a + (b + c) = (a + b) + c$
$a \cdot (b \cdot c) = (a \cdot b) \cdot c$

Distributive: $a(b + c) = ab + ac$
$a(b - c) = ab - ac$

Identity: $a + 0 = a$
$a \cdot 1 = a$

Inverse: $a + (-a) = 0$
$a \cdot \dfrac{1}{a} = 1 \; (a \neq 0)$

Properties of Inequality

Transitive: If $a < b$, and $b < c$, then $a < c$

Addition: If $a < b$, then $a + c < b + c$
If $a > b$, then $a + c > b + c$

Multiplication: If $c > 0$ and $a > b$, then $ac > bc$
If $c < 0$ and $a > b$, then $ac < bc$,
also if $a < b$, then $ac > bc$

Quadratic Equations

Standard form: $y = ax^2 + bx + c$

Vertex form: $y = a(x - h)^2 + k$
where (h, k) is the vertex of the parabola.
If a is positive the parabola opens up;
if a is negative the parabola opens down.
If $|a| < 1$, the parabola widens and if
$|a| > 1$, the parabola narrows.

Axis of symmetry: $x = -\dfrac{b}{2a}$

Steps for Solving Equations

1 Distribute to clear parentheses

2 Combine like terms on each side

3 Move variables to the same side

4 Undo + and −

5 Undo · and ÷ (reciprocals)

Quadratic Formula

$$\dfrac{-b \pm \sqrt{b^2 - 4ac}}{2a}$$

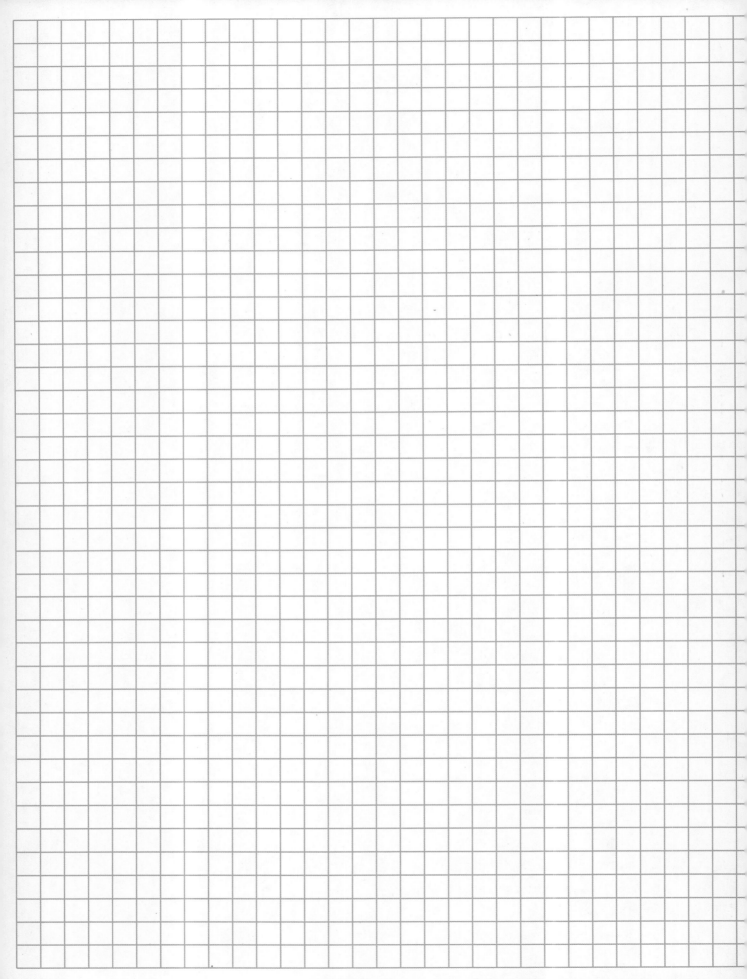

356

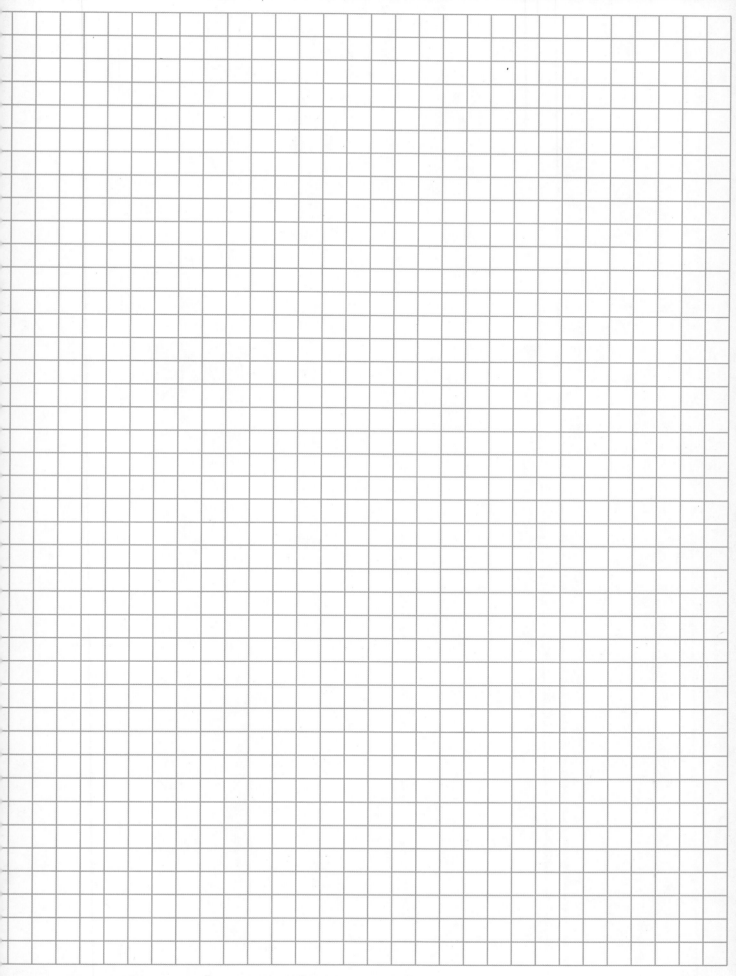

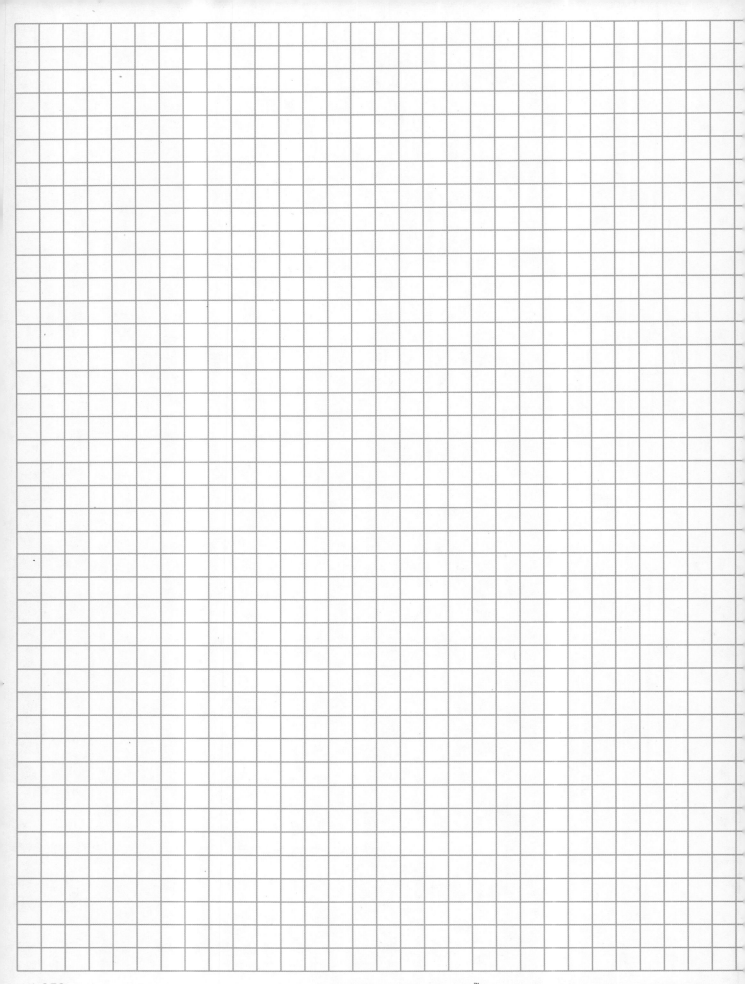

358

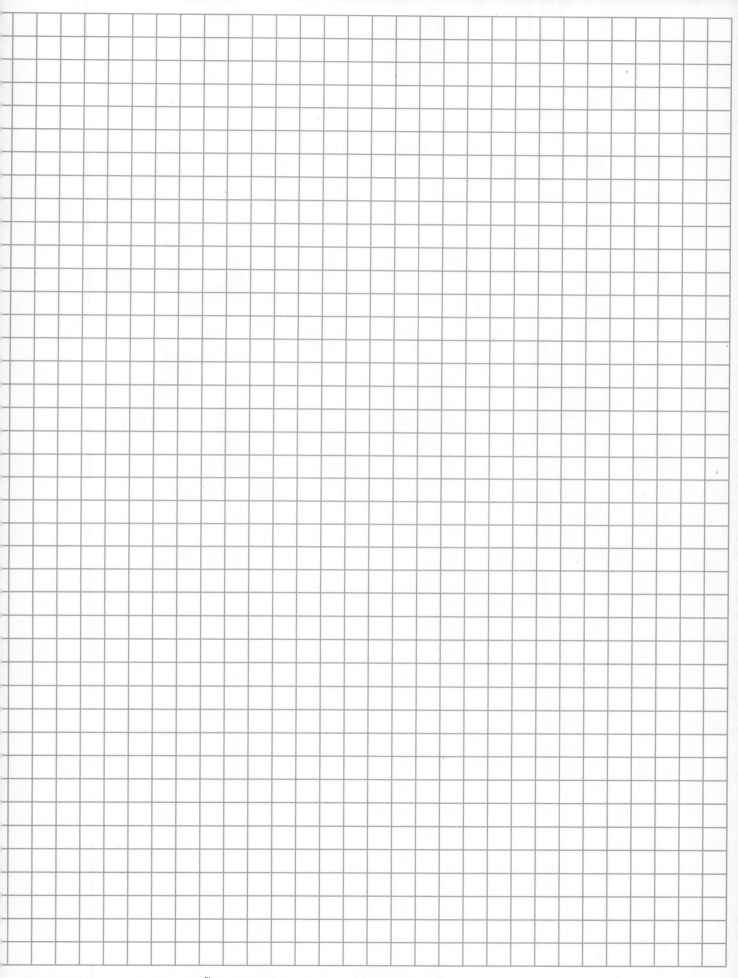

Balance Benders™

Which answer can replace the question mark?

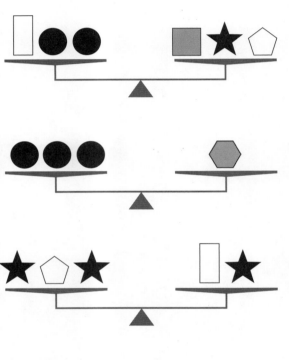

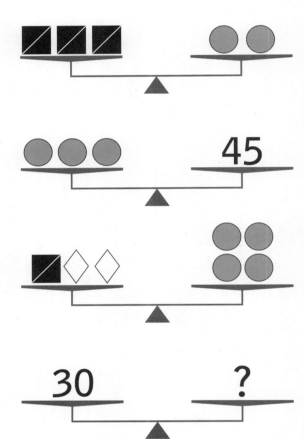

a. ⬠ ⬡   b. ▯ ⬡

c. ■ ⬡   d. ● ⬡

a. ◇ ◪   b. ◇ ●

c. ◇ ◣   d. ◪ ● ◪

Hint: On 3rd balance, remove ★ from both pans.

Hint: Divide 2nd balance in thirds.

Angles Puzzle 1

Use your *thinking skills* to find the missing angles and
record in degrees below. Figures are **not** to scale,
so do not measure.

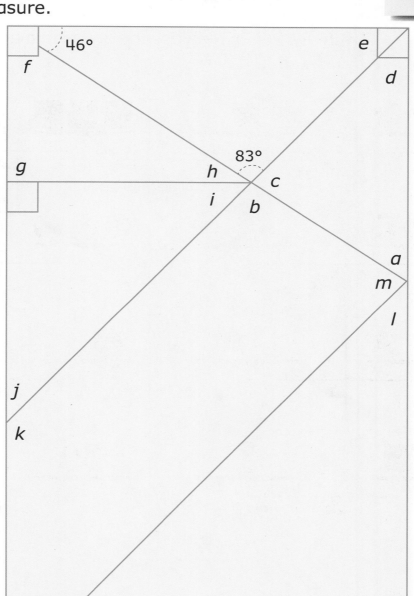

a _____ b _____ c _____ d _____ e _____ f _____ g _____

h _____ i _____ j _____ k _____ l _____ m _____

Special Binomial Products

- **Special binomial products – squaring binominals**

Special Products	Formula	Initial Expansion	Example
difference of squares	$(a + b)(a - b) = a^2 - b^2$ It does not matter if $(a - b)$ comes first	$(a + b)(a - b) = a^2 - ab + ba - b^2$ $= a^2 - b^2$	$(x + 2)(x - 2) = x^2 - 2^2 = x^2 - 4$ or $(x - 2)(x + 2) = x^2 - 2^2 = x^2 - 4$ $(a = x, b = 2)$
square of sum	$(a + b)^2 = a^2 + 2ab + b^2$ A perfect square trinomial	$(a + b)^2 = (a + b)(a + b)$ $= a^2 + ab + ba + b^2$ $= a^2 + 2ab + b^2$	$(x + 3)^2 = x^2 + 2 \cdot x \cdot 3 + 3^2$ $= x^2 + 6x + 9$
square of difference	$(a - b)^2 = a^2 - 2ab + b^2$ A perfect square trinomial	$(a - b)^2 = (a - b)(a - b)$ $= a^2 - ab - ba + b^2$ $= a^2 - 2ab + b^2$	$(x - 4)^2 = x^2 - 2 \cdot x \cdot 4 + 4^2$ $= x^2 - 8x + 16$

- **Special binomial products:** special forms of binomial products that are worth memorizing.

- **Memory aid:** $(a \pm b)^2 = (a^2 \pm 2ab + b^2)$

Example: Find the following products.

1. $(3y + 4)(3y - 4) = (3y)^2 - 4^2$ $(a + b)(a - b) = a^2 - b^2$
   $= 9y^2 - 16$ $a = 3y$, $b = 4$

2. $\left(5t + \dfrac{1}{2}\right)^2 = (5t)^2 + 2(5t)\left(\dfrac{1}{2}\right) + \left(\dfrac{1}{2}\right)^2$ $(a + b)^2 = a^2 + 2ab + b^2$
   $= 25t^2 + 5t + \dfrac{1}{4}$ $a = 5t$, $b = \dfrac{1}{2}$

3. $(3q - \dfrac{1}{6}p)^2 = (3q)^2 - 2(3q)\left(\dfrac{1}{6}p\right) + \left(\dfrac{1}{6}p\right)^2$ $(a - b)^2 = a^2 - 2ab + b^2$
   $= 9q^2 - qp + \dfrac{1}{36}p^2$ $a = 3q$, $b = \dfrac{1}{6}p$

4. $(t + 1)^3 = (t + 1)^2 (t + 1)$ $a^n a^m = a^{n+m}$
   $= (t^2 + 2t + 1)(t + 1)$ $(a + b)^2 = a^2 + 2ab + b^2$
   $= t^3 + t^2 + 2t^2 + 2t + t + 1$ Distribute
   $= t^3 + 3t^2 + 3t + 1$ Combine like terms.

5. $(2A - 3 + 4B)(2A - 3 - 4B) = (2A - 3)^2 - (4B)^2$ $(a + b)(a - b) = a^2 - b^2 : a = 2A - 3, b = 4B$
   $= (2A)^2 - 2(2A) \cdot 3 + 3^2 - 16B^2$ $(a - b)^2 = a^2 - 2ab + b^2 : a = 2A, b = 3$
   $= 4A^2 - 12A + 9 - 16B^2$ Simplify

- **Using function notation:**

Example: Given $f(x) = -3x + x^2$, find and simplify **1.** $f(u - 1)$, and **2.** $f(a + h) - f(a)$.

1. $f(u - 1) = -3(u - 1) + (u - 1)^2$ Replace x with $(u - 1)$
   $= -3u + 1 + u^2 - 2u + 1$ $(a - b)^2 = a^2 - 2ab + b^2$
   $= u^2 - 5u + 2$ Combine like terms.

2. $f(a + h) - f(a) = [-3(a + h) + (a + h)^2] - (-3a + a^2)$ Replace x with $(a + h)$ and a.
   $= -3a - 3h + a^2 + 2ah + h^2 + 3a - a^2$ Remove parentheses.
   $= h^2 + 2ah - 3h$ Combine like terms.